Half Blind
with
Full Vision

[signature]

2018

Half Blind with Full Vision

By
David Espinoza

E-BookTime, LLC
Montgomery, Alabama

Half Blind with Full Vision

Library of Congress Control Number: 2017958310

ISBN: 978-1-60862-712-7

First Edition
Published November 2017
E-BookTime, LLC
6598 Pumpkin Road
Montgomery, AL 36108
www.e-booktime.com

Dedications

To my mom, Gabriela Veliz Espinoza, there are no words that can express the gratitude I have for you. You sacrificed so much for us six kids. You cooked; you sewed; you washed clothes; you cleaned the house; you prayed for us; you made us go to church, and you showed us unconditional love. You were always there for us whether it was celebrating our birthdays or lifting us up when we were down. You introduced me to God, which was the best thing that ever happened to me. Thank you so much for being a good mom. You helped us survive a storm. I love you, Mom.

To my dad, Wenceslado Espinoza, growing up in Dimmitt, I was so blessed to have a dad like you. You taught me so much about cars and how they work. You taught me how to respect the law and to always do the right things. You instilled good values in me. You sacrificed for us every morning by going to work and setting an example. You provided for our family by working many hard-labor jobs throughout your life. Your family was priority over anything else. Thank you for being a good role model, I love you, Dad.

To Candi R. Espinoza, my high-school sweetheart who I deeply fell in love with. I was blessed to share a life with you for thirteen years. You taught me how to love and you introduced me to many Bible scriptures. I'll always be thankful for you being such a supportive wife, daughter to your parents, and an amazing mother to our two boys. We still keep you in our hearts every day of our lives.

To my two boys, Jake and Matt, I'm so honored and thankful that God gave me two talented children who became fine young men. Raising you two did not seem like work, it was fun, it was joy, and it was a true blessing. While I did my best to teach you about life, you two have taught me so much about many things. Thank you for always being there for me and for making life fun. Your mom would be very proud. Thanks for being my content editors. I love you both.

To Loni Espinoza, how lucky was I to have fallen in love again with another amazing lady? Our contrast backgrounds were a challenge since we met when we were much older. We had so many things in common, yet many differences. With Jesus in our lives, we came together and became one. Thank you for being my wife and for supporting me and standing by my side. Thanks for being my grammar-editing partner. I love you.

Acknowledgements

Gilberto, you were the oldest of six siblings. Thank you for always protecting me when I tagged along with you. You introduced us to different sports, new foods, and new activities. I learned so much from watching your practices and games. I love you, brother.

Loop, I'll never forget your undefeated team in the eighth grade. That was such an inspiration to me. To have a brother on the team was pretty cool. You also protected me from bullies. I was blessed to have a brother that was tough and stood up for what was right. Thank you, I love you, brother.

Louise, thank you for those summers at the FINA gas station. You helped my self-esteem which helped my confidence. I needed that after several harsh experiences with customers. I love you, sister.

Richard, I appreciated your friendship and your competitiveness while we were growing up in Texas. You were always a likeable brother to me and a good friend to others. Many of the kids you became friends with in Dimmitt looked up to you and followed your lead. Thank you for being my practice partner in the backyard. I love you, brother.

Diana, you were the youngest and you were always trying to keep up. I remember your enthusiasm and upbeat personality. Thank you for being the little sister that always enjoyed playing games with us. I love you, sister.

I have so many great memories of our Texas days. Before school started, we would all hop into the station wagon and drive to Amarillo to buy new clothes. On our way back to Dimmitt, we stopped at Hereford, Texas, to eat at McDonalds. Afterwards my parents would take us to the park. I also enjoyed playing basketball on our basketball court made out of dirt. Most of all, I'll never forget how blessed we were to have had such amazing parents.

Loop Espinoza

I remember seeing how dedicated my brothers were to sports. I always enjoyed Thanksgiving Day with my family in Texas. When we went to Amarillo, I enjoyed Wonderland Theme Park and the zoo next to it. Visiting our cousins was always a delightful adventure. Palo Duro Canyon was so much fun – a tourist place that I learned to love with my family. I will always treasure those memories.

Diana Espinoza West

Introduction

I'm fifty-eight years old and I've kept a secret for pretty much my entire life. For the longest time I wanted to be normal, just like everyone else around me. When you read my story you'll understand why. Deep inside I knew that I was different, physically. You wouldn't want to go through what I did as a child, as a grade-school kid, as a middle-school kid, or as a high-school kid. And then later as an athlete or as a young boy wanting to date a girl. My life has been one heck of a mess, one heck of a highlight, and one heck of a resilient story. I have felt depressed; I have felt embarrassed; I have felt scared; I have felt bullied; I have felt worthless, and I have felt cheated in life.

Things just didn't seem fair to me for a long time. Why God allowed this to happen to me, I'll never know. But when he closes half of my window, he opens other talents, possibilities, and joys for me. I never felt angry at God, but I felt angry at people who made fun of me. I felt angry at people that put me in uncomfortable situations throughout my life, especially when I was helpless and defenseless. I owe a big thanks to my dad, my sweet mom, and my two older brothers. They defended me whenever they could.

I can't imagine what my family went through, dealing with me and hearing how other kids or adults spoke about me. I've never asked them, and I don't think I ever will. One thing is for sure, they have always honored what I asked of them. They knew I didn't want anyone to know about my secret. I'm sure at times it leaked out, I understand they were not perfect. I knew that writing this would be difficult for me. I know this is what I needed to do to share with the world that despite a huge obstacle, people like me can still live a productive and joyful life. I didn't realize God was with me the entire time, guiding me and steering me in the right direction, but now I do. God loved me so much that He heard my prayers and He answered my prayers one at a time in His timing, and today He still hears my prayers.

I eventually overcame many things that happened to me during my youth life. I worked so hard at anything I did and mastered it – something drove me to want to be a perfectionist. During my adult life I lost someone very precious to me. Someone that I loved deeply. It would again affect me emotionally in a different way than what happened in my youth. I wasn't thinking about Jesus, and I was going to church every Sunday. I started thinking of myself only, selfishly. God was with me and heard my prayers, he brought people into my life that helped me along the way. Jesus restored me to the person that I once was before I lost someone very close to me. I owe a big thank you to Loni, Matt, Jake, and Darci. These special people, who display Jesus in life, helped me in many ways. You'll find out when you read my story.

I hope that my true story provides some useful information to someone that might be going through what I did. Just remember one thing, it's when things get the roughest and toughest that we must not give up, and we must continue the faith with the absence of doubting. Please sit back and enjoy my story, I'll do my best to tell it honestly and passionately.

1.

Traumatized My Early Childhood

I was a normal kid running outside and playing. My memory is lacking on what I was doing from age three to age four. When I was five years old, in a split second, my smile, my appearance, and my emotional state would change to one of the worst nightmares I would experience. The other nightmare came during my adult life.

My mom had this old-garage-sale washer that she used to wash our clothes in. She would hang the hose that drained the water onto the side of the washer. The hose had a thick wire with a sharp edge wrapped around it that was used to hang on the washer. I don't have a clue what my mom was doing in another room. She was probably cleaning the kitchen floor or ironing clothes for the wealthy people. They would often pay her for a batch of clothes at a time.

My brother, Richard, was four years old. We played together on a regular basis because he was close to my age – we were only a year apart. As we all know, it's impossible for a parent to watch their children constantly. I can't recall whose idea it was to play jump rope with the hose that was attached to the washer, but anyway, we each had a grip on the ends of the hose. My end of the hose had the wire on it. Richard begin to swing the hose like I was supposed to, unfortunately, somehow I lost my grip and he continued to swing the hose. All of a sudden, I felt the wire catch my left eye with a solid hit. My eye was immediately severely punctured and blood with white substance started gushing out splattering on the floor. I frantically started screaming from the top of my lungs as the pain started getting stronger and stronger. I was scared and in shock, what just happened?

My mom rushed from the other room and saw my brother standing there watching me, probably in shock as well. She started spanking him and I saw him start to cry. I kept thinking to myself, *why is she spanking him, it wasn't his fault, we were just playing.* She turned around and looked at me, I was covering my eye with one hand but could not stop the bleeding and the pain. If you've ever gotten hit in your eye with something, you might get an idea of what a wire in your eye would feel like. My mom did not drive a car at that time in my life, it was my dad that did the driving.

She rushed over to the neighbor's house across the street, she knew she had to rush me to the hospital. One of our cars was sitting outside, and my dad was at his job digging up a gas line with a backhoe just outside of town. The neighbors were not home. My mom ran back to the house, grabbed the keys and carried me to the car. She left the older kids in charge while she drove me to the Dimmitt Medical Clinic. I can't recall if we even had a hospital in Dimmitt at that time. I remember her driving as fast as she could while holding me next to her and blood still running down my shirt and pants.

I remember riding for two or three blocks standing next to her on the front seat of the Ford. I must have passed out because the next thing I knew I was flat on my back and there were two or three people around me talking. The room was cold, I don't get it, did anyone have heated rooms back then? Anyway, I could vaguely hear the doctors. One doctor said, *there's nothing we can do for him here, we need to get him to Amarillo as soon as possible.*

My mom knew how to drive a car, but had not driven in years. I don't know how she got me to the doctors, I feel it was God that guided her and held her hand. I can't explain it any other way.

I don't have a memory of how long I was in Dimmitt before being transported to Amarillo, but it did happen. My mom was able to contact our neighbors, Luther and Catherine Rogers. Luther drove out to my dad's worksite and notified him. According to my dad, when he found out, he left the heavy equipment he was operating and came home right away. By then I had been admitted to St. Anthony's Hospital in Amarillo, Texas. Amarillo is the largest city in the Texas Panhandle and sixty-six miles northwest of Dimmitt. Our neighbors had a phone, but we didn't. We often used theirs in emergencies. They were some of the nicest people I ever met in Dimmitt.

In 1964 I remember hearing muffled noises while I was lying on a hospital bed. I was only five years old. I had no clue what day or month it was, or what was going on. Why couldn't I see anyone with my vision? Everything was fuzzy and foggy. Why couldn't I hear anyone clearly? It sounded like someone had their mouth covered with tape as they were trying to talk to me. I didn't know anything at the time. I don't know how many days I had been lying on that bed after the surgery was performed, which was something that was not told to me. The doctors tried their best to save my left eye, but because of the infected optic nerve, they had to remove the eye. I lost half of my eyesight that year.

I cannot imagine what my mom must have felt like. I wish that she was still alive today so I could tell her how grateful I am for her courageous action. She managed to get me to a hospital doing whatever it took. I wish I could tell her that it was not her fault, or that it was not my brother's fault. Things happen and maybe God does allow things to happen for whatever reasons. I keep thinking about a verse in the Bible.

Proverbs 3:5-6, Trust in the Lord with all your heart and do not lean on your own understanding. In all your ways acknowledge Him and He will make straight your paths.

I truly don't have an idea of how many days it was before the sight of my one good eye was restored slightly. I remember those muffled sounds from nurses or doctors for several days. And then finally I was starting to see blurry people as I lied under the white sheets and white pillow under my head. I felt like I was in prison for a crime I did not commit. Every day the door was closed and locked. I was in solitary confinement as a five-year-old kid that did not know what was going on.

The doctors and nurses would continue to try and talk to me. There was a mixture of nuns and nurses that would come see me on a daily basis. The nurses would spoon-feed me since I was not able to move at all. They would talk to me, but I could not hear them very well nor could I see them very well. I had poor vision with the one good eye. I felt like a mummy with my entire head wrapped up in gauze except for the area of my one good eye and my mouth.

As the days passed by my healing began. It's so amazing how God made our bodies to heal. I have no doubt that the nuns at St. Anthony's Hospital were praying for me. I slowly started eating food, Lord knows how they fed me when I wasn't able to eat. My educated guess would be maybe, intravenously.

After several days of lying in a hospital bed, I heard a nurse. I opened my one eye very slow. I didn't know who this person was and I was afraid. All I could see was a lady in a white uniform wearing a white hat. It must have been a nurse hat of some kind.

I remember the nurses and doctors all being very kind to me. My body was so cold. All I had was a white sheet and a white blanket. I kept trying to tell them that I was very cold. The blanket was not enough. I had lost a lot of weight from not eating any food for days.

"I co," I said in a whisper.

"David, can you say that again ... what do you want?"

"Co."

"I don't know what he's trying to tell me," the nurse said to another nurse.

"I coal."

"You're cold?"

"Yes ma'am."

"Oh, he's cold! Well, let's take care of that."

The nurse grabbed another blanket and placed it on top of my entire body. That was such a relief, I felt so much better when I was warm. The nurse told the other nurses about me responding for the first time. Shortly after, the doctor came in with a small flashlight and started examining me. He said a few words to me, but like most of the staff, they probably didn't realize that my English was not that great at that age.

I was scared, I didn't know who all of these people were around my hospital bed. My eye was hurting and I was beginning to remember why I was here as I ignored the nurses and doctors. I kept replaying, in my memory, what happened to me over and over. The wire hitting my eye, my brother getting spanked by my mom, and the blood running down my clothes as I was standing on the car-bench seat next to my mom.

My vision started clearing up a little bit from my good eye. I did not see my mom or my dad. This was a place that I was not familiar with at all. My eye continued to hurt as it began to heal. Every movement I made I would cringe. I couldn't think very well, it was very difficult to think anymore, so I fell asleep.

The next day was a little better and again I would tell the nurses that I was cold. There was a certain nurse that always knew what I wanted, the rest of them struggled understanding me. Whether I was in pain or too cold, or just simply wanted the window blinds closed.

I was in a deep depression and angry. I didn't trust anyone there. One day I finally asked, "Where's my mommy and daddy? I want my mommy and daddy." I started crying and could not stop. A nurse was sitting next to me, she looked like a nun. I knew what she was from going to church on Sundays. She was very kind and talked to me in a quiet and friendly voice. She was wearing her habit – the black and white covering. I could only see her blurry face. She said, "Your mommy and daddy will be here tomorrow, okay?" I didn't say anything and my tears kept running down my right cheek.

No one told me what I had been through or how long the surgery took. I'll brief the event for you. There was an implant that was surgically placed inside the eye socket. This was to prepare for a future prosthetic eye. So naturally the healing time after the surgery had to be lengthy.

I was adjusting a day at a time. My mom and dad had not come up to the hospital yet. They did not have much money so it was difficult for them to drive to Amarillo during the week. There is no way in the world my parents could have possibly paid for my hospital stay or the surgery itself. The hospital knew we were poor and so did the doctors. My guess is that St. Anthony's had some kind of a scholarship program to help the needy. I think my parents paid for some, but only a small portion and by payments.

Here's a little history on St. Anthony's Hospital. In 2009, years later, my wife and I traveled to Amarillo, Texas. I wanted to show her where I was raised and the hospital that I was once admitted to back in 1964. I'm so glad I took a snap shot of this information.

This Marks the site of Potter County's first hospital organized by sisters of charity of the incarnate word on invitation of Father David H. Dunne, pastor of St. Mary's Church in Clarendon, Texas, and David Fly M.D. from Amarillo. The land was donated by W.M. H. Bush.

Four sisters opened the hospital as St. Anthony's Sanitarium, the original building. It was demolished to make room for a present school of nursing, which was a 14-room-red-brick structure without gas, electricity, or phone service.

A two-story addition in 1909 provided thirty beds and an operating room. Despite hard times, a school of nursing was also opened that year. In 1922 a third story was added to be used by the sisters as a convent.

In 1927 another addition enlarged the facility to a one-hundred bed capacity and provided a laboratory, delivery rooms, X-ray rooms, and more surgical suites. A third addition in 1949 brought the total capacity to 150 beds.

A $2,000,000.00 addition in 1960 making St. Anthony's a 250-bed general hospital, was made possible through funds raised by the Amarillo Area Foundation.

On my 2009 visit as an adult years later, I tried so hard to find out more about the hospital and what happened to it. They had built a new hospital in a different location and no one had any information on its history. I wanted to know more details about my patient history. What room did I stay in? What doctors and nurses helped me? What procedures were done to me? There was so much that I wanted to know. I'm grateful that my memory is good enough to remember some of what I experienced. And I am so thankful to God that He gave the hospital staff the skills to save my life.

Let's get back to when I was five-years old. After two weeks I started seeing the nurses' faces more clearly. I found out my parents were coming to the hospital to see me regularly during the early parts of my stay, but they had to return to Dimmitt to take care of the other kids. I had no knowledge because I couldn't hear or see very well for days. The nurse assured me that my parents were coming to see me on Friday and they would stay the weekend.

My Aunt Ninfa lived in Amarillo, and I remember my family staying with her several times when they visited on the weekends. They would bring all of my brothers and sisters to my aunt's house. The hospital would only allow my parents to see me, no other relatives were allowed.

The first time I saw my mom and dad, when I could actually talk and hear better, I was so excited and I thought I was going home that day. My mom broke down in tears as she sat next to me and rubbed my head with her hand. My dad was smiling but his expression was a worried one. My mom continued to smile while she was rubbing her tears off with her hand. The only words I recall that she spoke were, "It's gonna be okay mi hijo." I don't remember my parents saying, *I love you*, but I do remember what they did for me and how they displayed love so well.

Visits from my mom and dad were great for me, it helped my emotional wellness. I had that sense of them loving me. Before I realized they were visiting me, I felt like my family had abandoned me, I was so alone at this unfamiliar place. The first time my mom and dad tried leaving after visiting for a few hours, I broke down in tears. I was pleading with them, asking them not to leave. I did not want to be left at this hospital by myself.

It must have been an emotional wreck for my parents to see me the way I was ... and then to see me cry every time they had to leave. I'm pretty sure the hospital had visiting hours. Later on there were times that they allowed my mom to stay the night. My mom wore this coat that I still remember. Sometimes when it was time for them to get back to Dimmitt, they would wait until I fell asleep. I remember a few times seeing the backside of her coat as they exited the room. I started crying and yelling for them to come back, but they had already shut the door behind them.

The weeks passed by fast during my stay at St. Anthony's Hospital. And then the weeks became months. Sometimes when my parents would visit they brought a new toy for me to play with. My room was starting to look like a kid's nursery. I remember getting plastic trucks, bouncy balls, plastic Cowboys and Indians, and all sorts of little cars. When my parents weren't there I would get some of the nuns to play with me.

The nurses would often play with me for a little while. I'm thinking it was more of therapy exercises. The adjustment of seeing out of one eye had to be challenging. One nurse in particular would have me throw the ball to her and then she would toss it back to me and encourage me to catch it. I liked that game a lot. She told me something that's still fresh in my mind, *I can't believe how well you are picking things up!*

My dad had to continue working to support the family so it was my mom who normally would visit longer. I loved it when Mom showed up with another toy for me to play with. The nurses continued to play with me too, they would do their best to entertain me. I wish I could remember who they were, I would thank them. If you are reading this book and you were one of those nurses, I thank you from the bottom of my heart for all your care.

There were many days that it was just me in the room. No visitors, only the toys laying on a long table in my room. I would get so bored just staring at the ceiling, or at the walls.

One morning I woke up and I saw this spider on one of the ceiling corners. I started watching it. Back in Dimmitt I saw spiders in our house now and then. We would just kill them. I wasn't about to kill the only friend I had for many days. The room was so quiet that sometimes I felt like I could actually hear the spider talk to me. It moved so quick and stopped so quick. I saw this spider spin a web one morning. It's so funny how the Lord can find the smallest things that help us get through a day when we are in the darkest hours.

There were days where I could not remember what my brothers and sisters looked like, or for that matter, if they even cared about me anymore. I had no knowledge of who was allowed to visit. When the nurse would come by to check on me, I would always ask her, "When will my mommy and daddy be back?" The answer was always the same, *they'll be coming soon.*

I ran out of tears and I started realizing that this is just how it was going to be. When I saw my parents leave so much, I started getting conditioned to an isolated-life situation. Was I ever going to get well enough to leave this hospital? I began to believe that this was going to be my lonely home. My friends were, the spider, the doctor, the nuns, and the nurses. The one thing that kept me sane and not totally abandoned, was my mom and dad. They never gave up on me. They were with me for many weekends. The longest stretch that I didn't see them was roughly three weeks in a row. I didn't know better back then, but I'm sure they had things going on at home that I was totally ignorant about.

Some days the medical staff would put me in a stretcher and wheel me down the hall to an X-ray room, or a procedure room. And then I would be back in my prison cell, I mean, my hospital room. I hated the tests or procedures, or whatever they were doing to me. I remember being exhausted and in some pain on my left-eye area every time those medical procedures took place.

Months later, I was able to start walking and even jumping on the padded bench next to the window. The nurses would supervise me and warn me about being careful, since I only had half my vision. After a few weeks, they okayed me to get up on my own and walk around.

I remember during the summer when it got hot. I would look out of the window. I must have been on the fourth floor, because it was a long way down there. I would watch kids playing in a swimming pool. The water looked clear and the bottom of the pool was blue. There were oak trees all around the area. I could hear the kids screaming and laughing. I wanted to be there with them, having fun. I thought about my brothers and sisters and how we would play together.

My daily routine during the summer was walking over to the window and watching the kids swim and play. This was more entertaining than staring at the walls, or at a pet spider. Nothing against that pet spider, because it became a close friend. The nurses would come by from time to time to check on me, or if I needed anything I could push a red button on the side of the bed.

This experience was one of the hardest things I have ever gone through in my life. Some days I was in more pain than others, no one could understand except this little five-year-old boy. What did the wind feel like outside, or what did the sunlight feel like? I couldn't remember what my neighborhood was like back in the small town of Dimmitt.

There was one day that tore me up inside. I heard the door open and I woke up stirring a bit and pulling up the blanket, it was always cold in that room. The nurse had a broomstick with her. She walked to the corner and killed my spider friend.

"I finally got you little spider," she said.

"No!" I yelled.

"David, are you okay? It's just a spider."

I started crying once again. The spider was like my pet and an insect that I could watch when no one was in the room. The nurse did not understand, how could she? It took me a few days to recover from that loss. I never told the nurse why I started crying when she took my friend away. I did hear her talking to the other nurses, telling them about how sensitive I was.

As the days became weeks, and the weeks became months, I'm not going sit here and tell you that I made it through alone, because I didn't. Jesus Christ was with me to help me rise and to comfort me when I was in my lowest place as a child. Jesus strengthened my parents and the medical staff to be by this little boy who desperately needed much love.

My educated guess is that I was at the hospital anywhere from six to nine months recovering. Test after test, procedure after procedure. I truly thank God for being there holding my hand with highly-skilled medical people all around me, taking care of me.

Thank you St. Anthony's Hospital for all the medical expertise that you were blessed with to take care of me when I didn't know who you were or what you were doing. Thank you for helping a little kid that needed help so badly. I pray that someone from that hospital reads this book and that they know they were appreciated.

2.

I'm Coming Home!

I cannot express to you how excited I was to finally be able to step outside and breathe that fresh Texas air. I was close to six years old when I was released from St. Anthony's Hospital. The car ride was straight to McDonalds. I think my wife will laugh at this. It was more of a treat for us kids back then. We normally ate at home, plus we didn't have a McDonalds in Dimmitt. Before we exited Amarillo, my dad pulled over and treated me to a nice burger-fry feast.

Hospital food just didn't taste the same as tasty-filling food, maybe it's improved, but to be honest I got tired of the hospital food. I was treated like a king and with no brothers or sisters around it was nice just eating with my mom and dad. They even bought me a new toy for the ride back.

A new toy for any of us kids would cost a dime or a quarter back then. I never thought about the cost. Any new toy would bring a huge smile to any of us, whether it was worth $5.00 or just a quarter, it didn't matter. It was my toy and I was the first one to play with it.

The sixty-six-mile drive took a little over an hour. We drove past Hereford, Texas, on the freeway. Hereford sits in Deaf Smith County and is about twenty miles away from Dimmitt. I was excited to see my brothers and sisters again, but at the same time I was very nervous – hadn't seen them in months. A young kid forgets, have they grown some? What would they think of me now that I wasn't whole? I had this huge patch covering my left eye with adhesive tape and it was noticeable from a mile away.

The Ophthalmologist and his medical staff were making a prosthetic eye. I remember his name, Dr. Clamence. It was going to take them a few weeks before it was ready. I had blocked out all of the uncomfortable-sitting for hours while the doctors measured my good eye and then measured the socket for fitting. I felt like an experiment or something. They talked to themselves with technical terms I simply did not understand. The eye colors were documented. The rulers they used reminded me of a school ruler my older brother used for school. I hadn't even entered pre-school or kindergarten yet. I had not learned how to read yet.

The prosthetic eye would be made larger than my good eye. These doctors knew what they were doing. Their educated guess on how much I would grow, would determine how large they would make the eye. It was a concept of my good eye growing and catching up to the size of my prosthetic eye.

I was in for a challenging life of seeing my doctor every month to every six months to every year. They knew when it would be time to make another eye as I was growing.

All I had on my mind was getting home. I fell asleep before we arrived. My brothers and sisters were outside playing on this long alley behind our house. Our yard was dead from lack of water. There was nothing but hard dirt – it doesn't rain too much in Dimmitt, Texas. My mom carried me inside the house where she had prepared my own bed with a clean sheet, a blanket, and a toy-set of plastic Cowboys and Indians – I loved playing with stuff like that. I was so used to the clean hospital room and extra space that I noticed the difference right away. There's truth to, *there's no place like home.* I would rather be in a small crowded house with old blankets and no bedroom doors than at that hospital room with no one around, especially without my mom and dad.

I was finally home and as I was about to get some rest after playing with my plastic toys, I heard a bunch of kids talking outside. I hadn't heard a sound like that in months. The sound kept getting louder as they approached the house. They were all racing to see who could see me first. The two older boys won the race, of course, and the others followed. Mom was yelling at them to not be so loud because I needed to get rest.

They all were saying hi to me while smiling and giggling. Some were asking me if I needed anything or if I wanted to see what they made out of clay or what they drew while I was gone. They were all just staring at me and I was staring at them with a huge smile. My older brother had dirt all over his hair and it sure seemed like he grew an inch since I saw him. They were all full of dirt from playing outside. I remembered when I was that way too – it was so much fun to play outside. We would race sometimes, or play, "Kick the Can". Sometimes we would play cars, which consisted of making small roads on the dirt behind our small house. I missed this place so much while at the hospital, and it felt so good to be home again and to see the nice welcome my brothers and sisters gave me. My little sister was very tiny as she had just been born the previous year.

It didn't take me long to fall asleep, I was exhausted and the day had been full of new adventures that was anticipated months ago. I heard my mom praying from time to time. She was praying for me. I was still very young and didn't understand a lot of things like my mom praying and all. We did attend church on Sundays, so that helped a little.

Mom had instructions from the doctor on how to clean my wound from time to time. The opened wound had to be kept covered all the time except when being cleaned.

My poor mom, how did she manage taking care of me while being a wife to my dad and mother to her other children? It had to be the Lord guiding her. My dad went to work every day so I only saw him during the evenings. I remember the first thing he did every day after work. He would come directly to my room to see how I was doing.

I was adjusting fine until neighbors and relatives came over to see me. I didn't want anyone to see me like this. I was embarrassed. My mom would talk to them, I could hear her. I could also hear the people talk about me, expressing how sorry they were. All of them kept asking, "What happened?" My poor mom had to explain the whole story again and again. I couldn't wait until all of this settled down a bit. I certainly ate a lot of pies and dishes of food people brought over. That was very nice of them to do that for our family.

I knew I was now different and I knew that people were going to see me as different. I had lost a vital part of my body – half my sight. I didn't feel normal and I couldn't play like I did previous to the accident. My parents didn't allow me to do certain things, they wanted me to stay safe. I'm truly thankful for that because as a child I didn't know any better. I would have loved to play football, basketball, or baseball with my brothers outside. That was so hard for me to watch from the window. At least this time it was watching my brothers instead of watching kids swimming in an unfamiliar territory outside of St. Anthony's Hospital.

I can't recall how long it was before my parents drove me back to the doctor's clinic in Amarillo. I was told that the prosthetic eye had been completed and ready to be fitted into the socket. The flesh had been healed, thanks to my mom for doing all the right things for me at home. I remember being scared because I had worn this huge patch covering my left eye for days and I was conditioned to wearing it. Wait, this meant that maybe no one would ever ask me, *what happened to you?* Boy was I in for a huge surprise.

When we arrived at the clinic, for some reason my dad didn't want to come in. He stayed outside in the car – he always took advantage of sleep opportunities. I think you understand if you are a working parent, especially if you have a large family. My mom and I sat in the waiting room and stared at each other. I could hear some music in the background. She would make these funny faces and she would make me laugh. And then about twenty minutes later she would burst out in tears. I didn't know any better then, but now that I'm an adult and have kids and grandkids of my own, well, I can definitely relate to what she must have been feeling. I would not want my kids or grandkids to go through something like this.

At such a young age I wasn't totally sure what my mom was thinking. Maybe that I was her little boy and she felt so very sorry for me. Maybe she thought about the pain that I had gone through and the pain that I was about to go through. Or, maybe the questions she would have to answer to people in the future. What would people say about me or what would it be like entering kindergarten and then grade school? The financial debt because of my doctor visits had to be on her mind. They were already struggling financially with six kids in the family.

I'll never know exactly what she was thinking, but I will always remember the sacrifices she went through just for me. She would carry me to the car and back when I couldn't see very well. Mom prepared meals for me and watched for objects on my left side when I walked. It took her a few times before she discovered that knocking things over as I walked by was beginning to be a regular occurrence. I remember once at the grocery store, I knocked over an entire stack of canned beans. Another time I ran into the frame of a door and fell down pretty hard. She kept me from rubbing my eye socket when it itched so much. She helped train me to watch out for things by turning my head a little more. Oh, I could list a thousand things she did for me. I will always know that she was not alone, she had God holding her hand and giving her the strength that she needed to continue displaying that precious love that she displayed so well. I would often hear her pray when I was taking naps.

My dad had his work cut out. He provided for the family working long hours. He was a school bus driver and janitor for the school district. It didn't pay much for the work he did, but it was a secure job that paid for the bills and food for the family.

After sitting in the waiting room for about forty-five minutes, they finally called me. They sat me in this office chair with some nice padding. I had never seen such nice furniture and wall displays. The walls were light brown and the floor trimmings were dark brown and made out of wood. There were actual doors that opened and closed. At our house we had curtains in each room. Easy-listening music in the background was semi-relaxing, I had never heard that kind of music before. I liked the nice and clean atmosphere. I sat very still and very nervous as I didn't know what to expect. It was Doctor Clamence.

"Hi David, how are you?"

"Good."

I didn't know what to say, my English vocabulary was not very good at that time. It was an uncomfortable situation. This doctor was not familiar to me, but I trusted my mom and she was right next to me assuring me that it was okay.

"We got your eye made and we're ready to put it in so you don't have to wear that silly eye patch anymore."

He cleaned the eye off with warm water and then put some lubrication around it. I remember the light smell of cigarette, I'm thinking he was a smoker. Back in the 1960s and 1970s it was very common for people to smoke cigarettes in an office.

The moment of truth was about to happen. The doctor said, "Just relax, this is painless, it will be okay." I was tensed up and Dr. Clamence was struggling a bit getting the eye into the socket.

"David you have to relax otherwise this won't work."

So I tried my best to relax. I took a deep breath and my shoulders dropped a little. He finally got the eye into the socket.

"There we go!" The doctor smiled.

It felt so weird and different, and all I could think was, *how am I ever going to function with this thing that was placed in my eye socket?* If you want to get an idea of how it felt, try placing a safe object that's round in your ear for a few seconds. That's the best I can describe this. I felt different and I was scared and confused as a little boy.

The doctor promised me that after a few days of wearing the eye it would feel very normal and I wouldn't even know it was there. When I looked in the mirror, I was so impressed on how it resembled my right eye. The dark brown color with tints of purple were miraculously painted. The eye itself was made out of a special substance that hardened once put into a very hot tempera-ture. The result was like glass, but really it was hard plastic. If I were to drop the eye, it would not break. I didn't know this until years later, I thought it was made out of glass for the longest time.

The only thing I didn't like was that it was a little larger than my right eye, which was my good eye. The doctor told us that he had to make it that way to compensate for my growth, and in a few years he would have to make me another eye because I would be growing more. This is the best I can do to describe what I remember about this process, I hope you get the idea of what I went through as a young boy – not fun. As we were leaving, the doctor walked out into the hall with us.

"Can we pay you payments? We don't have the money to pay all of it," Mom said.

"No charge this time, see you next time." He smiled and walked away.

"Oh thank you Sir," Mom said.

At the time we had a 1957 red and white Ford, I can't remember the model though. My dad woke up and took one look at me. He couldn't believe how great the eye looked. He had this huge smile on his face. That made me feel pretty good and encouraged. They took me to McDonalds again. Back then it was this little dinky place just outside of Amarillo.

When we arrived home from our trip everyone wanted to take a glimpse of my newly implanted eye. All my siblings were nice to me and said good things. I began playing outside again. Throughout the week a neighbor or relative would stop by and their first comment would be something like, "You can't even tell, wow it looks so real!" This started making me feel uncomfortable and a little embarrassed. I knew they were trying to be nice, but I did not want that kind of attention. It wasn't like, *Wow that's a nice shirt!* It was about the accident I had and my imperfect body, at least that's how I felt. It was difficult back then to keep it a secret, since many neighbors and relatives heard about the accident.

I was comfortable around my brothers and sisters, but being around anyone else was terrifying for me. They all were curious and wanted to know what happened to me. My mom was one of those ladies that talked to the neighbor ladies while hanging the clothes to dry on a long wire outside the house. If any of our neighbors came over to see how I was doing, I would go to my room and hide. I didn't want anyone to see me because I knew where the conversation would go.

While making the big adjustment of wearing no patch on my left eye, I often stayed inside the house while my brothers and sisters played outside for hours. There were no video games, iPads, computers, nor did we own a TV. What we did have was a radio. It was brown and the top part looked like a half-circle cabinet with a curved dial in the middle. My mom would often listen to country music or just pop music. I started enjoying music and I was beginning to memorize the lyrics to many of the songs she listened to. She would also sing along with the radio while she cooked, or cleaned, or even did laundry. Now and then she would go check on the other kids outside. She would yell at them if they strayed too far from the house, or if it was time to eat lunch or dinner.

The first time I was allowed to play outside with my brothers and sisters, I was beginning to feel a little normal. To tell you the truth, the neighbor kids and my relatives forgot that I had an accident. I can't begin to tell you how relieved I was.

In Texas the weather was dry and the wind would blow with dust everywhere. As an eight-year-old kid I had no hint of the things I was about to experience playing outside.

I remember playing on the pasture behind our house on the other side of the alley. At the time that lot was empty. One of my brothers and myself were making a road on the dirt for our small cars that were made out of metal with dark plastic tires. We loved playing with those cars and also with those plastic horses and cattle. Anyway, my eye often got dry when I was outdoors playing with cars. I rubbed my eye because it itched so bad and then I went back to playing. I developed this eye-rubbing habit that took me a long time to break, well, I don't think I've ever completely stopped rubbing my eye, but it has improved over years.

We heard my mom call us. She would often yell out, "Vegan a cenar!", which means, *come eat dinner*. We all ran to the door and I was the last one. It was still difficult for me to see things as I was running, so I took it a little slower than everyone else. When I finally reached the house, my mom looked at me and she freaked out, "David, you don't have your eye ... where were you playing!" I didn't say anything. I was just looking at her speechless while covering the left side of my face.

"We were playing over there in the pasture!" my brother yelled out.

My mom turned off the stove and ran out to the pasture. We all followed her and we all started looking for the eye.

A neighbor was walking by. In our neighborhood there were always people that walked by, not many owned cars. The neighbor was curious.

"What are you looking for?"

"Oh nothing, it's just a very expensive toy, we'll find it, thanks!" Mom said.

He kept walking as he looked at us and then he waved as he continued walking. After a few more steps he would turn around and look again.

My mouth was dry and I was starting to panic, it felt weird not having that object inside the left side of my face. The funny thing is that I was standing right next to it. I looked down and picked up the eye, "Mommy!" Mom turned around and grabbed it from me, "Okay, come on, we have to clean it good and I'll try my best to put it back in." We all went back inside and my mom waited on serving everyone dinner. She went into the bedroom to clean me up first before cleaning the eye with soap and water.

She struggled putting the eye back into the socket. After twenty minutes of trying and getting frustrated, she finally got it back in. What a scare, I knew that from now on I had to be more careful and I had to try not to rub my eye. We definitely needed to talk to the doctor the next time we went in. My mom needed some instructions on what to do when things like this happened.

3.

Kindergarten Was a Culture Shock

In the summer of 1966, I was about to hit culture shock and the education world. I was probably the most uneducated kid in class even though I was starting school a year late. My mom put me in this summer-kindergarten program to get me ready for the first grade.

I knew very little English since most of the language we spoke at home was Spanish. I would often hear my mom talk in English to doctors or Caucasian people that came around trying to sell us products, door-to-door. When I was growing up as a little kid, both my parents knew how to speak in English, but their vocabulary was minimal. I was informed that I had to go to school to start learning just like my older brothers and sister.

My oldest brother, Gilberto (who we called Gilbert), was tall for his age. He was usually the kid that brought new ideas to the house, whether it be a game or a sport that he learned about. He was intelligent and optimistic – he always did well academically. Then next was Guadalupe (who we called Lupee). Lupee now goes by Loop. My oldest sister, Louise, and my younger siblings, Richard and Diana, we all just kind of followed what the two oldest kids did. We all played together and now it was time for me to start kindergarten.

In Dimmitt, Texas, that summer, the kindergarten program was held at the Dimmitt Junior High near S.W. 7th Street. This two-story building was roughly two miles away from our home across the tracks. The building was also full of classrooms on both floors.

My memory is not great enough to remember much about kindergarten, but the one thing I'll never forget is the first day of school. My mom drove me to school that day. After being her constant companion for two years, I wonder what she was thinking? My guess, it was going to be a good break for her to relax a bit without me being there to watch and to deal with. Or maybe she was going to miss me and understood that I had to start school – that was important to her. She was the one that pushed us to get up every morning for school.

I remember holding my mom's hand as we walked to the classroom. I had no idea that my mom was going to leave me there. I thought she was going to be there with me the entire time. It had to be like the doctor's office where we would wait in a waiting room for a long period of time. I was ignorant about what was going to happen, I had never been to school before.

We met the teacher and her aid. That is one name that I can't remember, my kindergarten teacher. I do remember my first-grade teacher's name and the rest all through my sixth-grade year, and some of the junior high school teachers. For some reason the kindergarten teacher's name or her aid's name is a blur.

After my mom and I met the teachers, I was instructed to go take a seat. I did not want to separate from my mom, and I did not want to go sit with a bunch of Caucasian little kids that were staring at me. I was very insecure and I was very nervous. My mom insisted that it would be okay and she kept trying to pull me to my assigned desk. This wooden desk had a gray-metal chair attached to it. The class probably had about twenty-five kids sitting on chairs.

My mom said that she would buy me a little truck after school if I was good and sat on the chair to learn. Well, I have to admit that sounded pretty good. So I went and sat down. Mom told me she was going to be standing at the back and not to worry. When the teacher started talking to the class I would turn around and check to see if my mom was still there. She would wave and smile, then I would turn and listen to the teacher. I was finally engaged a little. After ten minutes I turned around to see if my mom was still there. I caught the back of her coat as she walked out of the classroom. I got up from the chair and started running to the door, "Mommy!" The teacher's aide stopped me and assured me it was going to be okay and that my mom was going to be back after school to pick me up. She closed the door behind her to not disrupt the class anymore. I was crying loud in the hallway, I'm sure the other classes could hear. In my mind, my mom had left me again, it reminded me of St. Anthony's Hospital all over again. It was a flashback of when her and my dad would come visit on the weekends and then leave. I would see the back of her coat.

I cried for awhile as I looked down with my hands over my face. That poor teacher's aide, she was earning her money that's for sure. But what a nice lady she was, very compassionate and kind. She had a way to calm kids down making them feel better. I have this memory that will never be deleted from my brain. She started singing this song that I would often hear on the radio at home. The song was, "Downtown" by Petula Clark. I understood very few of the lyrics at the time, but when the teacher's aide sang it, I could relate and it made me feel good and safe. I'd like to share some of the lyrics of that song with you.

> *When you're alone, and life is making you lonely you can always go*
> *Downtown*
> *When you got worries, all the noise and the hurry seems to help, I know*
> *Downtown*
> *Just listen to the music of the traffic in the city*
> *Linger on the sidewalk where the neon signs are pretty*
> *How can you lose?*
> *The lights are much brighter there*
> *You can forget all your troubles, forget all your cares*
> *So go downtown, things'll be greater when you're*
> *Downtown, no finer place for sure*
> *Downtown everything's waiting for you*
> *Downtown*

When I hear that song today, and of course it's an oldie, that's the memory I have. I'll always remember that teacher's aide and I feel so bad that I can't remember what her name was. She helped me feel safe and eventually guided me back into the classroom.

The second day was much easier for me. I don't know how I made it through that summer, my memory is lacking other than a few things. Here's one incident that just plain embarrassed me. I had no indication of just how ignorant and uneducated I was. The teacher calls on me to come up to the front of the classroom. She wanted me to name this four-legged object that was displayed in front of the classroom. Every kid in there was focused on me walking up to the front of the class. I just stared at it thinking as hard as I could. What was it? I didn't know what you called this in English, but I knew what it was called in Spanish. I was a head taller than most of the kids in the class and I was under a lot of pressure, I should have known what this object was, but I didn't.

A kid raised his hand, he was pretty short, his head probably came up to my shoulder. He said, "I know ... I know!" The teacher had me take my seat again. The little kid walks up with great confidence, "This is a table!" He smiled and looked right at me as if he was trying to tell me, *I'm smarter than you.* After that day, I never forgot what a table was.

To me, kindergarten was a culture shock. I had never seen so many Caucasian kids, girls and boys. I was one of a few Hispanics in the classroom. They spoke different than I did, they ate different than I did. At naptime, I remember seeing some of the most beautiful towels that the Caucasian kids would use to place on the floor. My towel was pretty old and wasn't as appealing.

I can't remember having a best friend. I do remember only talking to the teachers at lunchtime. I was mostly alone and I was too young to understand why. It was as if the other kids already had their friends. I didn't give it much thought at all, I just accepted the fact that I was different. I know that I talked to a few kids now and then, but most of the time I was focused on doing what the teachers wanted, and learning as much as I could, it was all very new to me.

I remember watching a film strip on *Hansel and Gretel* and *The Gingerbread Man*, I enjoyed those stories, I had never seen a projected image on a screen. As far as what I learned in kindergarten, well, I do remember studying letters a lot and maybe the sounds, but that's about it. In kindergarten, I don't remember any kid making fun of me, they mostly just avoided me. They saw me as different. One of my eyes was a lot larger than the other.

We would have naptime every day, it must have been after two hours of class time because I know kindergarten was not a full day. I got tired of seeing other kids get a piece of candy because they fell asleep. I could never fall asleep, I had too much going through my mind. The floor was so uncomfortable, and I didn't have a nice padded towel to lie on. One day I got clever and decided to fake that I had fallen asleep. I wanted a piece of candy like the kids that would always fall asleep. When it was time to wake up, the teacher turned on the lights. I kept my eyes closed and pretended to be asleep. The teacher walked over and tapped my shoulder, "David ... David." I pretended to slowly wake up. She said, "David gets a piece of candy!" My face lit up because I knew I was getting a piece of candy. I didn't feel very good about cheating, but I guess a little white lie didn't hurt anyone.

During the kindergarten summer I remember my dad would take me with him on the nights he had to clean the field house. The field house was a place where the varsity football team dressed up for practices or games. There was a weight room, lockers, and showers. This place smelled like sweat and dirty clothes. He had a muddy mess to clean up when it rained after the team practiced or played a game. I was tired and wanted to go home, but I think my mom must have been busy with the other kids or maybe even working at this carrot-processing plant that was a few blocks from where we lived – who knows. I watched him hose down the locker room and I watched all of the football helmets and cleats hanging on hooks at each locker spot. I often fell asleep on the bench watching my dad work so hard to get that place cleaned up. I often think about how hard he worked to feed us kids.

I only have a few memories that stick out from my kindergarten summer. Academically, I must have done okay, because they advanced me to the first grade.

4.

First Grade

I attended Dimmitt Elementary School, which consisted of two different buildings separated by a large playground. First through third grade were in the south-grade building and fourth through sixth grade were in the north-grade building. The junior-high building was up on a small hill a block away. This grade school has since changed the name to Richardson Elementary, Mrs. Richardson was my principal back then.

I adjusted pretty well as far as going to school, thank God for the kindergarten days. I was very excited to be entering first grade. My oldest brother, Gilberto, was getting close to ending his grade-school days. Louise and Loop would soon follow Gilberto.

My first-grade teacher was Mrs. White. She was a Caucasian older lady that I enjoyed having as a teacher. I think this teacher was the oldest of any teacher I ever had while I was going to school. She had to be past retiring age.

We, as a class, discovered that first graders did not eat lunch at the cafeteria, only second and third graders had that luxury – there wasn't enough space. We had to bring our own lunch and we ate in the classroom before stepping outside for recess. Our recess time was between the first and second-grade building wings. There was a grass area and teachers monitored students so they wouldn't stray off to the road or to the other recess areas on the school grounds.

That year was when I discovered that I could actually make friends. My eye looked good, but you could still tell there was a difference. When I turned my eyes to look one way, the movement of both eyes was not equal. I was aware of this and tried to turn my head more than just using my eyes to look in one direction. Sometimes I would forget and that's when kids would laugh at me. They would ask me to do that again. I refused and just shied away.

It didn't take long for me to cause a stir. I ran into the corner of a shelf and knocked an entire set of books to the floor along with the shelf. All the kids started laughing at me. I couldn't see the left side and as I walked in the classroom I bumped the shelf with my left shoulder. The teacher asked, "David, didn't you see that shelf?"

I remember three Hispanic kids the best, Miguel, Baldomero, and Isabel (Baldomero's sister). We were the minorities of the class and we all came from poor families. I'll start with Miguel. I would always make him laugh by doing silly things in the classroom, whether it was impersonating the teacher, or just flipping a pencil and making a funny noise when it landed. He started hanging around me during recess and then sitting with me when lunchtime came around. I kept thinking, *wow this is different, I never had any kid wanting to spend time with me before.* My self-esteem jumped up a notch. One thing about Miguel is that he never asked me anything about my eye. I was so used to kids asking me every time they saw me. I appreciated that about Miguel.

Baldomero, who I started calling, Baldy, was another kid I became friends with in my early school age. Baldy was someone who I played football with outside during recess. He was an athletic kid that made it fun for me because I was pretty athletic too. I loved running and passing the football or the baseball with him. We played tag and it was fun because Baldy and I were two of the fastest kids in our class.

His sister, Isabel, would hang around us at times, but it was during class time that I got to know her better. There was something about Isabel that I liked. I've heard of boys not liking girls in the first grade, believe it or not I feel that boys fake it a little.

I started to like Isabel in a different way. I wanted to cut out art paper at the same table she did. Her smile was to kill for. Her dark hair and green eyes along with her almost-white skin made her one of the prettiest girls in class. Was I crazy in first grade? I don't know, but Isabel sure made me nervous any time I was around her. She would smile at me and laugh. I was shy around girls at that age, my confidence lacked. I didn't want her to notice that my eyes were different, so I kept my distance.

I remember once, we were working on puzzles during lunch. The teacher would bring out the puzzles on rainy days or if it was too cold to go outside. Isabel and I were in the mix of a few kids that played with puzzles. She was the person that I got into trouble with for the first time. Mrs. White asked us to put the puzzles away. The other kids did just that, we both ignored her and kept smiling placing pieces of puzzle together. I was trying to get mine done before she did and she was doing the same. Mrs. White warned us once more, but it was like we couldn't hear her, we were too engaged in each other. We ended up going out into the hall and getting punished with a board. Back then teachers were allowed to spank students with actual boards. Every teacher, bus driver, or principal had their own board. Some teachers would even give the board a name. They would have them cut in a certain shape and some would drill holes through the board to make them swifter when they swung it.

Isabel and I had never experienced this awful and painful episode. I remember being out in the hall and Mrs. White explained to us again why she was giving us licks. She also said that she didn't like doing this, and it would teach us to think about listening more carefully the next time. Isabel went first, she got one lick. She started crying and walked back into the classroom. I was getting a little alarmed because, for one, I knew what it felt like to get hit with a belt, but I had never experienced getting hit with a board before. I remember Mrs. White's words, "Okay David, you're next." I bent slightly and touched the wall like she instructed me to do – *bam!* That hurt so bad, my entire bottom was stinging and tears came out of my eyes, but I tried not to break down crying.

Isabel and I were so embarrassed, I don't think we ever played with the puzzles after that. I know that even though we were little kids, I was friends with a girl and I felt she liked being around me despite the difference she saw in my two eyes. Some of the other kids treated me differently and avoided me.

When it was time to eat lunch, the teacher always apologized for not having a cafeteria big enough for the entire school. My lunch would often consist of a luncheon-ham sandwich with mayonnaise and a banana. Sometimes my mom would also put potato chips in the brown bag. I remember we had a choice of chocolate milk or regular white milk. I always picked chocolate milk. To this day, if I ever eat a ham sandwich, it reminds me of my first-grade year.

Miguel continued to be my friend the rest of the year, that was such a blessing to me. I know God was working with me, molding me and handing me experiences that I could handle. I don't know how I could have made it at that age without Jesus next to me, even when I didn't know it.

I was sad when I found out the news about Baldy and Isabel. One day they did not show up for school. I asked Mrs. White why Baldy had not been coming to school. Her reply almost made me cry, it hit me hard. They moved to Spring-Lake Earth, Texas, a tiny town about twenty miles from Dimmitt. It was tough to learn that two of my best friends would not return to school. They made me feel accepted. They laughed with me every day. It was a tough loss and I was heartbroken. I didn't see them again until my high-school days.

The rest of the year is a blur to me, I just can't remember much. I do know that my dad was a bus driver and a janitor for the school, so it was nice to have him around. I saw him cleaning up messes in the hallways, or sometimes in the boiler room where he maintained the heating system for the school. He had to get that heat going every morning. If something went wrong with the heat, he was the one that fixed it. My dad was mechanically inclined. One of his favorite hobbies was working on cars. I remember all of the staff calling him, Benny. Some would call him, Ben. I don't recall how he acquired those nicknames, his real name is Wenceslado.

I'll wrap up my first-grade year by saying that I enjoyed learning how to read for the first time. We used this book called, *Tip*. The first sentence I ever read was, *See Tip run?* And then, *Jane, see Tip run?* In the first text book we used, the dog's name was, *Tip*. Other books used the name, *Spot*. When it was reading time, the class was structured in a way that you could tell the kids that were more advanced than the others. I was put in a circle with the kids that were not very bright. This was humiliating to me because I didn't feel smart and I wanted to be in the circle of smart kids. I think I started being competitive that year.

I was going to learn how to read so I could be in the smart-kid group. At least that's how I felt. My friend Miguel was in the smart circle. That made me want to be there even more. I was frustrated and I didn't feel like I was as advanced as most of the kids in the classroom, but at least I was ahead of a few students.

The good news, I did make progress in every subject. My favorite was reading and art. I could visualize Tip running and Jane yelling at him while running behind the dog.

In art, I could draw better than most of the kids in my class. I remember getting praise from some of the kids. They would say, "Look at Dave's – wow!" That made me feel good. I wanted that feeling when I read out loud in front of everyone in class, but I knew I had to work harder at getting there.

5.

Second, Third, and Fourth Grades

In the second grade I remember getting new clothes before school started. Wow, new jeans from J.C. Penney. My mom and dad would use a charge card to buy us Christmas presents or school clothes. We didn't have any large department stores in Dimmitt. My parents would travel to Amarillo or Hereford.

Dimmitt was too small, I'm guessing back then the population was roughly 3,700 people, give or take a few hundred. There were two main roads that crossed in downtown Dimmitt, W. Bedford St. and N. Broadway St. There were a few gas stations and two big grocery stores, the Dimmitt Supermarket and Taylor and Sons. We also had one movie theater in the downtown area. After watching the movie you would stick to the floor. It was easy to reach any destination, whether a toy or tire store.

My brothers, sisters, and myself often walked to the TG&Y store, I don't know if this toy store exists anymore. Toys and crafts are what they sold there and it was one of my favorite stores at the time. We had a Piggly Wiggly store, which was a grocery store with some added products similar to TG&Y's stock. Dimmitt had a city park close to the center of town. We would play there often and walking back home was always a tiring hike.

Every day before school, we would watch *Sesame Street* in the morning while my mom fixed breakfast, I never heard so much yelling from her. We were never excited about going to school so early in the morning. I have much respect for my mom who kept us going all those years. I mean, six kids!

At 7:00 a.m. we would walk two blocks down the dirt road to catch the bus on E. Halsell Street, a paved road that was pretty decent. The standard bus stops were all along that street, which was much wider than the dirt roads along our neighborhood. I always wondered why our roads weren't paved like E. Halsell Street. Now that I'm all grown up I figured it out. There were these huge metal barns owned by a company that stored hay bales, cotton bales, and possibly other crops. I'm not sure what these buildings were, maybe important facilities. My guess is that these people, that had money, paved that street to make it convenient to haul cotton or hay bales to the storage unit after the harvest. We would ride our bikes out there since the street was so nice with no dirt flying like brown powder everywhere.

To the opposite side of where we lived (E. 4th and N.E. Dulin Streets), was W. Bedford Street and again there was another facility where grain was processed and stored. This was about four blocks from our house. Sometimes I could see the grain piling up all day long while the loud-annoying machines ran, especially during the summer and fall.

The poverty neighborhood I lived in was surrounded by small industry. The homes were inconsistent on appearances. Some were maintained and others were falling apart and never painted or remodeled. Most of the people just didn't have the funds it took to upkeep their home. This is just the way it was on that side of town.

When we arrived at the bus stop, which was at the corner of two streets, it was pretty cool to see my dad open the bus door as we stepped up to take a seat. The mornings were pretty quiet as most of the kids inside the bus were sleepy and not ready to wake up just yet. I was tired and my eye was always a problem. It was often discharging because of the infection that would come and go. When my mom and dad took me to the doctor's office in Amarillo every few months, the doctor would clean it. The treatment cleared the infection, and in a couple of days it felt much better.

In the afternoons after school, the young crowd in the bus was much louder and fights would even break out. I saw my dad work very hard while being a bus driver. I would never dream of wanting to do his job, he didn't get paid enough money for dealing with problem children. I witnessed my dad punish kids on the bus. He would definitely warn them first. Back then it was a normal thing to punish using a board. Teachers, bus drivers, or any other staff members were allowed to put kids back into line when they violated rules.

Growing up during grade school I witnessed too many fights. I personally tried my best to avoid fighting, I was too concerned about my eye and how far it would set me back if I were to get hit there. But one thing is for sure, I always defended myself if anyone picked on me physically. Oh, there might have been a couple of times where a smaller kid called me cross-eyed or wooden-eyed. Kids like that would end up getting a couple of punches from me. If the person was a little bigger, I'd always try to talk my way out of it before exchanging punches. If the person was much bigger than I was, well, I couldn't do anything about it, I just had to get out of that situation soon.

I never told anyone about my incidents with kids. The girls never bothered me, they would just ask, *what's wrong with your eye?* Sometimes they just laughed at me amongst themselves and then moved on.

When my older brothers were around I felt safe because if anyone made fun of me, they would have to deal with Gilberto or Loop, they were pretty tough guys. When my brothers weren't around, well, that's when some of the neighborhood kids would make fun of me. On the bus ride to school, there was a prank that I used to hate. I would hear kids that were sitting behind me laugh and I didn't know what they were laughing about. It couldn't have been me, I was facing the front. As they continued to laugh, I turned around only to see a kid's hand covering my left eye. They all knew I couldn't see out of my left eye. This was very hard for me to handle. The kid went back to his seat before I could turn around and punch him. I was so mad, sad, frustrated, and my self-esteem and self-worth was diminishing rapidly. My two brothers were sitting at the far back of the bus and did not see this.

John B was a kid in the neighborhood that took it to the next level of bullying and joking in front of all his friends. John was about seven years older than I was. He never physically hit me or anything, but his words were very harmful to my soul – the words tainted me. He was a lot bigger and stronger than I was. He was a leader with a non-productive objective. He also had a useless pack of uneducated slime following him. They were all Hispanic kids and they all lived in the same rough neighborhood that I lived in. Two streets from my house there was an all-African-American section. There weren't any Caucasian people that lived on the north side of the tracks that I remember.

When I was outside playing by myself, throwing a rubber baseball against the house and then catching it, John B. would come around with all his friends following him on their bikes. Their bikes would have a piece of cardboard taped to the spokes to make motor-like noises. They had these colored streamers hanging from the handle bars. He would yell out, "There's the boy with a glass eye!" He sang out loud, calling me one-eye Jack. John would sing with made-up words calling me more names and then laughing. His mob (a crowd without a reason) also laughed as they rode their bikes behind him leaving a trail of dust. I was so angry, but there wasn't anything I could do. Getting away from the neighborhood and going to school was nice and a huge relief, especially if that meant John B. was going to be on our street.

During my second grade year is when this started and continued for several years. I was called many names. Some kids at school would ask me to turn around and look a certain way. When I did, they would start laughing at me. "Did you see his eye, ha-ha!" I felt like somebody that didn't belong. I didn't want to tell my mom or dad, I don't know why. I guess I thought that it would all go away and the kids would not bother me anymore.

One of the most humiliating words that I heard from certain kids was, "David can't do that, he ain't got but one eye." I never responded to any of those comments, because if I did I knew it would make them badger me more. I just wanted them to stop. I knew that my older brothers couldn't be around me all the time.

My second-grade teacher was Mrs. Diaz. She was a pretty darn good teacher and her straight forwardness pushed me to learn how to write words on paper. I enjoyed that. I remember the Christmas party the last fifteen minutes of class. It was so much fun with all of the decorations and refreshments.

As far as after school, I started working for my dad. I now know that God was not going to give me too much of what I couldn't handle, but at that time all I knew was that it was nice not to go home right away. I remember feeling caged up by my own choice. There were times that I cried when I was alone in the school playground areas with no one around. I kept saying to myself, *why did this have to happen to me?* The moisture from the tears would make my eye feel less dry on a windy day.

Lunchtime during grade school was when I first learned I didn't like foods like cheese, spinach, green beans, and more. I just liked the food my mom cooked at home. Mrs. Diaz told me that if I didn't eat the spinach and green beans, I could not go out for recess. Okay, so I thought maybe I could outsmart my teacher. After I drank my milk, I would put the spinach or green beans inside the milk carton. "Good job, David! You ate your spinach!" My teacher was proud of me until one day she caught me. Needless to say I spent many days inside the cafeteria while everyone else played outside. I mostly enjoyed Wednesdays, that's when we had hamburgers and chocolate milk with some cake.

After school, my job was to empty all of the trash cans in each classroom in the entire school. There were three large hallways, first, second, and third grades. I used this canvas bag that was hooked around a metal frame with wheels on the bottom. I would wheel that bag from class to class emptying out each garbage can. When the large bag was full, I would roll it outside to the big dumpster and empty it out. Then I would go back in and start on the next hallway. It took me a good hour and a half to complete my job. My dad paid me by giving me a dime to buy a coke from this vending machine in the staff room. Yes, a coke back then would only cost a dime – amazing how inflation works. I found out why they said, *things go better with Coke.* It tasted so good after working so hard.

I did that every day for my dad to help him, he was so overloaded with cleaning that school every day. I was pretty tall as a second grader and could do the job pretty well. If a classroom had raisins, well, I would help myself to some, I was hungry and hadn't eaten anything. No one told me I couldn't help myself. Hungry kids don't ask, they take. I didn't know any better, and I didn't say anything to my dad either. This job went on all through my second and third grade, and even fourth-grade years. After that, my dad's bus duties were a little more hectic and the school had hired more help to clean up the classrooms and hallways.

When my dad was little, he didn't make it past the fifth grade. On an upside, he did know how to read and he spoke English pretty well. He would often help me on some reading assignments. If I didn't pronounce a word correctly, he would make me say it again until I got it right. I enjoyed being around my dad. A lot of teachers liked him at the school. Sometimes when kids found out that the janitor was my dad, they would ask, "That's your dad? Wow!" I felt that because he operated these electric-powered cleaning machines and drove the bus, they all thought he was pretty cool. I have to agree with them, it was pretty cool to have my dad at the school I was attending. I just didn't like the late hours, it made it a long day for me.

When we got home we ate and then I did my homework and took a bath. Most of the meals I ate growing up were beans, rice with tomatoes, and tortillas. During the summers we ate more fruits and vegetables. We didn't have a shower and every night was a nightmare for the line of six kids taking baths. My mom would heat up some water and put it in a bucket. I poured cold water into the bucket to cool it down a bit, then used a cup to scoop water to pour over my head and wash up. This went on for the entire time I lived in Dimmitt, Texas. We never had a shower in our house. Sometimes my dad would take the entire family to the school at night, since he had the keys. We would use the showers there, that was such a nice treat. To be able to use a shower feeling that warm water spraying down, well, it was priceless. I only remember us doing that a few times, and when we did, it was like luxury. I would dream that some day I would have my own shower in my house.

During my younger years, us kids would spend a lot of time being creative outside with one thing or another. I can't remember who came up with this idea, it could have been my older brother, Gilberto, but I truly can't remember. The first time I remember shooting a basketball at anything was when we flattened a cardboard box. We opened this average size box. If you can visualize that it showed both ends wide open, then you can see how a ball could go through it. We somehow nailed it or stapled it to the porch rail. We used a small basketball that we bought at the TG&Y.

We watched the NBA on TV. We had a radio for the longest time, but we eventually bought a TV, it wasn't new or anything, but we were able to get reception in three channels, which were probably the only TV stations available in the late 1960s, when our TV worked – ABC, CBS, and NBC. We got clever and used foil paper on the rabbit-ears antenna on top of the TV. Players like John Havlicek; Nate Archibald; Wilt Chamberlain; Pistol Pete Maravich, and Bill Russell were a few of the players I remember watching as a little kid. In my opinion, Pistol Pete was one of the most exciting players to watch.

That cardboard box was our basket. We played a lot with this box. That's the first time I can remember picking up the basketball. All of us kids were outside playing for countless hours. My mom had to yell at us to come eat dinner. During football season, again, we would play football outside. It was usually Gilberto and Richard against Loop and myself for either sport. We tried to make the teams as even as possible, this would make it more fun and fair. The girls would normally play inside. Now and then they would come outside to play with the brothers.

When I entered third grade, my new teacher was Mrs. Keller. She was my favorite teacher of all grade-school-time. I'm guessing she was in her late twenties, thin, and attractive. She always greeted the students with a smile and she always seemed to be happy, but yet serious if needed. The world changed for me when I started reading better than ever. I was sent to a speed-reading class to learn how to read faster. I don't know if having one eye was a factor, but it must have been. I'm almost certain I could have been a faster reader with two eyes. There were a selected group of kids that would go to this thirty-minute session once a day. The teacher used this film-strip projector. She would insert a huge tape reel into the projector and we would read sentences on the screen against the wall. I remember having so much fun just challenging myself to read faster. I learned how to read well that year and it was fun the way the teacher taught us all.

I loved music and learned all about notes and half notes. I also sang songs and performed in school Christmas programs and spring programs. I looked forward to learning how to play the guitar on my own and singing.

I always wanted do the right thing. My mom and dad preached that often to us kids – some more than others. I never wanted to get into trouble. At church I had been taught that doing wrong was a sin. I started believing in God because of my mom and how much she always stressed the fact that there was a God. Not only that, but the board or the belt were awful painful. I still remember getting hit in the first grade when Isabel and I got into trouble.

My Uncle Jessie played instruments very well and so did my dad. They would often play the guitar and the accordion. I was intrigued and told myself, *I have to learn how to play the guitar.* My dad borrowed the guitar from my Uncle Jessie and I started practicing a lot. When my Uncle would drop by to visit, I would bug him about teaching me a song called, "La Bamba". He taught me the basic chords, but ironically it was John B. in later years that taught me how to play that song in more detail adding a few more notes and chords to the tune.

I played the guitar a lot, it was something I could do that filled my emptiness. It was very difficult because I couldn't make the chords sound right, my fingers were not placed correctly across the frets. Eventually in time, I mean weeks not just days, I learned how to play the guitar. It was my favorite instrument to play and still is today.

When I got tired of practicing the guitar, I would go out to the porch where the box was hanging, it was pretty beat up at that point. I would still shoot baskets imitating the NBA players on TV. I would pretend like I was playing in a game and there was an actual defender in front of me. And then I pretended like the crowd was going wild after I made a basket. It was my way of coping when no one wanted to be around me. I think that kids just got scared of my appearance, especially when one of my eyes was a lot bigger than the other. Until I grew a little, the eye sizes would be different, which made a lot of sense, just like the doctors told me.

If neighbor friends like Rudy, Freddy, or Ralph came over to play, they would always ask one of my older brothers, "What's wrong with his eye?" I didn't say anything despite the fact that I could hear them whispering. My older brothers would have to explain to them what happened to me. After that, they understood and never asked again. Those three friends would play with us, but they would never play when I was the only one there. I became used to having fun with the neighbors when my brothers were around, I guess the neighbors viewed me as so different that it was uncomfortable for them.

There were many times through my life that I felt like a misfit, like I didn't belong. I felt sad, and I knew there was nothing I could do about it. You can't make kids be your friends, they have to be willing to want to be around you. I remember just thinking about improving my skills in shooting the basketball or kicking the football. Playing the guitar was fun and when I actually got a chord or a note to sound right, it was like, accomplishment!

As a very young kid I learned that people appealed to me at times despite my appearance when I could do something they couldn't. My neighbor friends were super interested to watch me play the guitar. *Play that again!* they would say. And then soon they wanted me to teach them how to play a song on the guitar. This did some amazing things to my self-esteem. All of a sudden I felt important. It felt good for someone to look up to me and actually want to be around me. God was carrying me, even when I didn't know it.

Proverbs 24:12 If you say, "Behold, we did not know this," does not He who weighs the heart perceive it? Does not He who keeps watch over your soul know it?

Entering the fourth grade, to me, was a turning point. Previously, I had been a student that was placed in an average-academic class with average students. Back in those days, schools would place kids with the same academic-level students. This meant that slower students, average students, and smarter students would all be placed together in different classrooms. I don't think it's like that anymore, but it definitely used to be that way at my school.

My fourth-grade teacher, Mrs. Haulf, married during the school season and became Mrs. Story. She was in her early thirties and had a serious-type personality. This newly engaged teacher was assigned to teach the smart kids who could read well and had received excellent grades the previous year. It didn't take me long to figure out that I was placed in a smart classroom. Wow! from not being able to define what a "table" was during kindergarten to now being placed in the smart-student class, I was on cloud nine!

I was one of the few Hispanic kids in that class. Lupe was another Hispanic in there, she always treated me with respect. I felt her and I were about the same as far as academic performance. Again, there was maybe a total of four Hispanics in this class of maybe thirty kids, the rest were Caucasian kids.

This class was the first time I had a larger group of intelligent Caucasian kids. So I knew I was in a smart class for the first time in my life. What a great feeling it was to me, I didn't recognize any of the kids from my previous third-grade year. Those kids were all placed on an average or low-academic class.

In the fourth grade I started noticing the different ethnic types of kids and the different skin colors – mostly at recess time. The neighborhood that I lived in was definitely the poverty side of town. There were mostly African-Americans and Hispanics. I recognized several kids from my neighborhood as I scoped the playground, I just never associated with many of them. My parents kept us close to the house away from any negative influences or danger. I didn't understand all of this too much back then, but now that I'm older, it's pretty clear what my parents did for us kids.

This fourth-grade thing was all new to me and I was still learning a lot about many things. I was also emotionally dealing with my appearance and how other kids would treat me in this new class. My dad was no longer around since they had a new set of janitors for an entirely different building holding fourth through sixth-grade classes. I did continue to work for him at the south-grade section. After school I continued to do my job that I was trained well in, emptying classroom-garbage cans. I didn't want to ride the bus after school to avoid the kids that made fun of me. I felt safer working for my dad while he left the school to do his bus route. When he returned from his bus route, he would finish up sweeping the hallways and other required maintenance in the school. He would continue to give me a dime to buy a coke at the staff-room vending machine, but not all the time. Money was always tight in our family so that was always a treat for me.

When I wheeled out the garbage bag to the big dumpster outside of the school, I watched this kid that was a grade ahead of me. Johnny Hampton reminded me, of me. He would practice shooting the basketball on his driveway hoop. The difference, his hoop was a lot nicer and he didn't have to dribble on hard dirt like me. I often waved at him from a distance, and sometimes I would talk to him across the paved street. I never got brave enough to ask him if I could shoot baskets with him. But I definitely saw the passion he had for basketball. We both eventually became great basketball players, it was our passion. That moment was the first time I thought to myself, *some day I would love to have a basketball court in my backyard. I saw how Johnny could focus with no one else around, I wanted that some day.*

Sometimes I would sit in a classroom before taking the garbage out. My eye was bothering me and it would hurt. I would ask God, *why did this have to happen to me?* I would sit there and I would start crying, because I wanted to ride the bus in the afternoon to see some of the kids that I went to school with. Not all kids were mean – there were many that did not make fun of me. Sometimes all it took was for one kid to make fun of me and then it was like throwing gasoline on a small flame. A roadblock in my mind prevented me from riding the bus, because I would run into kids like, John B., and then other kids would hear and spread the jokes even further. Trust me, the afternoons were much worse than the mornings. Some kids would try to imitate me by squinting one eye and opening the other eye. They all would laugh. No thanks, I didn't want to be around any of that. It was too humiliating and demeaning. It was a very long day and I would often do my homework while waiting for my dad.

Throughout my life I have asked God that question, *why me?* And every time I think to myself, *would I rather that this happened to anyone else?* What if this happened to my brother who was holding the other end of that hose with that wire? The answer in my head was always the same. I would not want this to happen to anyone else. Another question I would often ask myself is, *if I had a wish to be someone else who would it be?* My answer in my head was always the same. I would not want to be anyone else, I would want to be me. Oh sure I admired certain people, I think most of us do at one time or another, but I was what God created, I was happy with me despite the hardship I was going through. I know I mentioned this passage before, and I'll mention it again, it is so strong and comforting.

Proverbs 3:5-6 Trust in the Lord with all your heart and do not lean on your own understanding. In all your ways acknowledge Him and He shall make your paths straight.

I started adjusting to the fact that I was different and yet wanting to prove that I could be just as normal as any kid in my classroom. I appreciated that none of the teachers throughout my grade-school years asked me about my eye. Did they even notice? I'm sure they did, adults treat people differently when they see something different, or I should say most adults.

Mrs. Story didn't treat me any different than any other student, I liked that about her. She was the type that made some kids cry because they couldn't get the right answer on the board – she was tough and it was important to her that all the kids learn. So I worked very hard to not put myself in a position where she would yell my head off. I'm not saying that this was good for all kids, I'm sure some were stressed to come to school because of her teaching style. I'm thinking she probably had things going on in her private life and maybe took it out on her students.

Sometimes we would read a story, heavens, I don't remember what stories, it's been way too long. What I do remember is each of us getting called on to read next after a student finished their turn reading. And trust me, you wouldn't want to lose your place in whatever paragraph we were on, because Mrs. Story would come down on you so hard – whew!

I enjoyed the spelling contests we had. Mrs. Story would always have competitions in spelling and it was always girls against the boys. I was a pretty good speller, I studied hard and in most of my tests I received one-hundred percent. I was getting to be very competitive and I didn't want to get a lower grade than others. Words for me came easy to spell once I saw them and had a chance to study. One thing that frustrated me is never being able to beat Tobin or Dana, they seemed to always be the last ones left in the competition, man were they sharp. I do believe that Mrs. Story could control who won every time based on the tough words she called out. This prevented one group from always winning. Fun time in the spelling world. That class was so much fun for me even though we had a crazy lady as a teacher, nothing personal Mrs. Story, much respect for your style of teaching that helped me become a smarter kid. I can't speak for some of the other kids, and there were a few things I would do differently, but all in all, I learned a lot that year.

There were a few wealthy kids in my class. I had a few embarrassing moments that didn't make me feel too good about wearing some of the clothes I wore. Yes, they were hand-me-downs or clothes given to my mom by wealthy people she ironed clothes for. Some of my pants were patched up and some of my shirts were sewn by my mom. They were used, and I have to hand it to my mom ... she never allowed us to go to school with torn clothes. Trust me, we played outside a lot. Tackle football with neighbor kids would result in torn clothes – especially on the knee area.

I'll fill you in on one story, and trust me, there were more. Please understand, that I would rather a wealthy person make fun of my clothes, the way I walked, my hair, my shoes, or me running into desk corners that I didn't see, than my physical appearance pertaining to my left eye.

I still remember her name and the way she looked at me. I vaguely have a memory of what was said to Jo Beth by one of her friends. It might have been something like, *what happened to your hair, did you forget to plug in your hair dryer?* The entire class started laughing. So naturally I started laughing too. I thought it was funny like everyone else. Jo Beth turned and looked at me, I was sitting on the aisle next to her.

"What are you laughing at? My mom was going to throw away those clothes you're wearing. She gave them to your mom ... you should be grateful."

She then gave me a snobby look and turned back around. As embarrassing as that was, I responded in the most honest way I could.

"Yeah, well my mom worked for these clothes, she ironed the clothes you're wearing, you should be grateful," I responded.

Some of the students cheered on my comment before the teacher settled us down. I was always nice to Jo Beth and I didn't know why she displaced her aggressions on me. I guess I was an easy target.

Some teachers chose to ask every student to stand up and share what they received as Christmas gifts the first day back from the holidays. Unfortunately, my fourth-grade teacher was one of those. I felt so envious of my wealthy friends. They stood up and spoke out proudly of the nice presents they got for Christmas. I heard, mini bikes, ten-speed bikes, skis, dogs, Dingo boots, and all sorts of electric games. After they were done sharing, some of the students would say, "Wow! That's groovy."

I dreaded standing up and sharing what Santa brought me, although I knew it was my parents that bought the gifts. I was tempted to lie and share things that my mind only dreamed of having. Instead, I was honest and made it sound good. I would say, *I got some new clothes, a record player, fireworks, oranges, and an electric football game.* I almost said that I got a Honda mini-bike, but I knew that would have been a lie.

We had physical education and choir outside of the classroom. Physical education was one of my favorite classes, I loved sports and learning about new sports. It was so nice to get out of the classroom and just run and be active. During P.E. the boys would go to one end of the gym and the girls would be at the other end. There were times that the girls would be together with the boys if there was some kind of fitness testing done.

I knew of boys having girlfriends in the fourth grade. I would hear, *who are you going with?* This meant, who is your girlfriend or boyfriend? There were a few of my classmates that had girlfriends, I think the most that happened was holding hands, or sitting next to each other. I never thought any girl would be interested in me, so I ruled that out and just accepted the fact that I would never have a girlfriend. Sports however, grabbed my undivided attention.

It was at recess one day that I was walking along this eight-foot fence that separated the football field where the varsity team practiced and the recess area. There was also this building called, the field house. I knew it well since my dad would take me there when I was a toddler. The fence was made out of metal with small squares as the design, but anyone could see right through it. The varsity team was practicing and I could see the practice jerseys with a label on the back that read, "Dimmitt Bobcats". The helmets were purple with a large "D" on both sides. When I heard the players grunt as they blocked for the runner, and the cheers as they got pumped up after a good play, well, naturally I was intrigued and the whole aspect caught my attention. The way the quarterback passed the ball and the way the receivers caught it for a long gain of yardage was impressive to me. That inspired me to want to be one of those guys some day.

We started attending the varsity games on Friday nights. My brothers and I would walk to the games. Early in the season the weather was warm, but later in the season during October and November, the weather got colder. Sometimes the team would play in a foot of snow.

I remember the first time I attended a varsity football game. It was us four brothers that walked across town from our neighborhood. Gilberto was usually the leader and somewhat responsible for the younger siblings. We decided to climb the fence from the backside. I felt a little guilty because I knew it was kind of like stealing, but Gilberto convinced us it would be okay. So we all climbed over that eight-foot fence and got in. I don't think anyone saw us. We were walking towards the bleachers when we were approached by this gentleman in a three-piece suit.

We were all a little alarmed and didn't know what to expect. Gilberto walked right up to the gentleman. I was thinking to myself, *what are you doing?* Gilberto asked the gentleman, "Could you tell us where we can pay? We haven't paid yet." The gentleman looked at us and said, "You know what, I like honest people, let me pay your way." He took out a ten-dollar bill and handed it to my brother. We all looked at each other and didn't say anything. We just kept walking to the gate to pay for our tickets. And, we had money to buy food at the concession stand as well. It's funny how I've passed that forward throughout my life because of that gentleman.

6.

Summer of 1970

The summers in Texas were hot and sometimes very humid. We're talking anywhere from 95 degrees to 110 degrees. When thunderstorms hit they brought gushing waters from the sky, it certainly cooled things down for a day or two. The tornadoes were scarier than any kind of ferocious weather we had, and I'm talking like golf-ball size hail too. Those horrible patterns were normally during June or July. Some summers we never saw a tornado, which was always a good thing. One of our neighbors had a cellar, during the tornado warning we would always run to it and walk down the steps. At the bottom we all stared at each other in fear. The room was solid concrete all around with a few cracks and spiders crawling everywhere. The older kids would always crack jokes once they knew we were out of danger. The Lord brings people together in strange ways sometimes.

After a week into the summer, my mom and dad had a talk with us kids. They informed us about a farmer that hired us to work for him. I remember the last name well, it was Roberts. There were several wealthy farmers with acres of land just outside of Dimmitt. We needed the money for school clothes and for a trip to see my mom's side of the family. As long as the farmer allowed the kids to work, it was going to happen. I think that year, I was the youngest of our family that became a labor worker. Richard and Diana were much too young. My mom, Gilberto, Louise, and Loop joined me for a sacrificial adventure that I would not want any kid to go through.

I woke up at 5:30 a.m. along with all my brothers and sisters on a summer day. My mom was adamant about being sure that we got an early start. "Time to get up, let's go!" Mom would yell at the top of her lungs. That was never fun for me since I was not a morning person at all. Both my mom and dad taught me great work ethics and it started with the field-work days chopping weeds.

My dad worked year-round at the school, he had many things to do as far as maintenance, like waxing all of the floors, cafeteria and all. Sometimes he would paint walls at the school, or fix broken boiler parts.

Mr. Roberts had several cotton, soybean, and cornfields – weeds grew all around the crop. The routine was quite simple, we would eat tacos with beans and bacon, sometimes eggs or potatoes in them, depending on what my mom had available. After eating breakfast, my dad would drive us all out to the field which was about fifteen miles outside of the town. He would drop us all off. The two youngest would go back with him. I don't know if my grandma watched them while he worked or if he actually took them to work with him. At any rate, we started working by chopping the weeds on this field with long-rows. The rows were half-mile long if we walked one way.

It was a true nightmare for me. I was tired after the first round of chopping weeds. We each had our own hoe and my mom taught me how to look for the weeds and to not cut the crop. It took practice on my part, but I finally got the hang of it. My mom was watching us, especially me, to make sure we didn't miss any weeds. She would yell at us, but in a joking way. She was happy that we would also get paid, her mood was uplifting whereas my mood was depressing and negative. I didn't want to be there. I wanted to be home punting the football or swimming at the local pool. We would often go swimming during summers and it only cost us twenty-five cents – definitely a place I would have preferred. Some of my school friends would talk about the camps they would have fun at. Others would share their Disneyland adventure.

The days were long and lunchtime was something we all looked forward to. My feet were tired from walking up and down the dirt rows of crop. My mom brought this huge container with cold ice tea that was sweetened with sugar – nothing tasted better on a hot day. We could only drink some when we made an entire round, one row to the end of the field and a different row returning for a drink of tea. We could hear the motor on a well that provided irrigation.

I forgot about my eye, the sweat gave it more moisture and it felt good. I leaned on the hoe to rest. After thirty seconds, my mom would yell, "Don't lean on the hoe ... the boss is watching us!" I just turned to her and gave her a mean look, "I'm tired!"

Now and then we would run into a snake or a field rat while chopping weeds. My brothers would kill it and then scare my sister, Louise, as they threatened to throw it at her. They would laugh and they enjoyed teasing her. My sister would scream and run to my mom. My mom got after my older brothers and made them go up farther ahead of us. Oh yeah, we had lots of excitement while working out on those fields.

At one end of the field there was an irrigation ditch with curved pipes laying on the ground. These aluminum pipes were used to squirt the water along the rows keeping the crop watered. Farm workers would go out and shake the pipes to create a suction that would force the water to continuously feed through the trenches of the rows. This was before farmers had automatic irrigation systems.

I remember taking dives into the ditch filled with cool-running water just to refresh myself with coolness. Sometimes there would be no wind blowing at all. It was hard to breath at times. And then finally there was a small breeze that cooled me because of the sweat pouring down my body. I would always wear a long-sleeved shirt and a hat. I didn't want to get sunburned from the scorching sun.

Each day became harder for me, it was not fun. Sometimes I would stand there and look up, and ask God, "Why?" I often thought what it would be like to live in a big house and to go on vacations like my friends at school did, at least the wealthy ones. It just didn't seem fair to me that I had to work like this at eleven-years old. When it rained, my mom would have to call the farmer to see if the field was too wet to work. Work was normally cancelled until the fields were dry enough to walk on. Those days were times I would celebrate because I would get to sleep all morning long and not think about those terrible fields.

We would start work at 6:30 a.m. and finish at 4:00 p.m. My dad wasn't always there on time to pick us up, so we had to wait for him. Finding some shade was always a challenge. Sometimes we would lie under a huge weed that looked like a small tree. Now and then we were working on a field that had a few trees next to the dirt road, which made a much better shade.

My mom would bring a large water jug that lasted all day long. Sometimes she would make cold-ice tea to pour in the jug. She was a pretty strong lady. I never thought about the weight of that jug. She picked it up and moved it to different locations on the field throughout the day. This was while supervising us and chopping weeds herself. She also made and packed all of the food we ate every day. Mom made some huge sacrifices for us kids.

I feel so bad about the times I complained because I had to wake up at 5:00 a.m. I never once thought about thanking my mom for cooking us breakfast every morning and for teaching us how to work. Now I thank God for blessing me with a lady like my mom, I was very lucky to have someone like her in my life.

Mom was firm with us, and yet had the talent to make us laugh out on the hot fields. She knew we were young and that we did not want to be out there working hard.

By the second week, I started to think about what my friends at school were doing for their summer. I'm sure some were at Disneyland or on a camping trip. Some would travel to a far away place to ski. I had no clue what they meant at the time, but I'm sure it was more fun than what I was doing.

Field-work pay was not good. We would walk and chop weeds on the dirt fields for $1.25 per hour. I was beginning to think that this was all there was in life for us. To be honest with you, I would rather be doing this than having a kid make fun of me and how my eyes looked. In that sense it was a blessing in disguise. I'm telling you, God works in mysterious ways.

One Friday, which was the last day of the work week, and a day we all looked forward to, there was a private plane flying over us spraying chemicals. I don't know if the pilot saw us or not, but he came awful close to hitting us. We all dived to the ground. My mom yelled out, "Close your eyes!" Throughout the many summers that we worked this happened often. I don't know what those chemicals did to me, I sure hope nothing serious.

The following year was much better since my dad purchased a 1955 Chevy Pickup. It was old, and with my dad's mechanical skills, not a problem. Gilberto drove it out to the fields while my dad was at work. Some of us rode in the back.

I started driving a stick-shift, or standard, when I was eleven – it was so much fun! I learned how to drive out on the farm fields and on the long dirt roads with no one around. In the Texas Panhandle you can see for miles, the land is flat.

After the fields were completed, my mom and dad drove out on a Saturday to collect our paycheck. My memory is so fresh. Mr. Roberts was not at home, his wife told us that he was out on the field in his truck. We drove out to the field that looked very clean – no weeds at all, thanks to my mom's training.

Mr. Roberts wrote us a check to include everyone's hours. My mom and dad had such huge smiles on their faces. I wish my brothers and sisters could have seen that. Mr. Roberts told other farmers about us and how we did excellent work. As you can imagine we had more farm work ahead of us. My dad gave us each a little money to spend, but most of it went for school clothes, and for the trip to Oregon that we were about to go on. We were a little excited since we had never seen the ocean before, we were told that it was amazing. I had seen ponds and small lakes, most of them with very little water. Buffalo Lake was close to Canyon, Texas, but it eventually went dry.

My mom was so excited to see her mom. Since we didn't have a telephone, my mom would ask our neighbors if she could use their phone. They were always very generous. Mom communicated with my Grandma Paula (pronounced Powla), and the visit was planned. The plan was to spend a couple of weeks visiting and then return to Texas. My dad had a secure job working for the school district, and cleverly he took some vacation time.

I grew up knowing my dad's side of the family. His brother Jessie and his family were closest to us. From my mom's side of the family there were two families. My Uncle Jose and his family, they lived in Friona, Texas.

The other family was my mom's sister, Olivia and her family. They lived in Brownfield, Texas, which was over 100 miles away from Dimmitt. When they came for a rare visit we would have a blast with them. If the Torres family would visit they would stay an entire week at our house. If we visited them, same thing. We would see them maybe once a year until they moved to the state of Washington. My mom and dad had other brothers and sisters, but we never saw them as much.

So it was set, and to us kids, this was an adventure that we all looked forward to. I kept thinking, *I'll be able to tell my friends at school that we went to Oregon.* At the same time I was a little nervous because I had not met my other grandma and to tell you the truth all I could think about was, *what are they going to say about my eye, am I going to hear my mom tell the whole story again?* I carried that thought with me for many years. When I met a new person, they would look at me like I was something from outer space. I learned slowly to adjust and give that person time to process the visual of a different-looking human being.

I remember leaving early in the morning. We had a navy blue 1963 Ford Galaxie and my dad had it all tuned up and ready to go. Most of the luggage was in the trunk, but the blankets and pillows were all around us inside the car. This was for our traveling comfort, if you want to call two adults and my sisters in the front seat and four boys in the back seat, comfort. This trip was my longest taken in a car.

Let's start with my older brothers, picking on me, or not letting me sleep. They were bullies at times. One brother used a feather and rubbed my ear with it to keep waking me up. That drove me crazy, they just laughed. We had no air conditioner so it was very hot. If the car broke down with a flat tire or an alternator problem, we would have a long wait until my dad could get a part at a close-by town and then install the part. He was a good mechanic so that was a true blessing for our family. I think we broke down in two places, Colorado and Utah. The other stops were just to rest or get some food, whether it be a fast-food place or a grocery store for sandwiches. We had to make our money last the entire trip.

My poor dad, he did the entire driving for three full days. We were finally in the northwest past Idaho and headed to visit my Aunt Olivia and family. My mom's sister moved her family to Moses Lake, Washington, years ago. We hadn't seen them in a very long time. We would stay with them a few days and then drive to Oregon, which is right next door to Washington.

My mom communicated with her sister previously, she took care of the arrangements. They had upgraded their house, it had three floors which made our house in Dimmitt look very small. With a large family like theirs, it was a great investment – they seemed to have done well. My Uncle Meliton landed a good job in Moses Lake and he was a very smart man financial-wise.

As we drove up to this big house, the first one out of the car was my mom. The first one out of the house was my aunt. Every time these two saw each other they would break down in tears. Growing up in their youth they were close, but now lived thousands of miles apart. Certainly now that I'm older I understand, but as an eleven-year-old kid, I didn't get it. I was so excited to see my cousins that I hadn't seen in so many years.

My cousin Paul walked up to me and literally looked up.

"Man you've grown, you're tall!"

I guess I never thought about it, but I had grown a few inches since the last time I saw Paul. My brother, Richard and I, mostly hung out with Paul and Jimmy anytime we would get together. Loop and Gilberto would hang out with Mel, they were close in age. The never-ending debates between Gilberto and Mel were entertaining, but got boring after awhile.

Baseball was my cousins' favorite sport. I learned a lot about baseball from my cousin, Paul. We'd play catch a lot. One of my favorite times with the Torres cousins was playing baseball, we had enough kids to make two teams. There was this pasture in front of their house, home plate and three bases, we wore it down.

I remember hearing the words, *who is the one that had that accident on his eye?* I never responded to that. I didn't want anyone to know it was me. It was always a matter of time when they would all look at me carefully and then they knew. Normally

I left the room or something. For some reason it was embarrassing and something I was ashamed about despite the fact that I shouldn't have been. I felt, deep inside, that I wanted to be normal, with two eyes that could see everything. I hated accidentally knocking over things in someone else's house. Throughout my lifetime I knocked over many things including stacks of cans at the grocery store as I walked by. It was quite embarrassing in a different way. It didn't affect me too much since people thought the incident was honest and it could have happened to anyone. If you're at a store, try closing one eye and walk around the place. You'll get an idea of what I was going through.

The week went by fast, and I knew we needed to get to Oregon to see my aunts, uncles, grandma, and grandpa. I had never met any of them. I was a little scared and nervous at the same time. We loaded up the car and said our goodbyes. It was so good to see my cousins again, it had been a very long time. I think my mom was grateful that she had this opportunity to spend with her older sister, Olivia.

It took us the entire day to arrive at our grandma's house in Oregon. The freeways were so packed with traffic. I had never seen that much traffic. Amarillo, Texas, the largest city in the Texas Panhandle wasn't close to the size of Portland, Oregon. I remember seeing so much that I had never seen before. The weather was much cooler in Oregon than it was in Texas. I noticed so many differences, not only culture-wise, but also how the people spoke. They all had a different accent where we had a little southern drawl. Texans say, *where y'all going?* Oregonians say, *where you guys going?* It was strange to me that in Oregon, people called boys and girls, guys. In Texas, guys were boys.

I couldn't get over the beautiful Columbia River that I was watching as we drove by Portland up high on a bridge that had three lanes on it going one way. I was in awe of the huge buildings that I had never seen in my entire life. The evergreens and the mountains were a sight that every kid should see, it was stunning. The air smelled clean and fresh. The cars, semi-trucks, and motorcycles would make nonstop noise the entire time we were on the freeway passing by Portland, the biggest city in Oregon.

As we headed south on I-5, a major freeway that never slept, I'd hear my mom reading each freeway sign out loud, "There's Woodburn, get off on that exit." She was getting excited, because she hadn't seen her mom in years. I don't ever remember my grandma coming to Dimmitt and I was eleven years old. My mom's brother, Uncle Pete flew to visit us in Dimmitt one time. He was married to Jan at the time. Pete was also able to visit his brother, Jose, in Friona, Texas. Other than that, I don't remember any of my mom's side of the family. All of us kids were about to meet some uncles, aunts, cousins, and our grandparents for the first time.

Once we were through Woodburn, we found our way to 99E, a two-lane paved road. In Oregon there are definitely more paved roads than in Texas where I was raised. It makes sense because it rains so much in Oregon.

My mom saw the sign that said, "Gervais." She raised her voice with an eager sound. I was actually starting to get excited myself, but it was more of, *great I can finally get out of this car*. I couldn't get over how green everything was, the lawns, the crop fields, and the trees. We finally drove up my grandma's driveway. Their house was a lot bigger than what we lived in. It had concrete steps in front that led you to the covered porch. The house was two stories, but the second story was more like a large attic. It was a cool older-looking house.

Never had I seen anyone jump out of a car as fast as my mom did, she ran up the porch steps and embraced my Grandma Paula. They were both in tears. Again, I was so young and to me it was strange. As we all walked up the steps my grandma had calmed down a little with a few tears still running down her face, "This is Gilberto? Come on in." Paula would ask my mom who each kid was as she wore a large smile on her face.

Mom knew that I didn't want anyone there to know about the accident I had, but it looked like some already knew. It wasn't too bad because in a couple days they would forget about it and things would be more relaxing for me. We met my Aunt Lydia who was a cheerleader for the Gervais High School football team. I thought she was pretty cool, she was athletic. She could outrun all of us except for Gilberto and Loop.

There was a baseball park across the street from their house, where we would often race and play tag. My Uncle Edward played for the football team at Gervais. He was short, but pretty quick. He mostly hung out with Gilberto during our stay. My Uncle Israel was planning on playing quarterback for the high school. My Aunt Delia was not as athletic as Lydia but she was a very nice girl and she hung out with Louise and Diana. It was a crazy time with many relatives around, I definitely was not used to that. We were always a private family with just us at home.

I experienced berry picking for the very first time with this family who I knew little about. My Grandpa insisted we go out and work in the berry fields. It was fun picking blackberries, marionberries, and boysenberries. It was not fun getting up early in the morning, especially in cold Oregon. I was fascinated about how fast my aunts were at picking berries.

My Step Grandpa Pedro was a veteran, he served for our country. My biological grandpa (Alijos Veliz) passed away before I ever met him. My mom told me he was a very tall man, 6' 8" or 6' 9". Pedro was also a gardener, he loved raising his own vegetables and fruits. The house sat on two large lots, one of the lots was used for gardening. Grandpa Pedro had a small tractor, and every morning you could find him working in his garden.

After spending a few days at my grandma's house we were all getting ready to experience the magical trip to the Oregon Coast. We were all very excited to see the ocean for the very first time. We took two cars, Uncle Edward drove and my dad drove. It took us a good hour and a half to arrive at Lincoln City. All of us kids were good swimmers except for Diana, she was much too young and had not swam yet. The anticipation was strong as we were eager to get out and into the water.

I can remember driving along highway 101 through Lincoln City and gazing at the gigantic body of water and the endless sand as the waves pounded the beach. What a beautiful sight that only God could create. This trip I could definitely take back with me and share with some of the kids from school that always told me about places they went during the summer. This was perfect and what was even better is that my entire family was there to experience the first time at the Oregon coast.

We parked and we all removed our socks and ran out to the beach screaming and laughing. My parents, my aunts and uncles, and several people that were there just watched us. I was probably the fourth person to make it to the water. I ran as my feet splashed water off the sand. As I got closer to the waves, the sand seemed a little more firm and it was easier to run. When the water was to my thighs I took a dive into the cold-ice water. Oh my goodness, not only was the water very cold, but I couldn't get over the taste of salt and the sand inside my shorts. It was more uncomfortable than I expected. I expected clean water like the Dimmitt public pool.

Aunt Lydia was close to Gilberto's age, she was the most active and joined us in the swimming fun. The Oregon coast is known to have an undertow, which can be very dangerous. People could be sucked into the ocean with a strong undertow. I never felt anything that strong that pulled me back. I just swam back with the waves. Like I said we were all pretty good swimmers, but I think if I knew back then what I know now, it probably wasn't the safest thing to do. I don't think my parents or my aunts and uncles were aware of that knowledge, or they would have told us.

We spent half the day there and then we grabbed some food before heading back to Gervais. I never thought I would ever see the ocean again. The weather was not too cold, maybe about sixty degrees. For swimming in the ocean though? I think a little cold. It was a memorable trip that I will never forget.

When we returned to Gervais, we planned to start packing the following day. I was excited to get back to Dimmitt to tell my neighborhood friends about Oregon. Kids like Rudy, Ralph Junior, and Freddy. Those were the kids that usually came over to our house.

My dad started feeling sick. It seemed like maybe the cold air at the beach or something might have affected his health. His face started changing formation. His lips were crooked and one side of his face was twisted like it was stretched. He went to the doctor but I don't think they knew what was wrong with him. So we waited another week hoping that he would get well. I'm not sure if the doctor gave him some medicine, or if his body just healed slowly. After one month at my grandma's house, we were finally ready to go back home.

I learned later that my dad came down with Bell's Palsy. Although the exact reason is unknown, it's often linked to some sort of viral infection. We were all happy to see my dad looking semi-normal again. Oregon was so much fun and we all loved the scenery, the ocean, and the friendly people we met. Other than a few issues with arguments amongst the younger kids, everything went pretty well. My mom was so thankful that she was able to spend quality time with her mom, brothers, and sisters.

7.

Fifth Grade

As I walked into my fifth-grade class the first day of school, I met my teacher, Mrs. Hughes, and I took my seat. Students started pouring in as she would greet them. There was no sign of smart kids from last year. I didn't get it, I thought for sure I would be in a smart-student class. Then, finally Jim walks in. Jim was in a smart class last year. I didn't feel too bad after that. Jim was not happy when he looked around. Not only that but he was pretty vocal about his disappointment. None of his smart-wealthy friends were in there. I felt exactly like Jim did, except I was very quiet and kept my thoughts to myself.

"Jim, does this mean it's going to be an easier class this year?"

Jim didn't say anything, he got up off his seat and went to talk to Mrs. Hughes, surely this was a huge mistake and he was in the wrong class. Mrs. Hughes went over her roll call and verified that Jim was in her class. This kid was disappointed because of the class he was in.

"I'm so glad you're in this class. It can't be that bad. Look at the bright side, it will be easier than the other class."

Again, Jim didn't respond as he turned his head slowly, looking at everyone in the classroom in an unhappy way.

I have educated guesses on this, now that I'm older and wiser. Sometimes parents that are involved with their child's academic success will talk to the school officials and request their kid be placed with a certain class. Maybe we got moved to this class to allow one of those kids to be in the above-average class.

It could have been that the smart-student class was overloaded and some had to be put in the average class with Mrs. Hughes. We'll never know what the process was.

Darenda was also in our class and she was a pretty sharp girl. This class was an average-student class, which isn't bad, but the kids in there were viewed as not above average, which was not true for Jim, Darenda, and myself. Whatever happened, it didn't bother me as much as it did Jim.

Jim became my classroom friend, but only in the classroom. At recess he would join his wealthy friends and avoid me or any other kid in our class. When we had P.E class things looked better, especially when basketball was the subject. We both loved basketball. I think that was a connection that started our semi-friendship in the classroom.

I was okay with that though. There were some challenging assignments during the year that he and I would work on together. I learned a lot from him, he was one of the smartest kids in this class. I was probably in the top three.

I enjoyed this class, not only because the teacher was so nice to me, but also because her husband would come in sometimes and he'd tell us these elementary jokes. Mrs. Hughes was against the idea, but all of the students seemed to pressure her into allowing him to tell us a joke before he left.

She would always tell me about the progress that I was making and how great of a student I was. No teacher had ever said things like that to me before. I think she knew that I had an issue going on with my left eye. It was difficult for me to do my school work at times because my eye would get so irritated from the dryness. I would rub it a lot which didn't help and I got tired of people asking me, *are you okay?* If it was warm, the sweat would always help with moisture. "Are you okay, David?" Mrs. Hughes asked quietly so no other student would hear. I asked her if I could go to the restroom to wash my eye, it was bugging me. She said, *yes*, every time. It helped to wash it with water, I did that often throughout my school years. I never removed it though, I would just splash water on it and softly wipe it with a paper towel.

On Friday nights my brothers and I attended every varsity football game. Dimmitt was a 3A school back then, I think it's 4A now. During my fifth-grade year I learned about a gift that I truly believe was from God. When I watched the punters during warm-ups, I was so fascinated by the way the football left the punter's foot and spiraled into the air up high. We're talking about high school kids that could make the football spin past the height of the stadium lights. I wanted to be able to do that, I wanted to start trying on Saturday morning. My brother Richard felt the same way.

After watching the game, which to me seemed like fifteen minutes, but really it was two-hours long, I told myself, *I want to be one of those guys one day.* God opened up a new adventure for me. I forgot that I was blind in one eye, all I wanted was to be able to punt the football like the varsity players. Those guys on the football field inspired me to learn how to punt the football. I remember two of the names, David Nino and Mark Wolgemuth.

The very next morning I started punting the football on Dulin Street, the dirt road next to our house. My first few tries were a disaster. I watched how the varsity players held the football and how they just let it drop on the top part of their foot. The tricky part was making the football spiral into the air verses a wobbly-crooked ball flying in the air. A wobbly action on the football would slow it down going against air dynamics, I could logically see that as a young kid. I practiced for hours every day, but I struggled hitting that spiral. After a few days, my brother started punting the football with me. This was nice since I didn't have to retrieve it on my own.

It was a couple of weeks later that I finally hit a nice spiral. I couldn't believe it! It felt great, I had such a huge smile on my face and chills all over my body. I figured out that by pointing my toe down as I punched the football, on the correct part of the foot, this created the spiral action and the football went farther. My brother was a year younger and he too eventually grasped the technique.

We started playing this game on Dulin Street within the block we lived in. Whoever punted the football past the block line on the dirt road, won the game. If we caught the football in the air it would prevent a score, this would prevent the football from rolling past the mark. We played this game a lot and we improved our punting skills. And then I went on to start practicing on how to kick the football correctly. I had a passion for this technique and I wanted to one day be the punter and kicker for the Dimmitt Bobcats.

I wanted to practice every day, so the following day I couldn't wait to get home to practice kicking and punting the football. I didn't even watch *The Brady Bunch*, which was one of my favorite TV shows to watch.

Oh wow, I had this old football made out of leather, it was given to my mom in a box full of toys. She would often iron clothes for the wealthy people. They would normally bring their clothes in a basket and then pick them up the next day. We were always glad when they brought us an extra box full of things they were getting rid of.

My first punt went a long ways down the dirt road. As I ran to retrieve it, John B. with his group of losers were riding by ... oh man! He yelled out, "There's the glass-eyed boy – ha-ha!" His goal was to make fun of me while he had an audience. Well, it worked and once again I was humiliated and embarrassed as they all rode by on their bikes.

I felt so mad, I walked over to where our garbage barrel was sitting next to the alley. I sat down on some bricks that my mom had lined up for the flowers. I started crying ... was this ever going to end? I decided to finally tell my mom, I just couldn't take this anymore, it was very painful and simply not right. When my mom found out about this, she asked me how long John B. had been picking on me. I told her it had been a few months, but really it was more like two years. Mom was furious, she grabbed my hand and said, "Come on, let's go." We walked across the old-beat-up pasture where we often played baseball. We went straight to John B's house. My parents knew his parents as neighbors but not ones they ever associated with. When we got there, Mom asked me to wait outside. She knocked on the door and John B's mom opened the door. The greeting was warm and welcoming, John B's parents were nice and they understood and apologized for their son's behavior. To tell you the truth, knowing my neighborhood, I thought there was going to be a family fight or something. Things went better than I expected.

To this day, I was never told what my mom said to John B's mom, but whatever it was, my life became much better outside my own home. At first I didn't know what to expect, but the next time John B. came around I was actually shocked. He was riding his bike with his obnoxious followers and one of them started yelling at me. John B. quickly yelled, "No! Don't call him names anymore, he's our neighbor. My mom knows his mom."

I appreciate so much of what my mom did for me and how much she cared for me while caring for the other siblings. I think some of you that come from a large family can certainly understand what moms go through, especially if you have a child with a certain disability or medical issue. I like to see it as a possibility instead of a disability though.

Back then, my mom would be the one that read the newspaper and informed us on anything that we could do to get prizes or win something. She told us that the Ford Dealer was having a Punt, Pass, and Kick Contest. She told us to go and sign up at the Ford Dealer. I jumped at that chance, I wanted to try at least, who knows, maybe I could place in the top five of my age group. My brothers, Loop and Richard, also signed up for this competition that would take place in a couple of weeks. I started practicing even harder to do well at this competition. Never had my parents introduced anything like this to us. I was very excited and could hardly wait.

At school the next day the P.E. teacher informed us about this Ford PPK contest and other kids were also excited about it. In Dimmitt it didn't take much to get people excited when a big event was happening. I guess I liked that about the small town.

When it was time for the competition we all showed up early to get registered. I didn't want to miss this. I mean, you could win a trophy and advance to the regional competition at West Texas State University. Everything was going great and then I saw Thompson. He was an amazing athlete and the fastest kid in my grade. Thompson won just about everything athletic-wise. Every kid wanted him to be on their team during recess, he was that good.

I was thinking to myself, *well, I'll just do the best I can.* The officials called out everyone's names and separated them out to the correct age-group. We were able to watch every kid punt, pass, and kick the football. They used a measuring tape to stretch out on the football field. If the football landed off to the side of the tape, then that's how much they would deduct from the distance and then record the distance in feet and inches. All of my throws, kicks, and punts felt good and went a far distance. My kick actually hit the tape right on the mark, so they didn't deduct anything from it. My punt was maybe five feet off. Although I lost five feet, the punt went pretty far. My pass was close to the tape, I lost maybe two feet.

When the competition was over, they told us to come back in the afternoon for the results. So we walked back home and we waited. Those hours were some of the longest ever. I wanted to know how I did. I had a pretty good feeling that I would place in the top three, but I didn't get a chance to watch Thompson. I thought for sure he would win the whole thing. My guess, there was about thirty kids per age group that signed up for this. There were spectators watching from the bleachers.

The afternoon finally came and we walked back to the football field. I saw the trophies, three for each age group, a first, a second, and a third. I was in the twelve-year-old group. I was hoping for second because I was sure that Thompson had the first place trophy. They called out the second-place winner, still not my name. There had to be some kind of mistake, because I thought I was better than him.

The announcer grabbed the gold trophy.

"And the winner and the one that will represent Dimmitt at the regional competition, with a combined score of three-hundred-twenty feet, David Espinoza!"

I was speechless. I never won anything before, was this really happening? I walked over to accept my first trophy ever. This was one of the gifts that the Lord had given me. I had the ability to connect with the football better than any kid in my age group.

That moment I realized that my hard work had paid off. Was it hard work? I enjoyed practicing and improving my technique –

it was fun not hard. My brother Loop also took the first-place trophy and my brother Richard took the silver trophy in his age group. I don't remember my parents being there watching. When we all got home we shared the news. My mom took us all out to the yard for a picture, thanks Mom, I still have that picture.

During my fifth-grade year I anticipated playing on a kids' basketball league that had started the previous year. I couldn't play in it because I was too young. It was a fifth and sixth-grade league and it was called Little Dribblers. The team names were Division I college mascots.

The kids' league was organized by volunteer parents, and the coaches were also volunteers. It was cool the way they picked teams. The tryout day was on a Saturday morning at the Dimmitt High School gym. Every fifth and sixth grader that wanted to be selected for a team had to attend, otherwise you could not play.

It was the best and the most fair way to divide the talent that existed in Dimmitt. They had all of us start with a lay-up exercise. Two lines were formed, one for shooting the basketball and the other for rebounding. I'm guessing there were about eight head coaches. The gym was packed with kids wanting to be on a team. The league was organized and they even had new uniforms for all the players.

The coaches took turns selecting a player for their team. I was the third pick over all, I was pretty tall for my age and I was coordinated. Dang, I think Thompson was the second pick, the only thing I had been able to beat him in was the Ford PPK Contest – he was a tough athlete. The tryouts went on all day until all the team rosters were full. Every team had at least ten or more players. The team names were, The Bears; Aggies; Razorbacks; Mustangs; Horned Frogs; Longhorns; Buffalos, and the Owls. I was selected to play with the Aggies, which was the mascot for Texas A&M. Our team colors were maroon, and get this, we even had cheerleaders. There was a youth girls' cheerleading program that picked us to cheer for at our games – that was cool.

After practicing one week, we all received our uniforms. I can't recall what my number was, normally I can remember that kind of detail, but for this team, I have no clue. I do remember some of the players on my team, both fifth and six graders mixed.

Jim Wright played forward with me, Matt Howell was our point guard, Jody Minnick was a guard, and we had about eight others that I can't recall.

I was so excited that when I got home after school, I put my uniform on and I went outside to shoot some baskets in the backyard. Our backyard was hard dirt, very dry weather in Texas. My dad had bolted a pipe against the house with a square piece of plywood clamped to it and the rim bolted on there. It was up to scale of ten feet high. That's all we needed to practice, because whatever rim we shot at, the height would be the same, dirt ground or gym floor, it didn't matter. I was so happy and excited at the same time. I was going to be playing in a real game with real referees and fans. I could not wait for that moment.

At the time the home court was called the North Grade Gymnasium – that's where all the games were played since that facility had more seating. The high school gym was smaller and more like a grade-school gym these days, which I always found bizarre. It worked out better for us because the gym was closer to our home than the high school. We normally walked or my dad would drop us off if the weather was wet or cold.

Varsity basketball games were so exciting to watch. We had one of the best coaches in the state. Coach Kenneth Cleveland was a coach that knew how to teach a zone defense. I learned so much about basketball watching him in action on the court.

At the basketball games, I remember having enough money to pay the ticket price to get in. I was always so hungry, but my choice was always to watch the game instead of eat food with the money. Many of the wealthy kids I knew came with their parents. I would vicariously enjoy the chili dogs they ate, or the Fritos with chili in a nice cardboard container. My dad couldn't afford more than the ticket price for all of us boys. The excitement of the game made my mind forget about food. There were a few other Hispanic kids from my neighborhood that attended the games, we all sat at the very top of the concrete bleachers.

To me it was so strange that some of the Caucasian kids, that I knew at school, would never join us or for that matter, never talk to us at all. They would isolate themselves to be around the other wealthy Caucasian kids. It was segregated by race – that's just how it was.

After the game, we would make our way home. Sleeping was always difficult for me as I was always replaying what happened at the varsity game. My brothers would all fall asleep rapidly. I heard them breathing as they slept. I had a game the next day and it was my first official game ever – so exciting! I finally dozed off and before I knew it, morning had arrived.

I put my uniform on, the bottom of the shorts came up to my thighs. They were about eight inches above the knees. In the 1970s the shorts were much shorter than in the 21st Century. It was the style back then, we just lived with it. The tops were just T-shirts with numbers on them.

I can't recall who we played first. I think it was the Mustangs. The coach put me guarding their point guard. It was effortless in my part to steal the ball, because the kid put it right in front of me. In the first two minutes I had six steals and twelve points. I couldn't believe that I was that much better than these Caucasian kids playing. I truly didn't get it.

After that sixth steal, the referees started calling a foul on me every time I stole the ball. I was frustrated and didn't feel it was fair. Now that I'm older, I can understand a little better. It wasn't fun for the kids that were learning if I stole the ball all game and racked up fifty points. So anytime I reached for the steal I heard the whistle. It didn't take me long to realize they didn't want me to get anymore steals. What I started doing is stepping back two feet and waiting for them to pass the ball. The passes were so telegraphed that I was able to get some easy steals that way. The referees didn't have a leg to stand on because it would have been pretty obvious that their calls were bad.

My fifth-grade year I probably averaged twenty points per game. A sixth grader on my team, Jim Wright, also averaged around twenty. At the end of the year I made the all-star team. What an amazing experience that was for me. The entire time I played basketball in this league I never had an issue with my eye, no one asked me anything about it. Both eyes were starting to look the same and the moisture from the sweat lubricated my eye giving it a healthy-normal look.

God was right there with me guiding me, allowing me to gain my self-esteem. Sports started becoming my counseling and my enjoyment. I felt so normal with my teammates looking up to me and their parents congratulating me after games. This had never happened before and I liked it.

There would be moments where a coach or a teammate saw me rubbing my eye if it was bothering me. They would ask, "Are you okay ... what's wrong with your eye?" Sometimes I would respond, "Oh, I just got some dust or something in it, I'll be okay." I always tried to think of excuses to prevent them from asking more questions or realizing that I could not see out of it.

In one of the games I had just come off the court for a breather. The coach had sent in a substitute for me. I sat down and wiped the sweat off my face with the towel. One of my teammates called me from the other side of the bench. I turned to look at him and the other players noticed that my eyes did not move equally, it was as if I was looking in a different direction. I was always cautious of that, but that time I forgot about everything, I was having so much fun and seemed as if no one knew there was something wrong with my eyes.

One kid laughed at me, and then some of the others did too.

"Hey Dave, you got a funny eye, what's wrong with it?"

"Oh, nothing, this is how I was born."

I just kept making things up. A few weeks later I learned that some people have what you call, lazy eye. The condition, lazy eye, is an imbalance of the muscles that repositions the eye. To me that sounded like a very logical answer if anyone ever asked me again. I used this answer throughout my life if anyone ever asked me about my eye. I didn't feel right about lying to people, I knew that lying was a sin. But in my position, I sure hoped that the good Lord would forgive me.

I guess when I told people I had a little bit of lazy eye, it diverted the unpleasant attention. I didn't like my teammates laughing at me or joking around about me for their enjoyment. I knew there wasn't anything I could do. The last thing I wanted them to know is that I had a prosthetic eye and that I was not a normal kid.

Little Dribblers was such a fun experience, I was hooked for life in this amazing game that Dr. James Naismith invented back in 1891. I was always looking forward to the next game. We normally had two practices a week, which I also enjoyed – I can't describe the joy and counsel this was for me.

My team looked up to me, the coaches depended on me to help our team. I loved having the basketball in my hands at crunch time and I loved to shoot the basketball. I even made a few friends that year.

Our team made it to the playoffs. We won our first two playoff games and we made it to the championship game. I was hyped and excited to play in the championship game.

All week I had talked about it with my brothers, sisters, and parents. I specifically asked my dad if he could give me a ride to the high school gym on Saturday, that's where the championship game was taking place at 11:00 a.m. He said he would give me a ride. We were playing Johnny's team. Johnny was a grade higher than I was and he was a smart basketball player that could shoot the ball very well. He wasn't real quick, but he was fast enough to be at the right place when he needed to be. My friend Tommy could drive to the basket and draw the foul. We knew that about those two and we were ready for them. I was the leading scorer of the team. I remember putting up thirty-five points in one of our games.

The big game was important, not just to me, but to the coaches and the players as well. On Saturday morning I was up early and I heard my mom and dad in the kitchen. I walked over and reminded my dad once more that I needed a ride to the high school. I told him we were playing for the league title. My dad looked at me and said, "Okay mi hijo, we'll be back, we have to go to the store." I don't think my mom and dad knew how important this was to me. I looked forward to this moment the entire Little Dribbler's season. There was a lot of talk that the Bears could beat the Aggies because Johnny and Tommy were on the team.

It was 10:30 a.m. and my parents were not back yet, in fact, there was no one at home but me. I had no idea where everyone was. I anxiously paced the rooms and looked at the clock and out of the window repeatedly. I put on my uniform and retrieved my shoes – I had some purple converse back then. I never wore them outside, only in the gym. When the clock turned to 10:40 a.m. I knew that my dad had forgotten. I wasn't too surprised because he did this now and then. I put on my old shoes, tied my converse together with the laces and hung them over my neck. I made a mad dash through the door and started running across the tracks through town and to the high school. The high school was a little over two miles away from our house. I didn't know if I would make it on time. My coaches, Gene King and Bob Murdock, were worried.

As I'm approaching this long field that was across the street from the high school, I saw a rattlesnake, the rattle was very loud as I ran by. I took a fast cut to the left to avoid it and kept running. From afar I saw a truck bounce over the curb onto the pasture and it was headed straight towards me. I knew it was Bob Murdock, my assistant coach. He spun a donut and yelled at me, "Come on David ... they're already warming up for the game!" Those words are still so fresh in my mind after all these years, it's crazy.

I was exhausted, the temperature was already 85 degrees that day and I had sweat pouring down my face. I was tired but I knew I couldn't miss the game. The coach drove up to the door and dropped me off before parking. It was so funny, he drove over the school lawn in front of the gym and said, "Get in there." So I rushed inside. Everyone was happy to see me and all I could hear was, *where were you?* I had dust all over me from running through a few pastures. Everyone was just looking at me.

Coach Gene King was relieved that I finally showed up. He had several players rebound for me while I took a few shots before the game began. When the game started I realized how good the Bears were. We were a good team too, but with me being so tired from the two-mile run in warm weather, well, our chance to win had diminished.

We kept the game close, but their plan of running smart plays and taking good shots helped them claim a victory over us. My defense wasn't as good and I think I only scored 14 points the whole game. After the buzzer went off I had a few tears running down my face. My coaches felt bad that I had to run so much before an important game, and they tried to cheer me up. I walked out of the gym and I was so angry at my dad. I walked home and cried all the way across the quarter-mile pasture. Once I reached the paved road I calmed down. My coach and his daughter, Debbie, drove up next to me and offered to give me a ride home. I agreed and thanked them.

That was the first time I experienced losing in an organized basketball league. We had not lost a game until the championship game. I didn't know where my parents were. I didn't know if they were helping my grandmother, or if they got caught up in something more important. What I do know is that when I got home my dad felt bad about forgetting. He apologized to me and was sincere. To me, I didn't believe him and I was mad at him. I was a kid and didn't understand all of the things my dad had going on supporting a family, maintaining the cars, working, etc. I did eventually forgive him but never again was I ever late for a game. I remembered this for a long time. The basketball season came to an end and it was way too short.

As far as girls, I did like a few girls that caught my attention in grade school. I envied my teammates that had girlfriends in the fifth grade. I had ruled out the possibility of me ever having a girlfriend, I just didn't see it, or maybe I just saw half of it. The girls might like one half of my face, but not the other half. All sorts of things went through my mind, but it was sports that distracted me from those thoughts – I felt more accepted on the basketball court.

Back in my neighborhood there was this dance hall, I still remember the name of it, La Estrellita. The loud music on a few Friday and Saturday nights, during scheduled days, was noticeable throughout our entire neighborhood. There was a lot of poverty in that section of Dimmitt. It was a Mexican-music dance and mostly Latinos would attend. Our neighborhood was populated heavily with people that drank beer and hard liquor. I learned early in my life that there was nothing good about excessively drinking alcohol.

I saw some fights in our neighborhood because of people drinking Coors beers or Budweiser beers. And then they would drink hard liquor on top of that, which did something to their minds. The mixture of the two brings huge problems to the mind and coordination.

I lived in fear on those weekend nights. Those evenings seemed to be the worst, especially during summer-dance nights. I'm sure some of my brothers and sisters lived through that fear as well, I just can't speak for them.

One night my older brother, Gilberto, was doing homework in the kitchen – it was past midnight. After the dance was over, we would often hear the vocal and irresponsible people walk by Dulin Street next to our house. They were heavily intoxicated and they would sing while they walked by, some with their hand around the can of beer, or a bottle of whiskey. We heard this loud sound come from the kitchen, our kitchen window was shattered to pieces. The glass just missed my older brother, who was doing some homework. It could have been tragic. We all rushed to the kitchen! My dad yelled, "No! Stay in your room."

My dad was already in bed before this loud sound startled everyone in the house. So he had to dress quickly before running outside. I don't remember if he grabbed his gun or not. We had a rifle with .22 bullets and maybe a six gun. I just heard the car take off. It was difficult to find anyone in the dark – they quickly disappeared.

When my dad returned, he called the police. Mr. Jones was the sheriff at that time, he came right away. He found a quart-size bottle of beer that was empty next to our house in a large dry bush. He thought they could check it out for finger prints.

Whoever threw that bottle at our house, not only kept me from getting sleep all night long, but he or she also added extra stress and work to my parents. They had to board up the window at 1:00 a.m. and they had to clean up all of the glass in the kitchen. We didn't have much money and we were barely pulling through each month. This person, whoever it was, not only shattered our window, but also shattered our budget that we didn't have.

On Sunday, at church, I felt more safe and my mind started to forget about that night. By Monday I was thinking that hopefully it would never happen again. My dad would drop us off every morning in front of the North Grade School – fourth through sixth grade. The older kids would walk to their destinations.

Another incident that occurred two blocks away from our house was even more frightening to me as a young kid. Our friend Rudy often had many relatives or friends over at his place. He had older brothers that were much older than he was. There was a huge family fight that took place. I was worried for Rudy and had no clue where he was. Several fist fights took place at the same time outside his house. One of Rudy's brothers even had a bottle of beer that he broke and used the top part to threaten his opponent. It was such an ugly mess and probably one of the scariest sights I had seen in our neighborhood. I just wanted it to end. I was scared and nervous and my parents were not home. I saw this altercation from our window, no way I was stepping outside.

After thirty minutes or so things were calming down. Some cars that were parked on the opposite side of Rudy's house peeled off leaving the dust hanging in the air for a few minutes.

We never did find out what caused the situation, it was a huge brawl with women and men involved. I was so glad when the whole episode ended. That definitely made other crazy things in our neighborhood seem more mild. That night, again, it was hard for me to sleep. I kept replaying the fight over and over until I finally just dozed off.

I witnessed so many things that happened because of alcohol. I'm almost positive that fight started due to a drunk person saying something and the other getting upset. It didn't take me very long, as a little kid, to avoid being around alcohol. It was a cool thing among some neighbors, my uncles, and even my dad.

They would often play music on Sunday afternoons outside of our house and they would drink beer while doing that. My mom did not like that at all and was always angry at my dad for doing that with his brother, Jessie, and sometimes friends who I didn't know. Sometimes I would go out there just to listen to the music and try to learn more about playing the guitar. They would also smoke cigarettes. All of us kids begged our dad to stop smoking cigarettes. He eventually got tired of us all coming down on him. It was a nasty habit and he eventually quit smoking.

A few blocks away where the dance hall was located there was a community of African-American people. I knew some of the kids from school, and they were all poor just like us. I was always scared to walk by that area because a lot of the African-American kids did not like the Hispanics. They would often throw rocks at us and yell out a few cuss words, and then they would all laugh together. These kids were neglected for different reasons. I understand now why they acted that way.

There was a tiny market that was owned by a Hispanic man named Frank. We used to call him Frank Highway, because we would have to go through a dirt highway to get to his store. This store happened to be located in the African-American neighborhood. We started riding our bikes there because it was much easier bypassing the dogs that would come after us or the African-American kids that would throw rocks at us. It was not a fun situation.

One time, my brother, myself, and our friends Rudy and Ralph, were all at the city park watching people play tennis and just hanging out. There were these three African-American kids. One of the African-American kids climbed the eight-foot fence and yelled at my friend Ralph, "Hey you in the red ... watch out!" He would spit at him. Then he would yell out again looking at the color of shirts we had on, "Hey you in the blue ... watch out!" He would spit again trying to hit the target. They would all laugh loudly – it was a joke to them at our expense. Just to let you know, most of the African-American kids in our neighborhood were pretty darn tough. My friend Rudy turns around. Knowing they would have to either climb the tall fence or run around the fence to get us, he yelled, "Hey you in the black ... watch out!" Rudy spit back at them. It was like stirring a bunch of hornets. The African-American kids started coming after us by running around the fence, but we got a head start and they couldn't catch us. I looked at Rudy, "What were you thinking?"

These are just a few of many stories that I recall about my neighborhood back in the days. I don't want to lead you on and give you a picture of total negativity, there were some fun times and productive things that happened in our neighborhood. We used to play "Tops". We would draw a circle in the dirt and then we'd string up our tops. Throwing a top down and making it spin on the dirt took much practice. I mastered that skill within days. I was one of the best top spinners. The objective to this game was to knock out the other tops that were already spinning inside the circle. If your top got knocked out you were out of the game. The last top remaining in the circle won.

We often played "Kick the Can" with the neighborhood kids or just us kids. I felt so bad for my sister, Diana, she was the youngest and always the one that was watching the can. The objective was to go tag someone so they'd have to sit out until someone that was hiding ran and kicked the can without being tagged. This would free up everyone else and the person guarding the can would have to continue trying to tag everyone. We would normally hide behind either side of the house.

There were also family barbecues that took place outside neighborhood backyards. Our neighbors, the Salinas' would often have outdoor eating during the summer.

We would fly kites on a windy day. We made our own kites out of newspaper. It was pretty easy. We basically needed two light sticks and some string. We would form a diamond with the newspaper glued to the sticks. Bending the stick that was horizontal would make the kite fly better. My family discovered different ways to have fun. We didn't need much money to entertain ourselves.

As far as sports, I grew up playing baseball in an unmaintained pasture. We'd get a whole bunch of neighborhood kids that would show up and before you knew it there was enough for two teams. This was the time that I received my first ever concussion.

I was playing catcher and my neighbor, Rachel, was batting. Rachel was a lot like my sister, a tomboy. She liked to play sports with the boys. The moms would not like that at all. They were protective of their daughters. I saw a lot of mother-daughter arguments due to that situation. Anyway, I was playing catcher and I didn't realize how close I was to Rachel. She swung the bat and hit me on the side of the head. All I remember was everyone calling me by my name. I didn't remember falling down after I got hit, I just remember lying on my back looking up as kids called my name. It was painful and I was helped back to the house. As I was walking back, I checked my eye to be sure it was still with me.

Fifth grade was so much fun for me, not only because I felt I was one of the smartest kids in class, but also because I was able to share a true vacation that my family went on. It definitely wasn't like Disneyland, skiing, or camping, but it was traveling farther than Palo Duro Canyon, Amarillo, or Lubbock. I was able to tell my friends about the Oregon coast and how wild it was to swim in the cold ocean. I also shared about how the mountains, the evergreens, and the rivers were so colorful and mesmerizing. It was a total contrast from the Texas Panhandle.

Fifth grade was flying by and I started learning so much. At home I would practice the guitar when I was tired of shooting baskets outside. At school I loved choir, and at the same time it was a little frustrating. My choir teacher, Mr. Dutton, would often have this solo-performance once a month at the end of class. He would pick one student to perform in front of the class. We all raised our hands, the ones who wanted that opportunity anyway.

Every month I would raise my hand and every month Mr. Dutton picked a kid he liked or a kid that was popular among the school. I was definitely not one of the popular kids. At recess I had to ask if I could play whatever game was being played. The kids wouldn't always let me play. I knew why they didn't want me to play. I once heard a kid say, "No don't let him play, his eyes are weird." In grade school I got used to the talk and how I was viewed. I also got used to the fact that I would probably never have a girlfriend like some of the kids in school.

One of the songs that the music teacher had for a solo performance was, "I'd Like to Teach the World to Sing (In Perfect Harmony)". This song was rerecorded by Susan Shirley and released in 1971. I memorized that song front and back and I practiced a lot. If Mr. Dutton ever picked me to do a solo at the end of class, I was going to be ready and I was going to deliver the best performance anyone could ever imagine. At least that's the way I felt about it. I still remember the first part of that song.

I'd like to build the world a home
And furnish it with love
Grow apple trees and honey bees
And snow white turtle doves

The last week of school there was one more chance that I could possibly be picked to sing a solo in front of the class. The microphone and the stand were both set up in front of the class. There were probably twenty-five students in there and only four of us raised our hands. I knew it was my last chance so I was jumping up and down and raising my hand as high as I could – I was no doubt the tallest kid in class.

Mr. Dutton said, "Raise your hand if you want to be picked to do a solo, it's our last one." I worked hard to prepare for this moment and I knew the other three kids had performed already earlier in the year. Everything came crashing down on my assumption. I predicted a result and it tore me up inside. Mr. Dutton picked a beautiful young lady, she was a brunette with long black hair and she wore glasses. I remember what she looked like, but I can't remember her name. I was almost in tears while watching her, not because of her performance, but because I was disappointed that I didn't get an opportunity. I was angry at Mr. Dutton for not giving me a chance.

The girl did a great job singing the song – I envied her. When the bell rung I just ran out of the class and headed toward the back of the building where no one could see me. I started crying for a few seconds, then I calmed down before running back to Mrs. Hughes' class.

My fifth-grade year was full of lessons learned. I believe that year was full of ups and downs. I was struggling with my identity as far as a person in a social environment. Being around other kids and being looked at differently was challenging. Again I would think to myself, *why God, why did this accident have to happen to me?*

8.

Summer Before Sixth Grade

My dad was being asked to produce more than one person could handle, but yet his boss kept hounding him on this. He finally quit his job and decided to start his own business by opening up a FINA gas station.

My dad was mechanically inclined and knew just about everything about cars and trucks. He had prior experience from working with his Uncle Lalo down in the Rio Grande Valley. Lalo had a shop where he repaired vehicles and my dad was one of his workers. He had also been a gas-station attendant in previous years.

Because Dad didn't have any kind of schooling, he paid an accountant to come by once a month to check on his bookkeeping – sales and receipts, etc. He also needed to do some remodeling on the old and small building. Stocking the shelves with candies, cigarettes, chips, and a few other things was a must for extra profit. He also bought a soda machine on a loan. It was a great investment because the customers loved to eat junk food and drink soda, especially when it was one-hundred degrees outside. The soda machine paid for itself quickly.

Gilberto and Loop were helpers in cleaning up the FINA station. The business was located on East Bedford Street on the outskirts of town towards Nazareth, Texas. I had never seen my dad so excited about work. He loved being his own boss and having to make decisions for his own business. He set the gas prices to be the lowest in town, which was 28 cents a gallon at the time. This was in 1971 and no other gas stations in town had anything below 30 cents a gallon.

While my dad was preparing to open his business, my mom was taking the younger kids to work at the fields for Mr. Roberts. I was dreading every day of working out at that field, it was not fun, it was boring and it was tiring work. I hated the hot weather and always looked forward to lunchtime. I still look forward to lunchtime to this day.

The field work continued unless the weather was too wet. If we had a downpour, my joyful spirit would glow as a few days off were anticipated. About mid-summer the field work was complete. I was so happy for that moment to come. And what was great about this, was that we were given more money to spend on whatever we wanted. The first store I hit was the TG&Y – toys and board games. We also bought clay to sculpture on the kitchen table. My brothers and sisters would always play with clay, Loop was the artist he always sculptured the best people or cars or anything. With six kids at a table playing, it seemed like there was always some kind of fight involving someone smashing others' pieces of art. And then everyone smashed everything. Diana would end up crying because she could never sculpture anything that looked half-way decent – she was too little and still learning by watching.

We even earned an opportunity to walk over to the Dimmitt Bobcat Drive-in. It was not an outdoor movie place, it was just a carhop place that served burgers, fries, shakes, and soda. The building was painted in purple and white, which were the mascot colors. Just walking by that place and smelling the food would put on three pounds on anyone's body. I loved to eat there and often begged my parents if we could go there. My parents would only stop there if they had one or two kids with them, otherwise it was too expensive.

On Sundays at church, I thanked God for the money and the treasures that we were able to earn. I attended church regularly with my mom, my brothers, and sisters. My dad was like a solar eclipse, it was very rare that we saw him in church, but when he did go, it was a special moment for all of us.

When the gas station finally opened for business, my two older brothers were the first ones working there with my dad. They were exhausted from pumping gas and fixing flat tires. My dad would do the oil changes and lubrication jobs for customer cars. If there was a semi-truck tire brought in, it would take Dad at least an hour to fix it. He fixed it manually, he didn't have special equipment. He didn't charge very much to fix a car tire, but the semi-truck tires were good money because of the amount of labor.

That summer was a celebration for me, not only because I no longer worked in the slave-hot fields, at least that's what I called them, but also because I started working for my dad. We were a very poor family struggling to make ends meet up to that point.

My dad's decision was genius, for the summertime anyway, because business was booming. There were some housing projects a mile down the road that were rented by migrant workers. Hispanics from the South would travel with their families for summer work out in the farm fields.

Many Latinos would head north to look for work. The pay was sometimes a little better, depending on the farmer. Some families had already established residency up in the north part of Texas and a connection was made with family members about farm work.

The Rio Grande Valley is in the southernmost part of Texas. There were many families that struggled financially. The lack of funds kept them from sending their kids to school. My dad dropped out of grade school in the 1940s for that same reason. He started working to help support the family. There were many families in similar situations in the valley.

My parents both came from that area and they both had large families, Wenceslado Espinoza, nickname "Vence" or "Wences" and Gabriela, maiden name, Veliz. Although my dad loved working with cars, he was once like the migrant workers that drove up north to find work. In the 1950's Dad held a job as a foreman, he would drive a group of Hispanics or Mexicans, up north to find work. Then after the season, he would drive them back south. Sometimes there wasn't enough work due to the influx of Mexicans crossing the border.

My dad's Uncle Lalo and his family would often migrate north for part of the summer. They would stay with us for a few weeks. It was fun having my Uncle Manual and Aunt Tao as guests. Tao would often help me with my homework during September before they left. She was very tall for a Hispanic girl and very bright. Manual was fun to joke around with while we worked in the farm fields. I remember both of them reading a lot, they were educated.

Most families from the South were wanting to work and to find a better life for their families. I heard many Hispanic adults talk about where the work was and what the pay was. The migrant workers that rented a room in the Dimmitt projects drove thousands of miles for work to provide for their families. They always looked eager to work during the summer.

The FINA gas station was in a perfect location. The migrant workers, in addition to several locals, were our customers day in and day out all summer long.

They would buy gas, junk food, sodas, you name it. My dad started selling Mexican music. He would buy eight-track cassettes from local artists or mainstream artists and he would sell them. These cassettes were the size of a standard book I'd say.

I had the morning shift, 6:00 a.m. to 3:00 p.m. Gilberto and Loop had the evening shift. During the summers we normally stayed open until 11:00 p.m. unless we had customers pouring in, then we would quit when it slowed down. For me it started out fun and exciting. I was always the type of person that could learn a skill and master it quickly. Pulling the pump nozzle off the pump hook was easy, and then setting it inside the tank-opening of the vehicle. Many old cars would have the opening just under the license plate at the rear.

The trucks would have the opening just to the left of the driver's side. I was pretty tall for almost being in the sixth grade. Our procedure was to clean the windshields unless the customer didn't want us to. We would also check the oil. If the customer's car needed oil, we would sell it to them. I remember our business carried Havoline and Pennzoil mostly. We also checked the transmission fluid. I was trained by my dad on how to help customers, even the rude ones.

My dad always told me to be nice to the customers, no matter what they said or how rude they were. I often complained about certain customers because of their bad attitude. My dad would always say, "Mi hijo, they are just words, as long as the money is coming in, they can say whatever they want ... just laugh and say, thank you."

There were certain customers that would come in and want a certain service done to their vehicle. My dad would always say, "Yes I can do that, but I need the money upfront." When the customer responded, "Okay, I'll think about it," my dad knew they probably weren't that serious about it or maybe planning on scamming him, like a few customers did. He learned quick that you can't trust customers with their word. After the customer left the gas station, my dad looked at me and said, "Money talks, B.S. walks." It was a phrase he would use often, but I never knew what he meant until I was much older.

My mom, Gabriela, was a supporter and a server for our family. She was there for whatever we needed, whether it was bringing us food, or buying material that my dad needed for the gas station. For example, we sometimes needed patches and glue to patch up flat tires, Mom would drive down to the hardware store and pick some up. She washed our clothes, cooked home meals and delivered them to us at lunchtime. And yes, she was the enforcer making sure we attended church every Sunday.

Deuteronomy 31:12-13 Assemble the people, men, women, and little ones, that they may hear and learn to fear the Lord your God.

I was flying, a young kid that could do it all at the gas station. I ran the cash till, and learned how to count back customer change. I learned how to manage debits and credits on the bookkeeping sheet. I felt powerful and important. The customers just watched me because they knew I was just a kid. I would hear all kinds of things that didn't bother me.

Two ladies drove up to fill up their car. I started pumping the gas and then I began to clean their car's windshield. One of them kept staring at me.

"Aren't you a little too young to be working here? Shouldn't you be playing outside with your toys?"

The other lady busted out laughing. I simply remembered what my dad said and just smiled and kept doing my work.

There were challenging times that reminded me I was not physically normal like everyone else. A group of guys in their late teens pulled in to put five dollars worth of gas in their tank. My eye had been bothering me that day, it was uncomfortable and I remember rubbing it because it itched so much, it was red and swollen. Sometimes I'd run water on it and close it for awhile. Anyway, I grabbed the sponge and dipped it in the soap to wash their windshield while the gas was pumping. I could hear them joking around and I could see them looking at me. I tried to just do my job and ignore them. They obviously knew there was something going on with my eye. The boy on the passenger side stuck his head out of the window.

"Hey, use your eye to clean the windshield!"

They all busted out laughing and could not stop. That moment was so humiliating to me. I just finished cleaning their windshield as fast as I could, took the nozzle off the gas tank and collected the five dollars. As the driver handed me the five dollars, he said, "Hey man, don't listen to them, they're just joking around." I grabbed the money and walked back inside. My dad was restocking the soda machine and I didn't say one word to him. I went in the back room where we kept a lot of our stock and sat down on a tire. I was tearing up a bit. I knew I had to be strong, there were more customers that would be driving in or walking from the projects during the noon hour. Again I would tell myself, *why me ... why did this have to happen to me?*

I believe that what I endured as a young kid made me tougher and made me want to be the best I could be at anything. I don't know what God's intentions were, but I know that He would not want any of us to suffer like this. He has the power to prevent things from happening or to allow things to happen, He's God. His plan is above all, I didn't know what it was, but I can guarantee it will be worth all the suffering and trials that I will ever experience in this tiny-temporary earth. Everlasting life in Paradise with Jesus sounds pretty darn good to me.

My dad wanted me to learn how to fix flat tires, he said I would get part of the profit. We normally charged $4.00 to fix a flat tire. If we had to jack up the car and remove the tire, then we charged a little more. I would get a $1.00 bonus for every flat I fixed. So I learned very quickly how to fix a flat tire. There was a piece of paper next to the till for me to log in the count of tires fixed that day. Many people would just bring in the flat tire because they knew it would save them money.

Dad hired someone to install a flat-tire machine that would allow us to remove the tire from the rim quickly. After that, we blew up the tire with air and dipped it in a water tank to find the nail or hole that was causing the leak. I got to where I could fix a flat tire in 8 minutes. The technique was very simple once you learned it. Sometimes there was a whole line of tires waiting to get fixed, especially on Saturdays and Sundays. It seemed like that's when everyone wanted their tires fixed. The more tires I fixed the more money I made for myself, because only my older brothers would get paid for working. Soon my brother Richard started working there with me, I trained him to do the work I did – he picked it up pretty fast as well.

At the end of the work day, I was tired. When my mom came to pick us up, my brother and I didn't have the energy to do much. Sometimes we would just take a bath and then a nap came after. I liked the food my mom fixed us. It was normally eggs with chorizo and potatoes, or beans and tortillas with Spanish rice and tomatoes. She would also make burger and fry runs and bring that to all of us who were working at the time. I always looked forward to lunch. We could never afford that kind of food before we had the gas station. Sometimes all we had at home were crackers and eggs, maybe some pinto beans. I was working hard and living a big dream of luxury, or at least it was to me!

I'll never forget the first time we had a dog as a pet. My older brothers were working at the gas station when they spotted a stray dog. This dog was a medium-sized German Sheppard. The dog seemed happy wagging its tail and begging for food. My parents were never ones to have pets around. Oh sure we had stray cats now and then that we fed and claimed as our pets, but never a dog.

My brother, Gilberto convinced my dad to bring the dog home with him. Wow! What a surprise that was. We had a pet dog, something I never expected. The rule was that we had to keep him outside. That was okay with all of us. So we fed him and he hung around outside our house. One thing about this dog is that he always wanted to jump on us and play when we came home. You can imagine our church clothes on Sundays. My mom would not like that at all, but he was our dog and we learned to love him. We decided to name him, "Jumper". This dog was the only dog we ever had for a pet. He was a great watch dog at night too, always watching out for our house. I learned that dogs can become part of a family, they have a lot of personality and they are easy to train. I'll never forget Jumper.

My dad bought a pickup and another used car, we needed those badly to transport car parts, tires, or whatever was needed. My brother Loop was able to buy a Yamaha 125. That was the first time I learned how to ride a motorcycle. Loop was generous in letting me ride it often. Gilberto was able to buy a Kawasaki 900, that motorcycle was one of the biggest bikes I had ever seen, he wanted to impress people.

I don't know to this day how my dad worked sixteen-hour days. He was always at the gas station. He managed to take a lunch break at times during the day. He'd have to go home for awhile and rest and then he would come back. I didn't like being there by myself longer than an hour. It was very scary, especially when rough crowds would stop by. Thankfully there was only a few times that I was sweating it.

Once I was working in the evening, my dad felt I had the confidence to handle a rush of people. He also had my sister Louise helping out by running the till and documenting sales or flat tires fixed. Louise was so awesome to work with. I'd have to say that those moments at the gas station were some of the most fun times with my older sister. We would laugh about stupid-little things when business slowed down. When we had massive customers, it was all business. I liked that I didn't have to run the till along with everything else. It's so funny because back then, girls were never seen pumping gas at a gas station. But now, I see girls pumping gas all the time at local gas stations.

Louise was the sister that made me feel good about myself. She would compliment me on how well I did things. She would tell me who the girls were that liked me when they stopped by the gas station. One girl in particular, she lived in the projects and would walk down to buy a soda or some kind of snack. She would smile at me and I would get nervous. Heck, no girl had ever smiled at me like that before. Louise would say that she would walk down just to see me. I still remember her name, Alicia. I never knew her last name, but I did learn that she was from Del Rio, Texas. Her parents were migrant workers. She was a Latina that had white skin with reddish hair and a few freckles on both cheeks. She wore this black collar around her neck sometimes, it was like a leather necklace I guess.

The entire summer, I knew she liked me, but I never gained the courage to actually talk to her. When she bought something and I helped her at the till, I just looked down as I handed her the change. Deep inside I didn't want her to see my eyes, I was so self-conscious because of how I looked and I wanted her to return. All I know is that I enjoyed when she came by, and what my sister told me, is that Alicia liked me a lot.

I think the only words I ever said to her were, *where are you from? You look nice today.* My sister would always ask me why I was so nervous to talk to any girls. She would tell me that I was a nice looking guy. I guess I didn't have that kind of confidence at that age and I was very insecure about my looks.

Alicia eventually moved back to Del Rio with her family when the field work was completed. I never saw her again, but only hoped she would return next summer. Maybe I would have the confidence by then to talk to her.

One of the funniest things I saw at our gas station was a man that had been drinking alcohol. He had just left the dance and was with a few of his friends. I was exposed to so many different things when I was growing up, it's mind-boggling. Anyway, this man stepped out of his car and came in to buy a bag of potato chips. First he hands me a twenty-dollar bill with some change – the change fell everywhere on the ground as he handed it to me. When he grabbed the chips from the shelf, he tore the bag open and the chips scattered all over the concrete floor that had been stepped on all day. He squatted down and started eating them from the floor. We were all just watching him and his friends were laughing hard. I wanted to laugh too, but I didn't want to offend the drunk person. I'm sure if you asked my brothers and sisters about our gas-station days, they would have some stories too.

One evening I was working late and I was all by myself. My dad had to take care of a problem at home. Something was broke and he was fixing it. I don't remember where everyone else was. A blue Dodge truck pulled up for some gas. I walked out like I normally did to help any customer. I was about to say, "Can I help you?" Before I could speak, this person hops out of the truck. He had long black hair and he looked a little like a Native American.

It was John B. I took a big swallow as he walked toward me ... and to my surprise, I had grown taller than him. I was about three inches taller. I was probably stronger than him as well due to all of the flats I had fixed – I just felt strong and was hoping so bad that he would make fun of me. He looked tiny compared to me. He must have been 5' 3" and I was probably about 5' 6" at the time. Oh wow, my adrenalin was going. I had a quick flash-back of all the things he said to me back in the days when I was little. John B. took one look at me.

"David! Man you've grown. How you been?"

"I've been good, how 'bout you?"

"Staying busy, I'm a foreman for a group of people at a field."

He started asking for a fill up and he wanted me to put some motor oil in his truck. I had never seen John B. being so nice to me. All of my anxiety and stress just flew away. From that day on he was like a friend that showed so much respect to our business and to me. He became one of our best customers and he often recommended our gas station to his friends.

This was about the time that I learned to forgive John B. for all the things he said to me and for all of the hurt he caused in the previous years. It didn't take me long to forgive him when I saw the fruits he was producing every time he stopped by the gas station.

Mark 11:25 And whenever you stand praying, forgive, if you have anything against anyone, so that your Father also who is in heaven may forgive you your trespasses.

That summer he even took us brothers to hunt rabbits. I had never tasted cottontail rabbit before. Gilberto was closer to John B's age so he learned a lot about different adventures with John B. His family barbecued rabbits, and believe it or not, cottontail rabbits tasted just like chicken. We told my dad about this and he was leery of us going out shooting rabbits with a .22 rifle.

One night we brought back a few rabbits. I learned how to skin a rabbit and gut it out. After the rabbit was skinned, the instructions were, first boil the rabbit, add a little flour, and then fry it in a pan. My dad took a bite of a cooked cottontail rabbit with barbecue sauce dripping down one of the rabbit legs. We all just watched him in hopes that he would like it. After he took a big bite of the rabbit, his eyebrows raised and his eyes were wide open, "When are y'all going hunting again!" The rabbit did taste like chicken, except it was free and it was fun hunting out on the dry fields with miles of empty space – that's just how a lot of Texas was and still is today.

John B's dad managed the landfill which was located a few miles out of town. John would take us out there at night to shoot rats. These rats were as big as a cat – huge rodents. We'd park the truck in front of the gigantic holes with tons of used parts, whether bike parts or car parts or furniture that people threw out – a lot of junk. We would shine the lights and we would see hundreds of rats squirming and squealing all over like they were panicking. We all had a .22 rifle and immediately began shooting these creatures. Every now and then I got one, but it was hard. Talk about a fun time on a summer Friday night. And no, we didn't eat the rats, we just hunted them for fun. The rabbits we did eat, they were good!

Toward the end of the summer, we were becoming financially stable. It wasn't like we were middle class or anything like that, but we could at least eat well, and pay the bills without any collectors calling all the time. We had money to buy things that normally we couldn't.

At the end of July it was getting close to going-back-to-school time. My Grandma Matilda was in Edinburg, Texas, and we heard that she had lung cancer – she was a heavy smoker. She was in the hospital and my dad was notified. Dad decided to close the gas station for one week to travel south. He would leave Gilberto, Loop, and myself in Dimmitt. Louise, Diana, and Richard would go with them.

It was Friday night and my parents were planning on leaving early in the morning. There was this carnival that had set up in a huge pasture just three blocks from our house. Carnivals in Dimmitt were like Disneyland to us, we only saw events like this once every summer. My older brothers and I asked if we could go, since we had money from working at the gas station. My dad said it was fine. So we went to the carnival that Friday evening.

What a blessing in disguise this carnival turned out to be. I magically came up with a lot of money by accident. This would help my dad cover some expenses for the long trip. The Lord works in mysterious ways. My dad knew that the trip was going to set us back financially, but it was his mom and he needed to go see her at the hospital.

When we arrived at the carnival, I walked over to this game where many people were circled around. This rope was holding a curtain that draped down. There was a large table in the middle with dishes. If a player threw a quarter and it landed inside the dish, they were awarded that dish. Quarters were flying everywhere and the only worker was an old man, which I assume was the vendor for that game.

This Hispanic lady looked at me.

"Ask him if he needs help."

"Excuse me sir ... do you need help?" I asked.

"Yes come on in and put on one of these aprons ... if you see a quarter in the dish, give it to the person that made it."

I put on the apron and started working. It was actually pretty stressful since I had never done this before. I just came to the carnival to have fun, I wasn't expecting to work. I put myself in this situation and I just went for it since the pay was $1.25 per hour. Tons of quarters were landing on the canvas that was laid out on the ground. My job was to also pick them up and put them into the apron. When my apron got full I started putting them in my coat pockets, and then my pants pockets.

It was crazy how all of these ladies were telling me to give them the dish even if they didn't make it in the dish. They would speak to me in Spanish so the old man couldn't understand since he was Caucasian. I was too honest and was raised that way. I resisted their persuasive nature, and we don't need to get into what they did to try and get me to budge.

They finally gave up and moved on to another game. There were rides going on and I saw friends from school that came to talk to me while I was working. My friend Rudy asked, "How did you get this job?" I responded, "Oh man, I have no idea, I just fell into it." I wanted to go have fun with them but I was stuck for the long haul. The old man was tired, he must have not expected a big crowd in Dimmitt. The migrant workers wanted to have fun spending their money and they heard about the carnival. There was a massive amount of people that stomped the pasture flat all night. You could hear the screams of joy on the rides all night long, and the food smelled so good. I hadn't eaten anything yet – I was starved.

It was nearing midnight and my brothers left for home. The old man asked if I wanted to help him tear down his tent, he would pay me extra. I agreed, and when the carnival ended we started tearing down the tent. I started picking up even more quarters and my coat pockets were loaded with quarters as the apron was overflowing.

All of a sudden, I heard my dad's voice.

"David!"

"I've been working all night."

"Oh mi hijo, we have to go. We've been looking all over for you."

"I'm sorry sir, I have to go ... that's my dad." I looked at the old man.

The vendor thanked me and paid me for the hours worked, he gave me extra for helping him clean up a little after closing. I took my apron off and handed it to him filled with quarters.

My dad was not mad at me he just felt bad and knew they were leaving early in the morning. I apologized for staying so late. I was so tired and he knew I had exhausted myself just to help the old man. On the way home my dad was very compassionate, he felt bad that I didn't have any fun at all. He told me that he was going to buy me a bike when they returned from the Rio Grande Valley.

When we got home, my dad explained to my mom what I was doing at the carnival and that it was okay. My mom had been so worried about me. As a kid I didn't know how much worry I caused her, but now that I have kids and grandkids, I can imagine how she felt.

I walked over to the kitchen where my dad was talking to my mom. I had forgotten about all the quarters in my pants and coat pockets. The old man had already packed up and left by now. I said, "Dad, look what I have for your trip." I started pulling out all of the quarters from my pants and coat pockets and I placed them on the kitchen table. That was the most money I had ever made in one night as a twelve-year-old kid.

My mom and dad just looked at each other and then looked at me and smiled something special. They had money for their trip and I would like to think that they slept pretty good that night before leaving in the morning. My dad let me keep the quarters that I had in one of my coat pockets, which amounted to about thirty dollars.

This was the first time I remember having so much money. The next day I walked over to TG&Y and bought a BB gun. I enjoyed shooting sparrows with my brother's gun, but never had my own. Then I walked over to the Bobcat Drive-In and ordered a hamburger and fry with a large cherry coke. And after I finished that delightful meal, I ordered a strawberry milkshake. I was so full I could hardly move. I thought to myself, *wow, so this is what it's like to have money?*

9.

Sixth Grade

The summer was over and my sixth-grade year was about to begin. I had purchased some cowboy boots and some nice clothes to start the school year, thanks to that lady that suggested I help the old man at the carnival. I had my clothes all laid out in the order I was going to wear them – none of them had patches, they were brand new! Three pair of jeans, three T-shirts, and four dress shirts. White socks were always on sale and what I would normally wear. I was tired of wearing hand-me-down clothes, or donated clothes from the wealthy people across the tracks.

The only Christian music I would listen to in this era was the music at church on Sundays and it was normally in Spanish. I can still strum those guitar chords – they were pretty simple. Most of the tunes I listened to were 1970's soft rock and rock. Some country music was okay, Hank Williams, Dolly Parton, Loretta Lynn, Johnny Cash, and others. It was mostly my mom that liked country music so I picked some up at home on the radio.

I knew it was a sin to think of girls in a certain way, or to view inappropriate pictures and movies. Until my first day of school in the sixth grade I had never paid so much attention to what girls were wearing. I don't know, maybe I started growing and I was at that place where boys take a bigger interest in girls. The mini-skirt days were a hot style and many of the girls were wearing short dresses that exposed most of their thighs. I would often watch girls grabbing the bottom part of their dresses and pulling it down with their hands. I never got that, because if you don't want anyone seeing your entire set of legs and even your underwear at times, why are you wearing it?

I'm so thankful that Jesus forgives, because I know I sinned many times by looking and having sinful thoughts. I asked for forgiveness many times.

> *Matthew 18:21-22 Then Peter came up and said to him, "Lord, how often will my brother sin against me, and I forgive him? As many as seven times?" Jesus said to him, "I do not say to you seven times, but seventy-seven times."*

At our school the lockers were split up in two. There was a top half and a bottom half which both required a combination lock that we had to provide. We also had to memorize our combination – like a manual password. There was this blonde-blue-eyed girl. I wouldn't say she was like a beauty-queen model, but she was pretty and had a very nice figure.

While I was putting my lock on my locker, she walks up to me.

"Hi, y'all work for my daddy, I'm Sheryn Roberts."

"Hi, I'm David Espinoza."

The entire sixth-grade year every morning, I had to face this nice girl that we worked for, and I had to fight the desire to watch her in a mini-skirt while she was getting her books from her locker above my locker.

I became friends with Sheryn that year. She even invited me to her house after school one day. She had it all planned out. She knew that we chopped weeds for her dad during the summer. I was totally unaware of this. She had a little brother, I just can't remember his name.

This wealthy-Caucasian girl was not discriminatory toward me, she actually looked up to me and I don't know why. She did mention P.E. class and how I did things during that class that were athletic, but truly, I think we had a connection from the summer fieldwork at her dad's farm.

She never once asked me about why my left eye was different. I appreciated that about Sheryn. I didn't know whether we were just friends or if she was interested in me being her boyfriend. I never asked her about that, I just enjoyed talking to her when she approached me during class, during recess, or in the hallway.

Sheryn wasn't shy, when some of the kids asked how she knew me, and this was during class, she would respond, *he works for my daddy during the summers.* I didn't want anyone to know that I worked for her dad during the summers. It was just the way it was and I admitted that I was poor and had to work in the fields. I was sure to mention that I no longer had to since my dad started a gas station business. I guess that lifted up my pride. It felt so good to say that my dad owned his own business.

When my brothers found out that I knew the bosses daughter, they would make fun of me and laugh at me. They would say that Sheryn was my girlfriend. They would say stuff like, *ha-ha! David has a girlfriend.* Well, she wasn't, because as much as I wanted to hold her hand, or try to kiss her, or even ask her if she would *go with me*, it just wasn't going to happen. I was too nervous to even ask her if that was even a possibility. Why would a wealthy girl want to *go with* a poverty-Hispanic kid from the other side of the tracks?

During the sixth grade, Sheryn made me feel like I was a normal kid. She also made me feel special. It was heart-warming to see that a nice girl so complete would take an interest in me, a kid with imperfections, a kid with low self-esteem. The most fun I had with a girl during the sixth grade, was with Sheryn Roberts.

My mom asked my brothers and I if we would come work at the Roberts to finish a field that was incomplete. It was four hours worth of work and it was happening on Friday after school.

Sheryn approached me at our lockers in the hallway. She knew about us doing field work for her dad on Friday. She asked me if I wanted to come over after school on the country bus she and her brother rode. Goodness gracious, she invited me to come to her house! She said that after we played some games at her house, I could go out to the field and meet up with my mom and brothers.

I was already done with fieldwork and had put that behind me, since the FINA gas station kept me busy, but an opportunity like this one was unheard of for me. This was the first time any girl from school asked me to do anything.

At home that evening I asked my mom and dad if I could go to the Roberts' house on the bus with Sheryn. They didn't seem to have a problem with that, so it was settled. And of course my brothers made fun of me again, "David's got a girlfriend!" I hated that, I didn't have a girlfriend, she was just a friend. Deep inside I thought to myself, *I wish she was my girlfriend, I really like her.*

That Friday, I didn't work at the gas station, instead I rode the bus with Sheryn. I asked her if I could sit on the window seat, I didn't want any of the rich farm kids to see me or to talk to me. I was nervous about bus rides and how kids would make fun of me. I was surprised when I discovered these kids were not like my neighborhood kids. They talked different, I didn't hear the F word or any kind of bad language. They seemed to be more calm in a way.

Sheryn was full of information sharing, I just listened to her and all of the things she had to say about her farm. I learned early on that girls love to talk forever. She asked me so many questions about what I did and where I lived. When I turned to look at her, she was on the side that was easy for my left eye to move evenly with my good eye. I paid close attention to these details about myself. I told her about the FINA gas station and how my dad owned it. I filled her in on all kinds of tasks I learned and excelled at during the summer ... that impressed her.

When we arrived at her house, we mostly did cartwheels in her garage with her brother. Her garage was as big as our entire house – wow! We didn't have a garage so I couldn't relate to her luxuries. At our house we parked our cars outside on the dirt. She asked me if I wanted a soda. She walked over to the huge refrigerator in her garage and opened the door. It was full of drinks like sodas and juices. Sheryn handed me a Dr. Pepper. This tasted so good on a perfect day.

Before I headed to the field to join my family for some chopping weeds on the soybean field, I kept thinking to myself that I should ask her, *are we boyfriend-girlfriend?* I never got that courage, I was too nervous and scared that she might reject that idea. I had friends in the sixth grade that were "Going steady with a girl," meaning they were a couple. I had not held a girl's hand, which is what most couples did at that age – I never knew otherwise. I couldn't hide that feeling I had for Sheryn. The entire year we were just friends, and I'll never know how she felt about me. Could I have been a boy she would have held hands with?

There is a Bible scripture that comes to mind, and I love this part of it.

Luke 22: 42-44 And there appeared to him an angel from heaven.

I know there's more to these verses, but with Sheryn during my sixth-grade year, this is what I felt. She was my angel that gave me self-esteem and confidence. I thank God for Sheryn that year.

Sheryn continued to say hi to me and I would say hi to her even past the grade-school days. Our friends were in different groups as the years went by in school. I'll never forget the adventure to her house and how I thought to myself how different I lived at home than her family. I loved seeing her nice-clean house with expensive furniture and all. I wanted that some day. I just had no idea how I would get there, I was too young and still learning so much.

Our teacher was Mrs. Allsup, she was a short lady with a chunky build and a face that always looked like she was mad. She was one of the toughest teachers I had in grade school. I was joyful and full of confidence that year. I was placed in the smart class ... Jim was also happy. There were many other smart kids in this class. If Tobin was in your class, you knew you were in the smart class – the kid was a genius.

Being in a smart class meant doing tougher work, which I wasn't too excited about. Mrs. Allsup would make us memorize poems once a week. Every Monday she assigned each of us a short poem to memorize. I can't even remember what poems or who the authors were. The only poem I can remember from that class was, *The Road Not Taken*. Being in a smart class was nerve-racking with Mrs. Allsup. Why did we have to memorize poems and then recite them in front of the class? That was her thing, she loved poetry and wanted to introduce that to us. There were some kids that handled speaking in front of class better than others. I normally did okay if I knew my material.

The teacher did help us if we got stuck and couldn't remember the next line. It was still stressful at times. I found that if I studied hard and knew my lines by heart, I wasn't as nervous as when I didn't study hard. All year long the homework was tough. I normally worked on homework in-between customers at the FINA gas station. The days were tiring and sometimes I would end up finishing my homework in the hallway before school the next morning. With work after school and watching some TV before getting ready for bed, there just wasn't enough time. Heaven forbid I give up watching *The Brady Bunch; Gilligan's Island; Batman; Superman; The Lone Ranger; The Virginian; Bonanza,* or *Lost in Space.*

I would often ask Sheryn what her result was for an answer to a math problem or any other assignments. If she came up with a different answer, I'd ask her to explain it to me. She would do that – it helped me understand it better. Sometimes when I didn't understand how teachers explained things to me, I would ask one of my smart friends, and most of the time they could explain it better to me.

What sticks to my mind is watching four sixth graders that were in my class do something I would have never done. Some of them, although very intelligent, would do stuff as a joke. I'm not sure what kind of attention they were trying to get, but it never ended positive. I witnessed them lifting up the front part of Mrs. Allsup's Volkswagen – they straddled the curb with this car! The curb was a few inches higher than most. Volkswagens were known to have the engine on the rear part of the car. Wow, that was a crazy thing to do. I just watched and then went back inside. I stayed away from that prank.

When Mrs. Allsup found out, she asked the class if anyone knew who had done this to her car. No one said anything. She must have found out from another source because the kids that did that were definitely in trouble. I'm not sure how it was handled, but they all learned a lesson and paid their price. One punishment could have been licks with a board by the principal and a conference with the parents. These kids were all from good families and just did something stupid without thinking how dangerous it could have been if the car fell on one of them.

Sports to me were priority, I loved football, basketball, track and field, and baseball. Although our schools never had soccer as a sports program, we did play it at recess. I remember getting hit by the soccer ball on my stomach – knocked the wind out of me. I finally recovered after gasping for air for twenty seconds or so. The group of kids were all around me and asking, *are you okay?* That was the first time I had ever experienced that – what a horrible and scary experience.

When we picked teams at recess, it was mostly Thompson and Leon that got picked first. These two African-American kids were very athletic and no one messed with them. Leon and Thompson lived in the same side of town that I did, although it was rare that I associated with them off school hours. I was normally picked third or fourth for whatever game we were playing. It drove me crazy that I would never be picked first. I still remembered beating Thompson in the Ford Punt, Pass, and Kick Contest. I'm sure he was aware of it. I never brought it up because I didn't want to get in a fight with Thompson, he was one of the toughest kids in school. He would get angry at me if he saw any sign of me beating him at anything.

Thompson and I had much in common, we were friends throughout the school years, but just not real close friends. We were both very competitive and driven to be perfect at something – no matter how hard we had to practice. We played sports together for many years. We had our good times and our bad times. We also enjoyed hanging around the wealthy-Caucasian kids, somehow we could relate with them better than our own race. I was Hispanic and he was African-American. Sometimes kids would call him Oreo and me, brown Oreo.

A great memory for me was a shooting contest in our physical education class. Mr. Lind was the P.E. teacher and he pretty much allowed us to play whatever games we wanted. He would take a vote for what games we would play in P.E. He stayed with the sport in season, whether football, basketball, or track and field. During basketball season, P.E. had to do with basketball-shooting drills, scrimmaging, or some kind of contest.

There were several classes grouped into one physical education class. We always looked forward to exiting the classroom for some exercise. Mr. Lind promised to buy a milkshake for the boy that won the shooting contest. I knew I had a chance because of the hard work I had put in practicing at home. It was like Johnny Hampton on his driveway, I practiced a lot. Thompson was not as good of a shooter and this was my time to shine. Leon was okay but not as good as I was. Rocky, Jeff, and Jim were also good shooters. I knew I had my work cut out. In result, I ended up winning the competition. Thompson was never happy for me when he lost. I still remember what his response was, *Espinoza you got lucky.*

I wasn't ever physically stronger or speed-wise faster than Thompson or Leon, but I did master certain skills better which gained their respect. I don't know how they truly felt, but that's the impression I got many times.

Sixth grade was also a fearful time for me. I was in a position where I started being friends with a few Caucasian kids. At school, I had some Hispanic friends but not as many as Caucasian friends. I was harassed by some of my Hispanic friends because I would hang around with Caucasian kids. *How come you're always hanging around White Crackers? You should be with us Chicanos man.* I don't want to dwell too much on the reverse discrimination because for a while I was trying to figure out how I could hang out with both races and not offend anyone.

I saw many fights out on the playground. It was rare that two Caucasian kids were fighting. It was mostly Hispanics and African-Americans in some kind of a brawl. I watched and hoped that no one picked on me. I was one of the bigger kids for my age and I didn't normally put myself in a situation to cause a fight. I was always planning on what I would do if someone picked a fight with me.

I was at a disadvantage because I did not want a fist to connect with my left eye. The serious hospitalization would have been a never-ending nightmare, not just for me, but for my parents as well. There were a few times where I got into scuffles with kids, but they were smaller than I was and it was not an issue. A lot of these smaller kids ran from me if they made fun of me. I could never imagine getting into a fight with someone like Leon, or Thompson.

Teachers would always break up the fights and then for the remainder of the school day, that would be the news at every class. Students would get the inside scoop on who got whipped by who. Sixth grade was mild compared to my junior high days. God was with me during these trying times when I was still learning. And as a young kid, despite the fact that I went to church every Sunday, I still didn't know how much God loved me and how much freedom He was giving me to make mistakes and learn from them.

My dad bought us some used boxing gloves. He showed us how to protect ourselves. I learned pretty fast. I also watched the professional boxers and learned from them. Sugar Ray Leonard was quick and one of the best. I watched how he protected his face. All of my brothers started boxing in the backyard. I even saw my Uncle Jessie box my dad once. My dad did well with his defense. Uncle Jessie wasted punches where my dad was smart and connected with good timing. All in good fun though.

I got pretty good at boxing against my neighbors, Rudy, Freddy, and this one kid called Tito. I also boxed against my brother Richard many times. I learned how to protect my eye with my left-hand glove. I conditioned myself to close the eye tight, not just during boxing matches, but also when I went swimming at the public pool. The boxing gloves were 16 oz. gloves, padded well, but you could still feel a good punch.

Tito was short and about four years older than I was. He was a friend of my brother, Gilberto. When I boxed him I was pretty confident because I had beaten Rudy and Freddy, who were also a little older than I was. No one told me Tito was a lot older. I'll never forget the beating he gave me. I was a head taller than he was, so I thought, *this should be a piece of cake*. Once we started boxing, I blocked a couple of his hooks and I was focused on protecting my left eye. I caught him with a left hook after dodging his right-hand punch. His eye was red and started swelling a bit.

We kept boxing for a few more minutes, you could hear the rose-colored gloves pound against each other. I knew this kid had boxed before, maybe Golden Gloves or something. I was over-protecting my left eye, no way I wanted to get hit there. He threw a right-hand blow right into my left-hand glove that was protecting my left eye, and then he threw two quick combinations. I stopped his first one, but he got me good with the second one. I started crying and I said I didn't want to fight anymore. I was mad because I was a head taller and felt a little embarrassed that Tito had prevailed. I didn't realize my dad was watching. He told me to get back out there and finish one more round with Tito.

His objective was to teach me not to quit. I didn't want to continue, but my dad insisted that I needed to do it. So I went back after wiping my tears with my shirt. Again I came at Tito because I was angry. I caught him with a jab and then a right-hand punch. After that he had tears in his eyes, but came right back at me anyway. I couldn't match his skills and my brother, Gilberto, who was officiating the fight, stopped it and said, "It's over! Good fight." Tito apologized to me after the fight, I was still in tears and accepted a defeat. He was stronger and more experienced at boxing than I was.

That day I learned a valuable lesson. Don't judge a person by their cover. Tito was a short kid, but my strength could not measure to his. He was also more coordinated than I was. I also learned what it was like to fight. My brother Gilberto loved boxing against me, but I knew he took it easy on me. He never went all out on me, it was fun for him to box against me.

After all the boxing in the backyard, I started wanting to join Golden Gloves to become a fighter in the ring. I even used to go watch some of my friends. People like Ernie Reyes who was a grade higher than me, and a good friend. This guy was always nice to me no matter where we were, the basketball court, the boxing ring, the pool hall, or even at church. Ernie was a good boxer and wanted me to join Golden Gloves with him.

I asked my parents if I could join Golden Gloves. The definite answer from my mom was, no. She knew what could happen if I got hit on my left eye. I was a kid and I didn't think about that – I just knew I wanted to get into the nice ring with red ropes. I wanted to be part of Golden Gloves like my friends – it looked exciting to me. What I didn't know is that I would be fighting kids that were in junior high and high school. The categories were by weight and I was pretty tall for my age. The Golden Gloves idea was put to rest when I saw the guys I had to box, plus there was no way my mom would ever approve of this sport, especially for me. I learned how to fight in my backyard and I was ready for anyone that might want to pick on me at school. The only difference was that in school, there would be no gloves, just bare fists – yikes.

Luckily I was able to avoid any fights during my sixth-grade year. I discovered a hidden skill I had, talking the person into not fighting. Whether it was, *I don't know who told you that but I never said that, you're a good friend of mine.* Or maybe I'd say, *I have to get back to class I'm late man, let's not worry about this.* I would always think of something. It was mostly with the kids that were much bigger than I was that I'd find a way to get out of the situation. I always told myself that I would defend myself only if it was the last resort, and never did I tell any of those bully kids that it was because of my eye. This system worked for me, until I got to junior high, which you'll read about a little later.

While my boxing dreams vanished, my basketball dreams resonated to a higher level. I watched my older brothers, Gilberto and Loop, play on their respective teams. Loop was in the eighth grade and Gilberto was already in high school – Gilberto had a passion for basketball. I had never seen anyone practice as much as he did. I watched as many games that I could since they were a close walking-distance from our house. I attended every home game and I only hoped that I could go to the away games – that would never happen.

Loop's junior high team went undefeated that entire year. They had some great athletes. Loop was one of the best athletes around our neighborhood and he was also one of the toughest kids in our neighborhood – kids just didn't mess with Loop. He looked after me when I hung around with him and his friends.

I still remember the five starters on his team, Ronnie Lawson, Loop Espinoza, Leon Sandoval, Jerry Schaffer, and Edward Nino. Three Hispanic kids and two Caucasian kids. They were all athletes and hard workers. All through my career in sports there were only a few times that my teams came close to being undefeated, but I never experienced what Loop did. Wow! I mean, it's very difficult to go undefeated when you're playing ten teams in the district. That was a huge inspiration to me, watching my brother be part of this historical eighth-grade team. The Bobcats were rolling and for many years Dimmitt had great basketball teams while I was there.

10.

Seventh Grade

My parents would take us to Palo Duro Canyon. This place was so cool, and reasonable as far as cost. It was a place our family could get away from Dimmitt for a day. It was mostly on Easter Sunday that we drove there after church. We wore our church clothes to the canyon – never understood that logic.

Palo Duro Canyon is located just outside of Canyon, Texas. At the bottom of this huge canyon there is a famous tourist attraction. The actual play "Texas" goes on all summer long. The entire time I lived in Texas we never went to this play. I think that we just couldn't afford it – the ticket price for each of us would run my dad a pretty big bill. I did finally watch this play, but it was years later. It was amazing, the actors were great and they used real horses and all on this large-stadium-seating amphitheater.

We managed to run in the canyon trails and we also discovered another tourist attraction called, Six Gun City. That was a place that I could have spent all day just watching the Cowboys and hanging out at this make-believe Cowboy town. They had a saloon, a jail, a mercantile, a restaurant, and twice a day they would hold a show with live actors on the street. All of the shows ended in a gun fight. It was so much fun and we always looked forward to a trip to Palo Duro Canyon.

Every time we took a vacation trip there we learned something new. I learned how to ride a horse at Six Gun City. You could rent them for $3.60 per hour. There was normally a tour guide unless you were an experienced rider, then you could just go on your own riding trails. They had overnight-stay cabins down in the canyon. It was so much fun and I felt like the Cowboys in the western movies I'd watch on TV. I felt blessed that my parents did that for us despite the financial situation.

My two older brothers had the opportunity to work there during a couple of summers when they were in high school. It was cool seeing them in some gunfights on the Cowboy-town street performing in front of tourists. In one of the gun fights I was even an extra by no choice. I happened to be at the right place at the right time. One of the Cowboys picked me when I was watching next to a fence post. I think the cowboy actor said, *this young man saw you shoot my friend!* He grabbed my arm and continued, *I guess we need to take him to jail!* I was in a little bit of a stardom feeling when I noticed everyone looking at me during the show.

We had fun growing up together in Texas, and Six Gun City was definitely an escape we all looked forward to. What would have been cool, was staying one night down in the canyon, but we could never afford to do that with a large family. I did ask my parents several times if we could stay in the cabins, but the answer was always the same, *no*.

The weather was also scary living in Texas. Every year we would hear the sirens. If we heard three of them, that meant a tornado warning. The news on TV was always a big help to inform us of any weather-destructive pattern.

Things got pretty crazy in our neighborhood. People in cars were driving everywhere like maniacs. When those loud sirens went off and the strong winds were screaming with dark clouds surrounding the area, we all knew that a tornado could possibly hit. I witnessed several instances where I actually saw the funnel cloud come down and touch the ground only a few blocks away. Tornadoes were the scariest thing I ever saw. I remember praying to God as a kid. I wanted my family to be safe, we didn't have a cellar, in fact not many of our neighbors had cellars. There were a few that had a hole dug up with steps leading down to a small concrete room. Ralph and Sara, our neighbors, had a relative close by with a cellar. It was two blocks away from our house. No questions asked, we always loaded up our car and drove there –

the winds were too strong to walk or run. It was possible to get hit with an object flying by. Everyone in our family would freak out except my dad, he was always calm.

I remember once, a huge cyclone touched down about a mile away. We were all yelling at my dad, "Hurry up!" Some of the younger kids were crying because my dad went back in the house to open the windows and grab some valuables. If you don't open your home windows and a tornado hits, well, your house could possibly explode with the pressure. When he came out he was walking fast, but not running. He then stepped on the gas pedal and drove through the alley straight to the neighbor cellar.

Sometimes I think God allows these things to happen for reasons. I don't know, but just maybe, He wants us to know the kind of power He has. When we made it to the cellar, there were several neighbors there. Some that we didn't know and some that we did know. Tornadoes to me were always like an emergency-neighborhood meeting. We never got together unless there was a tornado adventure happening.

Everyone seemed to be nice. One kid was cracking jokes and his mom would come down on him. It was easy to joke around once we were in a safe place. Some of my wealthy friends would just spend the night in their large basements – worry free. I knew that some of my friends had their bedrooms below ground level.

Once every few years we would fear that our roof would cave down on us. Hail as big as softballs had been reported in certain areas of the Texas Panhandle. The biggest hailstorm I ever witnessed was golf-ball-size hail with some scattered baseball size. I thought our house was going to come down while I kept cringing through the massive episode of these white bombs pounding on our roof. My mom would tell us to keep away from the windows. Three feet away from the window I watched the white mass of solid ice falling from the sky. My heart was pounding and I remember the ten minutes that hailstorm lasted, but it was more like two hours to me. I just wanted it to go away – I was so scared and full of fear for all my family.

Dust storms were not threatening, but such a huge nuisance and very uncomfortable. The strong winds and the dust from all the dirt roads and farm fields kept us captive inside. The dryness during the summer contributed to these dust storms. There was no visibility when you were driving. I remember a few times my dad pulled over to the side of the road until the dust let off a little.

One year we had a teacher give us kids a ride to a basketball tournament in Leveland, Texas. We hit a dust storm on the way. She pulled over because of poor visibility. We waited an hour on the side of the road with the car lights on. When we got back home late that day, our house was full of dust. As sealed as we had the windows and doors, the dust managed to find its way inside our house. Those times were horrible for me, and I felt like just wearing a patch over my left eye again. The dryness it caused was unbearable. I had no eye drops – they would've helped. It hurt a lot but what could I do? It was always a relief when the dust storms went away.

Summers were all too short before school started once again. I wished summers could have gone on forever. We made it through another year operating the FINA gas station and we were able to afford more things and more trips to different places. My dad started closing the business on Sundays, it got to be over-whelming and he needed that break as we kids did too.

When I entered the seventh grade I was super nervous about many things. In grade school I saw those kids all year long, they were used to me and I felt comfortable around them. In junior high I would face new kids that I never met before. There would be seven periods throughout the day and a different teacher at each class.

I liked the fact that if you made the football team, the prac-tices would substitute for a P.E. class. That meant no physical education class for me in junior high. English was one of my favorite classes. I still remember my English-class teachers, Mrs. Rake and Mrs. Brooks.

The previous week, Mom and Dad took me to Amarillo to see the doctor for my eye-cleaning appointment and checkup. I hated every one of those appointments and still do today. I never got excited about going to the doctor for a cleaning or checkup. I was always relieved when it was over. The ophthalmologist told me that I was growing fast, he couldn't believe it. My eyes were starting to match size-wise, and the color was precise. I was glad to hear that, but the real test would come when I started school.

I talked to my mom about trying out for football – the Dimmitt Bobcat seventh grade team. My mom looked at me with a worried look.

"David, it's too dangerous, I don't think I want you playing football."

I asked my dad as well. He also did not want me playing football. They were thinking of my safety. What if I got hit in the eye? I explained to them that the helmets had faceguards which would protect me and I would always close my eye when I hit someone or when I got hit. For the next week before football tryouts started, I begged my parents day and night.

"Please can I play football, I really want to play football. Gilberto and Loop played, why can't I?"

The answer was always, no. I cried and I cried, I wanted to be on the team, I was good at football and I had a gift to punt and kick the football. It was difficult for me to accept what had happened to me and that I would not be able to do the things my brothers did. It just wasn't fair. I would hear Thompson, Tommy, and some of my other friends always talk about how much fun it was going to be when we played on a real team with helmets and pads.

My dad explained to me about working at the gas station. He needed me to work right after school. This was a frustrating time in my life. Because of this horrible accident I was controlled as to what I could do and what I couldn't do. It was not fair and I wasn't about to give up.

I wore my parents down after four days of begging and crying. I couldn't sleep at night so I would go stand outside their bedroom curtain and tell them I couldn't sleep. My mom would come out to the living room and she would pray for me. She did that for me often throughout my childhood life. Whether it was because of a neighborhood incident that was on my mind and I couldn't shake it, or whether it was because of me wanting to play football. Baseball was not even a question despite my passion for wanting to play on a team with my friends. I got over baseball because I was allowed to do track and field.

My dad kept asking me, *what are you going to do if you get hurt?* I kept telling him that I would still help him after practices and I was hoping not to get hurt. He could tell that I was very passionate about playing football. I wanted to be one of those players in uniforms playing in a real game. I had no doubts in my mind that I would make the team. My dad would get mad at me and he would tell me that I was wasting my time playing football. He was clear on what he wanted of me, which was going to work at the gas station right after school.

I totally respect my parents for their concerns. They wanted me to stay safe and to not get injured. I got tired of not being allowed to do something because I could not see out of one eye and because I could get hurt. The fact was that I wanted to play on the team with my friends. To me it was fun, rewarding, and fulfilling. I also felt more normal than ever when I accomplished something like the normal kids in my grade. I asked my parents in tears one more time.

"Mommy, Daddy, why am I the only one that can't do certain things in my family?"

"Mi hijo, are you sure you want to take that chance of going back to the hospital?"

"Mommy, yes, I'm willing to take that chance. I want to play that bad."

My parents both looked at each other.

"Well it's up to you, I guess it's okay with me," Mom said.

"What about work after school?" Dad asked.

"I'll be there right after practice every day, I promise, Dad."

They finally gave me the approval – wow! The happiness rushed to my brain, and it was like a huge weight lifted off of my shoulders. I can't believe how many days I had to beg my parents for their permission. I remember going to church the following Sunday. I kneeled in front of the cross and I thanked God for helping me convince my parents. I knew there was a God, I felt like He was listening to me when I talked to Him.

The first day of football practice was basically instructional. Long hours of standing listening to the coaches talk about what was expected of us. I looked around at the team and I saw R. Ewing, Thompson, Leon, Eddie, and Reggie. These four African-

American kids were tough and I was glad they were finally on my team for once. We would be playing against other towns. I never thought I would get this opportunity.

One of the first things the coach mentioned was that we needed to get a sports physical. I immediately went into a concerned-mode again. What would the doctor say? Would he not allow me to play football when he found out about my left eye? There was only one way to find out. During the first few practices there was no kind of contact. The coaches were waiting for every player to complete their sports physical.

The next day, my mom took me to get a physical. What a nerve-racking experience. If you're a boy and you've had a sports physical, you know exactly what I'm talking about. I won't go into the details of what the doctors do. I will say this though, the doctor never asked me about my eye and I didn't bring it up. I completed the physical and was approved to play football!

From that day on, each year, I went in for a physical. I no longer worried about that issue. If the doctors noticed my eye and asked about the danger if I got hit while playing football, I always reverted to the previous year. I would respond, "Yes sir, last year the doctor approved me to play." I found a way for all doctors to approve my physicals. It never became an issue like I thought it would. A few doctors did recommend I wear athletic glasses, but I never bought any until years later, they were too expensive.

Seventh grade was an eye-awakening experience for me, no pun intended. Every day my dad or mom would drop us off in front of the Dimmitt Junior High building. At the time it was my sister Louise and I that were dropped off. She was in the eighth grade and I was in the seventh grade. The mornings were great as far as bullies staying away. After school was always a stressful adventure when there was no football practice.

There were fights that took place after school and sporadically during lunch and recess times on a regular basis. The reasons for these fights were so stupid. It was usually because someone said something and then the person it was said about didn't like it. Girl or boy, it didn't matter, they would approach each other and trash talk in front of the entire student body. Then they went on to say, *after school, meet me after school in front of the busses*. And sure enough, after school there was bunches of students in a huge circle watching these two students go at it. I watched a few fights after school. We had a few minutes before football practice so if I heard of a fight after school, I would want to watch like most of the kids in school.

I feared that one day it could be me fighting. My sister Louise beat up a few girls during her school days in Dimmitt – she was a tough girl. I never saw her fight, but everyone told me about it. Most of the time she would say a few words to the girls and they would run from her.

At church I had to memorize the ten commandments, I knew what a sin was. Fighting was a sin, stealing, killing, disobeying your mom or dad was a sin, and so on – there are many ways to sin and it's easy. Following what Jesus Christ taught us is not an easy thing to do, to follow a narrow path to the gate of paradise.

Why were kids so angry at this school I attended? I didn't know then, but now that I'm a lot older, I have a few ideas. I think many kids in junior high had a mindset of, *it's about me*. They also didn't want the student body to think someone else was tougher than them. There were several dysfunctional families and poor kids that brought their anger to school. Another reason fights broke out was because someone got jealous over a girl. Or if it was a girl, someone got jealous for a guy.

I knew Oscar, a kid that had one of the prettiest girlfriends in school. I remember being in the bathroom. Oscar told another kid, who was minding his own business, to not look at his girlfriend and say things about her. This kid was pretty strong, he lived a few blocks from my house. He turned around and looked at Oscar. I remember them arguing about the matter. He told Oscar to meet him after school so he could have a chance to shut him up. Oscar agreed and it was a done deal – a fight after school. I looked at Oscar and asked, "Are you crazy, Oscar? He's a lot stronger than you are ... don't do it." Oscar said he wasn't going to let him talk about his girl like that.

I was sitting there thinking, *oh my goodness, is this guy serious about getting his head beat in?* Pretty soon it was all over the school, we didn't need social media back then, word of mouth at Dimmitt Junior High traveled like lightning. During my seventh period, the last class of the day, I tried convincing Oscar one more time. It didn't do any good, he thought he could beat this kid in a fight. He was going to prove it in front of his girlfriend.

The bell rang, and sure enough I followed Oscar, maybe ten steps behind him, to the back of the school where they agreed to meet. I'm just going to call this kid, "G". G was waiting for Oscar. Before you knew it there was a big circle of kids surrounding the two and Oscar's girlfriend pleading for him not to fight. Oscar didn't have a chance. He tried to take a punch at G, but it was no use. G smacked him right in the face and broke the nice glasses he was wearing. Oscar fell back on the ground and as he started to get back up, G kicked him on the face and blood started gushing everywhere. It was such a sad scene. I wanted to jump in so bad to stop this senseless fight, but at that school you just didn't stop fights unless it was by a teacher. G's sisters were watching and after Oscar was full of blood and lying defenseless, they started telling G to stop it. G was just kicking him and punching him even after he broke Oscar's nose. I felt so bad for Oscar, he put himself in a horrible situation. He not only embarrassed himself by his poor decision, but he also put his girlfriend in an awkward position. It caused problems the rest of the school year.

My seventh grade year was one of the years I witnessed so many fights after school and sometimes during school. I avoided fights anyway I could, not just because of my eye, but because punches hurt. I knew what it felt like to get hit with a 16 oz. glove, I didn't want to get hit by a bare fist. My brother Richard and I had a few fist fights at home during our childhood days, so I had a small taste of it. I was ready in case someone didn't give me a chance to avoid a fight.

In-between classes there were students everywhere, and it wasn't unusual that I would literally bump into someone walking in the opposite direction – half my vision was lacking. I was headed to my English class and I accidentally bumped into this eighth grader. He was a tough kid, I wasn't sure if I could take him or not. I didn't want to find out either. At Dimmitt Junior High, there was a lot of pressure, it would not look good if you backed down from a fight. It would make one look like a scared chicken, or a coward. I had that in the back of my mind and I also had my left eye on my mind. So this kid, his name was Jessie, came at me using verbal-abuse language. He stood there talking trash at me with some of his friends behind him watching. Immediately afterwards, a pile of kids circled around us.

Oh my, I had such a bad feeling about this. Jessie was running his mouth inches away from me and looking up at me because I was four inches taller. I thought to myself, *If he touches me in any way, I'm defending myself. I'm closing my left eye and I will protect it while I start punching just like I did against Tito, and I'm pretty sure Tito is tougher than Jessie.* We stood there for about three minutes, I didn't say one word. He kept asking me, *come on ... you scared?* He was spitting out the F word and many others at me, but I was strong and didn't make the first move. I came awful close to losing it – I was getting angry.

I was relieved when the bell rang and it was time to go to class. Jessie never hit me or pushed me. I think in a way, when he saw how big I actually was, he might have had second thoughts. He walked off with his friends following him and he continued to throw cuss words at me. I just looked at him one more time and shook my head as I walked into class. I think the crowd was disappointed that there wasn't a fight.

I was sweating it because I also knew that fighting could get you suspended from school and that would not go well with my football coaches. I was so relieved that I did not get into a fight with Jessie. Believe it or not, I was proud of myself for yet avoiding another fight. I had no suspicion that God was with me in times like this, I never thanked God for being with me when I was that age. I have thanked Him since for all the things He guided me through. Even when I didn't know it, He was there for me.

The adjustment for this type of environment was challenging, but I was able to overcome many challenges that came my way. Discrimination was minimal I would say, but it did happen. Not only African-American kids but also Caucasian kids. I got plenty of dirty looks from both races. At times, even Hispanics would discriminate against me because of who I would hang out with at school. I did the best I could, but sometimes I felt so out of place. My eyes were looking pretty good, and unless someone looked close, they could not tell that I had a prosthetic eye. If they did recognize that, I'd always say, *yeah I have what you call, lazy eye, I was born like this.* That answer was working for me, I felt normal avoiding the island of the misfits.

I remember watching *Rudolph the Red-nosed Reindeer* during Christmas time. In that part where they talk about the island of the misfits, well, I pictured myself being one of those characters. I felt sad and no one could relate to what I was feeling or going through at school. I never talked about these things with my parents, I didn't want them to feel bad for me. They had enough stress in their lives already.

The gas station business was hanging in there and my dad was starting to slowly show losses. The migrant workers left for the season and business slowed way down. There was a gas crunch in the 1970s and he was starting to have problems getting fuel delivered to the large gas tanks underground. Dad also hired, Luis, one of our neighbors, to work for him. With all of us kids in school, he needed help during the daytime.

The financial problems hit our family again, we were all on the free-lunch program and I was embarrassed when some of the rich kids saw me pull out my lunch ticket. They knew I was a poor kid from the other side of the tracks. To them I was cool despite my poverty life because I was the starting fullback on the football team, and I could boot the football a long way.

Leon and Thompson played halfback, and Matt played quarterback. I always wanted to play quarterback but it was not possible. The coaches determined what position everyone would be assigned. I started seeing the pattern of how some parents were more involved than others, I'll just leave it at that.

It was sports that turned my whole life around. In addition to being the fullback, I was with no question the best kicker and punter on the team. All season long we kept winning games, we were undefeated, with Leon and Thompson I never thought about losing a game. Sure I got the football now and then and ran for a few yards, maybe scored a couple of touchdowns, but Thompson and Leon were the reason for our success.

Toward the end of the season, what I anticipated at this school became a reality. Fortunately, I only got into one fight the entire time I was in Dimmitt. Oh sure we played around a lot, my friends and I, punching at each other or wrestling outside, but it was never like a real fist fight. There were many times after this that I did avoid them, but this one fight was unavoidable.

We were preparing to play the Tulia Hornets. The practices were long and hard. Tulia was over thirty miles away from Dimmitt. We had just finished practicing, we were in the dressing room removing our equipment and getting ready to shower. Leon had been picking on a small-framed Caucasian kid. I was on the opposite side minding my own business when I heard this kid say, *why don't you pick on someone your own size like Espinoza? I bet he could kick your butt.* I just took a big swallow when Leon looked at me and came over. I said, "Come on Leon, don't listen to him ... I don't wanna fight ya."

That didn't slow Leon down, he came right at me and I knew he wasn't a Jessie. I put up my guard when he started throwing punches hitting the side of my shoulder and then my stomach. I was protecting my eye as I swung back at him and smacked him with a right hook. We were throwing punches so fast I couldn't keep up with how many punches we threw. A couple of punches grazed my head, but my defense helped keep my face protected. In about thirty seconds, in walks the coach. I thought to myself, *thank you God.*

The coach stopped the fight and took us to his office. I was surprised that I went thirty seconds with Leon – this kid was three inches taller than I was and one of the toughest kids in school. We were both supposed to get hit with a board. I took my three licks with the board for fighting – that was the school policy. Leon refused to get hit with the board. The coach sent him to the office as he would eventually get suspended from school.

Needless to say, we got beat by the Tulia Hornets – our first loss. Our second loss was against Hereford, Texas, they were a bigger school than us.

My coach told me that I did the right thing, and he knew that it was not my fault. I told him what happened and he understood. The coach also told me that because I stood up to Leon, he would never bother me again. He was right because Leon never bothered me again. The board hurt so much, but the school policy stated that if you get into a fight you earn three licks as punishment, or a suspension.

In the 1970s that kind of punishment was allowed in schools. Our school also had dress codes. If a girl wore a dress, it had to be a certain length to meet the requirement, I just can't remember how many inches above the knee. If we wore pants that had loops on them, we were required to wear a belt. As athletes our hair had to be cut above the ears. Every summer I would grow out my hair. It was the style in the 1970s, long hair. The coaches did not like it and we had to cut our hair or we would not be allowed to play. I wanted to play so bad that it was an easy decision. Did I like it? No, of course not. My friends that didn't play sports all had hair just below the ears. School code did not allow students to have it longer than that. Sports were very important to me, I started thinking about playing in the NFL some day. I also started thinking of how great it felt to be treated like a normal kid.

During basketball season, things were looking up for me as I was once again one of the top players on the team. The hours of practice that I put in developing all my skill sets paid off big time. I only remember our team losing two games the entire season. We were stacked with great athletes. I earned the opportunity to play in my first official tournament in Canyon, Texas.

I remember riding with my friend, David Gregory, and his mom. They had this brand new Cadillac, it was so comfortable and smooth. I thought, *wow, how lucky my friend was to have such a nice car and a nice brick home.* After that tournament we became friends. We both had the same first name and he would always treat me with respect. At recess time we played football together or just hung out and talked about sports or girls. We also competed on who got the better grade on a test. He pushed me to excel at school work.

After another basketball tournament on a different weekend, we returned home and it was late at night. I knew my friend would see where I lived on the dirt-road neighborhood. I was a little embarrassed because I knew I was poor and he was rich. His house had a paved road, with a long driveway leading to a triple-wide garage. My house was a small shack with dirt all around, or mud when it rained. I'm sure David's mom explained to him why my neighborhood was so different than theirs. They were nice to me and I appreciated that. I could always tell which wealthy families were prejudiced, and there were a few in Dimmitt. The Gregory's were not, I could tell the way they treated me.

My friend had an older brother that was playing basketball on the varsity team with my older brother, Gilberto. My brother would tell me how Bill Gregory would defend him when some of the rich kids made fun of him at the high school.

Before our games, the school would hold a pep rally, which is like an assembly to start the spirit of the game coming up. They were normally held the last half hour of school. The seventh and eighth grade cheerleaders would invite people to decorate the day before the pep rally. I was invited to help decorate. I had never done that before and thought it might be fun. I was about to learn that some wealthy-Caucasian girls did not like Hispanics. For some reason, because I was a good athlete and some of my friends were Caucasian, I must have been an exception to be invited to this decoration party.

It was basketball season, and one of my friends from that year's football team was walking along with me outside of the school. He asked me where I was going. I told him and even invited him to join us at the decorating party. We walk up the steps at the front door and we were greeted by three cheerleaders.

They opened the door and said, *David, you made it... come on in.* I said, "Yeah, I brought Florentino along, is it okay if he joins us?" They told me he wasn't invited and he could not come in. Florentino had such a disappointed look on his face.

"I'm sorry Florentino."

"It's okay."

The way he walked away with his head down and almost in tears, made me feel bad. I didn't know what to do, I had never been to an event like this and I was excited to be part of it. I went in and saw that Florentino could have helped and would've had fun. It was not too full and it was wrong what those cheerleaders did. And yes, they were the little rich group that hung out together – not to say that all rich girls were like that. I knew plenty of rich-

Caucasian girls that were very nice. I didn't see any Hispanics in there. I was so frustrated and I felt like I let Florentino down.

I know this event should have been fun for me, but instead I felt sad for my teammate and how he was treated. Oh sure, I went through the motions and laughed with some of the students in there, but I struggled with the entire situation. The least I could have done was walked away with Florentino and not join the pep-rally party. As a young boy I was excited to get invited to any-thing – no cheerleader had ever invited me to anything.

Later on in life, I heard that Florentino made it to the state championships in the mile run. I was so happy for him, I guess because of my own knowledge that he was smiling and having fun in school. I just thought to myself, *good for him*!

Everything was going great for me in seventh-grade basket-ball. I was inspired by some of the varsity players and how well they played the game. I watched the NBA and learned from them how to create my own shot. It was a drive that I had. Not only did I enjoy basketball, the better I got the more friends I made and the less I was made fun of.

God didn't let me get too overconfident, just because I was an athlete and one of the tallest kids on the team. Leon was the only kid taller than I was. An incident put me in check, this scared me and I was caught in an awkward situation. We were playing in a tournament and I don't remember what team it was.

We were up by ten points nearing the half, and they had a pretty big kid that I was guarding. We both went up for a key rebound, I was able to take the ball from him, and when we came down he swung his elbow and hit my left eye! I yelled loud and fell to the ground, and then I noticed blood starting to run down and drop on the gym floor. I didn't want anyone to know. I covered my eye with my hand, but the blood was starting to run down my hand. I was panicking and didn't know what to do. Before the referee could see me, I got up and ran into the dressing room. I don't know what everyone was thinking and that was the last thing on my mind.

When I made it to the dressing room I looked in the mirror and turned the water faucet on. I did my best to wash off the blood and then I took a paper towel and held it over my eye. By that time the coach walked into the dressing room, "David, you okay?" I remember thinking, *what am I going to say, they don't know about my eye.* I noticed the bleeding slowing down and I calmed down.

My flesh was cut with the prosthetic eye after the opponent's elbow connected. I explained to Coach Reese what had happened to me and why I didn't tell anyone about it. He understood but informed me that I should have come to him before the season. I told him I was afraid they wouldn't let me play basketball. That was the last conversation, about this issue, I had with my coach the rest of the season.

I stayed home two days to heal, my mom wasn't too happy, but she felt bad for me and understood. She was so supportive of me in whatever I wanted to do. She had a way of being firm when she didn't want me to do something for safety reasons. When I did them anyway and I ended up injured, like this situation, she was full of compassion. I loved that about my mom. My dad was the same way, full of compassion for something like this.

During the track and field season I found a love for the hurdles and high jump. The hurdles were challenging and every day after school I would work on technique getting over that hurdle. At the time we ran sixty-yard hurdles. I could not make three steps between hurdles, so I would alternate legs. The high jump event was my passion, I watched my older brother Gilberto high jump in the previous years and he taught me how to practice high jumping. I was so exciting to high jump.

There was only one problem, Coach Reese did not pick me to be one of the high jumpers on the seventh-grade team. I asked him several times but he wouldn't give me a chance. The African-American kids were the high jumpers, Leon, Eddie, and Reggie. The coach never once had us do a jump off to see who would earn the spots.

Back in those days we used these huge bundles of sponges as a high-jump pit. I went out to the high school to practice with my older brother every day – I wanted to master the Fosbury Flop technique. A technique that was popularized and perfected by American Dick Fosbury. I wanted to high jump and I knew that if I got that chance I was going to be ready.

My coach was watching me during practice one day. I think the bar was at 4' 10" or something like that. I did exactly what my brother taught me as far as running up to the bar and throwing up my right leg as I was flying over the bar arching my back. As I was coming down my heels clipped the bar and it fell to the ground. I remember Coach's words perfectly, "Espinoza you'll never be a high jumper – give it up." I was so mad at my coach. I was going to work even harder now, because I knew I would have to at least clear 4' 11" to get his attention.

Halfway through the season, we were headed to the Boys Ranch Invitational. It was about seventy miles away from Dimmitt. For some reason, Leon did not show up before our bus left the school. He was one of the high jumpers. The coach stood up in front of the bus, "Leon didn't show up, can anyone else here high jump?" I raised my hand up and firmly asked, "Coach, can I high jump?" He looked at me in a not-so-excited way and answered, "I guess, just this one time since Leon's not here." I not only lucked out to do the high jump, but I also ran in the 4 X 100 relay and I threw the discus for the first time.

I was ready, especially in the high jump. When the meet was over, I had cleared 5' 1" in the high jump and earned the gold medal! I placed second in the discus, and we placed second in the 4 X 100 relay. Two of the African-American kids didn't make the trip, so Scott Armstrong and I were the substitutes. I'm sure that's why we got second – with Leon there it would have been first for sure. I was happy though. This was the first gold medal I ever won. All I have to say about that is, *thank you Coach Reese for telling me I would never be a high jumper.*

I made it through the seventh grade. The year was full of fear, laughter, academic challenges, and sports. The fact was that I overcame and I made it. My grades were good and I made a few friends. I learned many things about ethnic types and how one race can discriminate against another. I also learned that there were more kids struggling financially than what our family was dealing with. I was excited about coming back for my eighth-grade year and I was so glad that summer was approaching again. God was with me even when I didn't know it.

11.

Eighth Grade

The summer before my eighth-grade year was the last summer I worked at our gas station. There was talk about a gas shortage and our FINA station was pretty small – it was in trouble. FINA trucks had to travel a long way to deliver gas.

The franchise cut us off and we had to shut down. My dad sold a lot of his equipment. I now know how difficult that must have been for him. I loved working there and seeing all of the people come by. I especially loved working there with my sister Louise and my brother Richard. We had some amazing times laughing at the many funny things customers did.

It was a sad day for all of us, especially for my dad. Losing this business that we all had embraced was heart-breaking in more ways than one. It put a strain on us financially and emotionally. We were struggling again and my dad began to look for another job.

John B. had a group of people that he supervised in the fields. We went out to work for the farmer he worked with. A few weeks of work during that summer was a blessing – it helped bring more income to our family.

We also spent a lot of time swimming at the public pool. I never saw some of my wealthy friends at the public pool. I never knew why until my friend Ralph told me they swam at the Country Club. I had never been to that place. It was a club where you could play golf. It was a beautiful brick building with golf carts and all. They had a nice swimming pool and the members there were definitely in a different income class.

We paid a quarter to swim all day at the public pool. My brothers and I would walk there. During this long hike across the tracks we would often find things on the ground. The trail was used by so many kids from our neighborhood that sometimes we would find a penny, a nickel, or a dime on the trail. Next to the train tracks were these metal belts with holes in them. Shipment was wrapped with these belts. There were so many laying on the ground. We discovered that we could make whistles out of these metal belts. We just folded a small piece of the belt making a whistle. When we blew through it you could hear a loud-high-pitched sound. It was so much fun discovering so many things on such a simple thing as a walk to the swimming pool.

I normally closed my eyes before I dived into the water. I was careful because I did not want my eye to fall out while underwater – that would have been a nightmare. Holding my breath with my eyes closed, I knew where I was as I swam under-water and then made my way to the top for a gasp of air. My swimming-pool days were always fun, I didn't realize how much exercise I got when I was a little kid.

One day we were in the dressing room changing after a long day of swimming. The chlorine would make our eyes tired and sometimes a little red. My brother Gilberto was in there with me, everyone else left. Two bullies came into the dressing room and noticed that one of my eyes was red and the other one was pure white. They started making fun of me and laughing. They even wanted to see my eye up close. I said no, and I just looked down. These guys were in their twenties. They threatened to throw me in the shower with all my dry clothes I had just put on. I started crying and yelling, "Leave me alone!"

My brother was still in high school and much younger than these bullies. They were such big losers I don't even remember their names, but I can still see their faces in my memory. Gilberto yelled at them, "Leave him alone, if you want to throw someone in the shower, throw me in there!" So the bullies walked over to my brother and picked him up and threw him in the shower clothes and all. I was screaming at the top of my lungs for them to leave us alone. They finally did after they saw me crying and pleading.

My brother comforted me and he told me it was okay. His words were, *those guys are a couple of punks, they won't bother us again.* Shortly after that incident I saw my brother start a weightlifting program. There were a few kids that used to pick on him because he was always a skinny kid. That all changed when he completed his weightlifting program. During his junior and senior years of high school, no kids picked on him. He had developed into this body-building stud, and with his boxing experience, I would say any kid in school would have been crazy to mess with him. I always heard the news when he had beaten up a kid that made fun of him, whether in sports or in the hallway.

Hanging around Loop was the same, I always felt protected when my brothers were around. I remember all kinds of punks trying to pick a fight with Loop, but I never saw any of them actually follow through with it. One time I saw Loop outside the fence at the swimming pool. This kid and Loop were standing there staring at each other. There was a circle of kids around them – everyone knew there was a fight about to start. After they stared at each other and exchanged a few words, the kid said, "It's not fair because you have shoes on and I don't." Loop didn't say anything, he just took his shoes off and threw them to the side. The kid started walking away and said he wasn't going to fight Loop.

Growing up with me they knew what I had gone through. I never thanked them for looking out for me. Loop and Gilberto, if you are reading this book, thank you for always being there for your little brother. Thank you for making me feel safe wherever I was, whether the bus or the swimming pool, whether walking through a crowd of rough kids or whether at church among other kids. You showed your love as brothers in more than one way and I truly am grateful for that. It's so cool that both my older brothers are believers in Jesus Christ to this day.

God was with me even when I didn't know it. It was up to me to start acknowledging Him, and to be honest it took me a very long time before I was at that point. I was young and still learning so many things. I knew that I had to go to confession on Fridays and church was a must on Sundays. I grew up Catholic and was taught that it was a sin to attend a church other than the

Catholic Church. I didn't quite understand it, but that's how it was. I was always nervous about going into a confessional and listening to the priest behind a screen. I was scared and anxious. I mean, I would rather get into a fight with Leon Glover than go into this closed box with only the priest and myself there and me telling him my sins. It was not a good feeling.

I used to count my sins and jot them down on a piece of paper. I memorized how many times I said "damn it" after I missed a lay-up in basketball, or how many times I saw girls in mini-skirts and thought sinful things in my mind. Or maybe how many times I disobeyed my mom or dad, and possibly how many times I fought with my brothers or sisters. I learned early on that the Catholic religion was probably one of the toughest religions around. My mom was strict with us when it came to church.

I never bought into some of the rules the Catholic religion has. I do believe that Catholics worship the same God that I do. The processes they have in place and some of the interpretations from scriptures are a little different than what I understand. I don't want to offend anyone, and I am speaking for myself. I always had topics that I believed with the Catholic Church and topics that I would just throw out if I didn't agree. It wasn't until much later in my life that I started developing my own religious beliefs, thanks to some of the people that came into my life. More on this in a later chapter.

Like I was saying before, it never crossed my mind that I would ever in my lifetime have a girlfriend, or for that matter even hold a girl's hand. My eighth grade year, the good Lord put all kinds of things in front of me, it was up to me to make decisions to decide whether I wanted my life to grow or to just give up and admit defeat.

I never looked at myself in the mirror, I usually didn't like what I saw. Most of my grade-school days and during my the seventh grade year, I combed my hair quickly and skipped looking at myself. I had no idea how God was about to transform my face. I was about to find out during the eighth grade.

Football season started once again, I was once again selected to be the kicker and the punter of the team. I also played defensive end and fullback. Tommy was the quarterback and we were going to run out of the wishbone formation. Leon and Thompson were the two halfbacks. We were having another great year and I was having a lot of fun.

During our pep rallies the coaches always picked one kid on the team to speak in front of the school. I always wanted to be that kid. It seemed to me that you either had to be very popular or you had to be from a rich family. At least at the time, that's the kind of message I got. I don't know, maybe the kids that had parents super involved also had that opportunity. All I know is that I wanted to be one of those kids, I envied them. I never once got that opportunity the entire time I was in Dimmitt. It did make me sad, but that's just how it was, we can't always get what we want.

Football was a hot sport in Texas and my younger brother, Richard, was making his own mark as a punter in the seventh grade. It didn't take long for word to get out that I had a younger brother that could punt the ball as good as I could. I knew that already from playing the punting game on Dulin Street. My brother helped me become a great punter and kicker. We were both very competitive.

My brother, Loop, was struggling a little in high school. I'm not sure what he was dealing with. I was busy with my own world in junior high and didn't see him or Gilberto very much. Loop was a heck of an athlete in track and field and he was good at football and basketball. He wanted to help out my mom and dad by getting a job. The coaches didn't comply with him wanting to work after school because of practices. Loop wanted to remove himself from Dimmitt High School. He was afraid he was going to hurt someone and that was the last thing he would want to do to any kid. Some of the rich kids made fun of him at times and the instructors would not help with support. When he got into a fight with this one kid, it scared him. He had trained himself from a karate book he bought. He was worried that he would break someone's leg or arm at school and he didn't want to do that.

To be honest with you, Loop had a couple of God-given gifts. He could run the 440-yard dash in 50.1 seconds as a freshman in high school. He would always place second behind Randy Finch, an African-American kid that had long legs and ran the 440 in 49.9 seconds. All of the track meets were invitational meets, we didn't have duel meets in Texas. The second God-given gift my brother had was art. He could model anything out of clay. He could also draw anything and it would always look so realistic – especially horses or any western piece.

So many things happened during my eighth-grade year. Loop was working for a retail store and he found out that you needed a GED to get better paying jobs. He found out about a program in Roswell, New Mexico. He could complete his high school education in a few months and he could start working. This was a solution for him to get out of Dimmitt High School and to get a job to help our parents. This was the start of my family not having everyone around. When Loop left, he left us his stereo system that he purchased a few weeks earlier. We loved listening to music on that stereo.

Some of the groups we listened to were Stevie Wonder; Three Dog Night; Olivia Newton John; Paul McCartney and Wings; Elton John; The Partridge Family; The Doobie Brothers; Grand Funk Railroad; Boston; Captain and Tennille; Karen Carpenter; Jim Croce, The Temptations, and Michael Jackson. The music was good and a lot of kids always carried their transistor radios around. One of the popular stations we'd tune into was KOMA, we would get reception all the way from Oklahoma City. We managed to buy a few records, but we didn't have much money to buy more. The radio sure was a blessing.

Gilberto was a senior and he had narrowed down his sport to be basketball. He wanted to focus on one sport and he wanted to play on the varsity team. I felt bad for him because he had some pretty talented players he was competing against for playing time. So he normally came off the bench during games. I never missed any of his home games.

Gilberto spent a lot of time away from home, I didn't see him much during his senior year. It was mostly Richard and I and my sisters, Louise and Diana. I only saw my sisters at home and rarely spent much time with them. We had different groups of friends and we would share information about each other in the evenings or in the mornings.

My dad landed a job driving a Ready-mix truck. He would deliver cement to areas outside of town and in town. He would pour it as well. He was tired of all the mud and the dust and the crime at our old neighborhood. Even after a petition that our neighbor Sara started, the neighbors refused to sign it for a paved road. My dad found a small house next to the city park and we moved there – he took out a mortgage and began making payments on it. We were three blocks from the Dimmitt Supermarket. This store offered an apple for every "A" on a kid's report card. I normally got a bag full of apples and shared them with my family.

It was an easy walk to this store for groceries, and we had paved roads! The downfall was living in a bit smaller house. It only had two bedrooms, a small living room, a kitchen, and one bathroom – and again, no shower. We had to fill up a bucket of hot water from the kitchen sink and mix it with the cold water from the bathtub. We never had a shower the entire time I lived in Dimmitt. Thank God for football practices and the showers afterward.

My mom and dad always had their own bedroom in our previous house. In this house the boys had one bedroom and the girls had the other bedroom. My parents leaned a mattress against the kitchen wall. When it was time to go to sleep they would place it on the floor and that's where they slept. In the morning they would lean it up against the wall again. The sacrifices that were made for us were over and beyond and I am so thankful that I had parents like them despite our financial difficulties.

The summer nights were warm, calm, and full of hanging out at the city park, which was right next to our house. Summer nights in Texas were the best, crystal clear skies and stars shining bright.

The good news was that we only had about six blocks to walk to school – a lot closer. The house had a pretty large backyard that was fenced in. We had an outdoor dog, Jumper, that we brought with us as well. We kept him in the backyard.

Jumper's life ended shortly after we moved. We found him close to the back fence near the alley. Someone had shot him – we saw the bullet hole. We never found out who did this. It was a sad day for all of us. I never had another dog as a pet after that. He was a good dog and full of life. I still remember Jumper, a medium-sized German Shepherd.

Yes indeed a lot of things happened during that year, some were very good and others were very sad. God was throwing all kinds of things at me and I was taking them in. God was allowing me to make decisions, because of Jesus dying on the cross for me, I had that free will.

Football season was going and we had won our third game. I finally scored a touchdown and I kicked my first field goal. I think it was a thirty-yard field goal. Thompson and Leon would score most of the touchdowns, they were amazing athletes and I was glad to be part of a winning team.

On a Saturday morning, my brother, who was in the seventh grade, delivered a letter to me from a nice-looking rich girl. He explained to me that she was hot and that I was lucky because she liked me. He handed me the note, and my first thought was, *what?* What girl in her right mind would be interested in me? I didn't know how to react because I was convinced that I would never have a girlfriend, I had accepted that and I was focusing on my sports and school work.

The first thing I did when I opened the letter was opposite than the normal. I looked at the end of it to see who this girl was. I saw the name, Kylene Collins. My brother assured me that she was a blue-eyed blonde with a killer figure and she lived on the west side of town in a brick house. I scrolled up to the beginning of the letter. I want to share with you the best I can, what Kylene wrote me. It may not be exactly what she wrote, but it will be pretty close.

Hi David, I know you don't know me. I just want to say that I really like you a lot. I hear some of your friends talk about you in band class. Wow! You are a great athlete. I enjoy watching you play and I think you are so cute! Please let me know if you could ever ask me to go steady with you. I hope you ask me because I would say yes. Please write back to me soon.

Love, Kylene Collins

What in the world would I do with this? Here's a girl that I haven't even seen and I have no kind of experience with girls at all. This was flattering to me and such a huge surprise. I was so excited for Monday to see who she was. I kept thinking to myself, *is this really happening to me?*

It was between periods in the long hallway when I asked one of my friends, "Who is Kylene Collins?" He responded, *oh, she's in my band class ... look over there ... she's wearing that black and white checkered coat.* I turned around and I saw her placing her books in the locker. I was so nervous, she was indeed a nice looking girl. Her skin was white as snow and her hair was very blonde. As I walked closer to her she turned around and smiled as she waved. I noticed her blue eyes instantly. I said very few words to her and I told her I would write to her. She said that would be great, and then the first bell rang and we both walked to our classes. She was a seventh grader and I was an eighth grader.

Kylene had a mad crush on me and I can't describe how great that made me feel. Talk about my self-esteem jumping up ten levels. The following day I had a letter for her and I asked her if she would "go steady with me", again, that meant, *will you be my girlfriend?* I don't know what kids use now days.

At school the next day I handed her the letter between classes and even walked with her for a bit before departing to my class. That was one of my longest days in school. Football practice went by pretty fast and before you knew it, I was at home sleeping and thinking about what she would write back.

The next day Kylene was full of smiles but yet very quiet. I think she was just as shy as I was about talking to the opposite sex. It was a new experience for me, and when she handed her letter to me, I noticed the hearts drawn on it.

I was the first one that walked into math class. I wanted to hurry up and read the letter to see if she said yes to my request. Sure enough, she said yes. The excitement and joy that I kept inside while other students walked into my classroom was beyond measure.

In junior high, I didn't dare talk about my feelings toward Kylene to anyone. When I read those words, *yes David, I'd love to go steady with you!*, I instantly had a case of puppy love or whatever you want to call it. I had a girlfriend for the first time in my life. I never thought for a second that this would happen.

When I walked down the hallway, some of my wealthy friends already heard. They would tell me things like, *hey, heard you're going with Kylene ... right on!* Or, *is Kylene your girlfriend, dude?* I starting feeling like a normal popular kid, not only because of my athletic abilities, but now because I had a rich girl as my girlfriend. That, to me, was a total shock for awhile. This was unheard of if you were me, a kid that struggled with a physical look that kids made fun of.

I didn't realize how lucky I was, and I didn't realize how much I had changed as far as my eyes looking closer to the same size. Turning and looking toward my right would definitely affect the movement of my left eye, it would not move equally with the right eye. I was overcautious about that and tried not to look that way unless I turned my entire body that direction. Sometimes I would forget and that's when kids would take a second look at me. Some kids would ask me to look at them again. I usually ignored them unless they were persistent. The same question would come up, *what's wrong with your eye?* I would answer, *oh, I just have a little bit of a lazy eye ... I was born like this.*

I lived with that lie for many years, even to this day as I'm writing my story. It was a lot easier and it avoided people from continuing the badgering and the curiosity of what was wrong with me. I didn't want anyone to know that I had a prosthetic eye. I was embarrassed and I didn't feel normal. When these moments came up, and believe me they came up all through my life, it made me feel very uncomfortable. If there was a photo taken of me with an old Polaroid, one of my eyes would always be red and the other one clear. Some of the kids would say, *hey Dave, you got a funny eye ... what's wrong with your eye?* I didn't say anything, I just raised my shoulders and opened my hands.

Now that I had my first girlfriend, another level of stress would affect my emotional well-being. Would Kylene notice this about me? How would she react? I had all sorts of questions flying through my head. Sports were my counseling, I truly believe that God placed sports in front of me to help me deal with my insecurities.

The school I attended was diverse, there were definitely more Caucasian kids than Hispanic kids, and we also had several African-American kids. Just taking a wild guess, I'd say 60% Caucasian, 30% Hispanics, and 10% African-Americans. Most of the rich kids ate at the snack bar in the upstairs area of Dimmitt Jr. High. The free-lunch kids, which I was one of, ate at the south grade cafeteria. I always rushed through my free lunch. I loved it when we had hamburgers with chocolate milk, which was usually on Wednesdays. After eating my lunch, I would hustle back to the upstairs snack bar at the junior high. I enjoyed hanging out with some of my friends. I often wished I had money so I could eat at the snack bar.

On away games it was nice that the coaches stopped to eat at a burger place or a restaurant. My experience growing up in a poor family made me want to do better for myself and my future. There were times when we would win some tough games, whether it be basketball or football, the team would stop at a burger place. I was full of pride, sometimes I would sit in the bus and not go in to eat with the team. I told my coaches I wasn't hungry, sometimes there would be one or two Hispanics or African-Americans in the bus with me. I'm pretty sure it was for the same reason. I didn't want to ask anyone for money nor did I want them to know that I was poor.

I learned that year to start a savings account at the bank. All of my summer earnings would be used for away-game trips and for clothes. I wanted to get some new cowboy boots. The ones I wore were falling apart. My parents bought them for me one Christmas with a charge card. In Dimmitt, Texas, it was common for boys and girls to wear cowboy boots to school. Rodeos were big and some kids even worked in the feedlots, where cattle grazed. There were many feedlots around Dimmitt. You could always tell by the smell when you drove by a cattle facility, let's just say the smell wasn't pleasant.

Sometimes I would come home after school and turn the TV on, that worked most of the time. I'd watch *The Brady Bunch* and then *Gilligan's Island*. There was usually some cereal with milk, but to tell you the truth many times the cupboards were empty just like my stomach. All I had eaten was eggs and tortillas for breakfast and the free lunch at school. I was getting pretty thin from football practices and not eating enough.

My mom had applied for a minimum-wage job at a nursing home and was hired. That helped support the family a little. She loved working in the kitchen. My dad was still working for Killingsworth, a Ready-mix company.

I often thought about what it would be like to have my own room and a big house like my wealthy friends. I'm sure Kylene had her own room and a big house. She once told me where she lived, so I rode my bike by there just to see where she lived. She had a beautiful red-brick house with a garage, a nice green lawn, and a big driveway. I heard that her dad owned a big farm.

When basketball season started, Kylene and I would attend the varsity games. I loved watching the varsity boys, they inspired me to become a better basketball player. Coach Kenneth Cleveland was one of the best coaches I ever knew in Texas. He mastered how to coach the zone defense and he could relate to just about any kid. My brother, Gilberto, was a senior on the team. I looked forward to these games for many reasons, the excitement, the great plays, and my education about the game. The team uniforms were so cool with purple and white. I also enjoyed watching the visiting teams that came to play us at our home.

I often sat with my girlfriend, Kylene. It was the first time I had ever held hands with a girl. Kylene had a friend, Leanne Crozier. Leanne would talk more, she stretched her neck around her friend to talk to me. Kylene and I were definitely people of a few words. I think we were both just a little nervous. I knew that she didn't want her parents to find out for some reason. Kylene told me that she didn't want her parents to see us together. I was clueless and I didn't understand, but I honored her request and sat next to her when her parents weren't at the game. I guess I was ignorant to the fact that her parents might not appreciate her holding hands with a Hispanic kid originally from the other side of the tracks.

We were going together through football season and the first part of the basketball season – I started liking her a lot, but I was only in the eighth grade. She never once questioned me about my eye. It looked great and I remember once looking in the mirror and seeing myself as a more attractive kid. God had transformed me into a handsome young boy, or at least that's what I kept hearing from several girls at school and at church.

I had never kissed a girl before and I was a little nervous because I didn't know how Kylene felt about this. It was after a varsity game on the steps of the north grade gym, where the games were played, that I finally kissed Kylene. I remember asking her if it was okay, she was looking around to make sure no one she knew was watching. She said, *maybe a small kiss, I don't want word to get to my parents.*

I could tell that Kylene liked me a lot, but yet was fearful of her parents finding out. I didn't get it because there were couples at that age where parents knew about them and they were okay with it. The problem was that she was Caucasian and I was Hispanic. I would hear people talk. The two cultures just didn't match and the wealthy-Caucasian dads and moms would not accept the fact that their daughters were with Hispanics or African-Americans. I'm not speaking for all Caucasian people there, because there were many friendly and loving Caucasian people in Dimmitt.

With Kylene it was a tough situation. We were young and it could be that her parents felt she was too young to be getting involved with a boy. In a realistic opinion, I felt that me being a poor-Hispanic kid and only in the eighth grade, and her being a wealthy-Caucasian girl and only in the seventh grade, things were not looking good for our young-puppy-love adventure. As much as I wanted this to continue, I didn't know how long it would.

I normally didn't discuss any girl situation with my parents. I did point her out to my dad once when he was dropping me off at school. He just smiled and shook his head up and down. I never told my mom, I'm not sure how she would have reacted. This was the time she was pretty strict with my sister Louise. Mom didn't like the idea of us dating anyone at such a young age. My brother, Gilberto, started dating at a young age. Him and my mom would argue about those times. Nope, I don't think I was going to bring up Kylene.

Christmas was here once again and our whole family was together for the holidays. Christmas has always been my favorite time of the year. We celebrate the birth of our Savior, Jesus Christ. No one knows when His exact birthday was. I like the fact that we celebrated on December 25th. My dad would always buy the boys some firecrackers and skyrockets. We would all get one or two gifts and some clothes. Us brothers and sisters would wrap up gifts for each other – nothing too expensive. My mom liked the Christmas lights and she would decorate our silver-artificial tree. It was too expensive to buy a real tree – the artificial tree worked for our family.

I dreaded going to midnight mass. I would fall asleep sometimes – it was way too late and I was always tired because of my active sports life. I liked it better when we attended church in the early morning on Christmas day.

On Christmas morning we would have cinnamon rolls or Spanish sweetbread with hot chocolate. The entire atmosphere was relaxing and fun. Some of our relatives would stop by later in the day. My Uncle Jessie and his family was a definite, yes. My twin cousins, Joe and Jessie and their brothers Junior and Johnny would sometimes come by. In the evening, we would all go to my Grandma Matilda's house – they usually had a small gift waiting for us. It was what Christmas was all about, Jesus Christ and family time. We never sang Christmas carols as a family, we just opened our presents and enjoyed a new game or whatever we got.

I missed the last day of school before the Christmas break, and I had this bracelet that I bought at the TG&Y store. I had it engraved with Kylene's name on it. I used some of the money I saved up from my summer job.

My sister Louise was a freshman in high school and she had her driver's license. I asked her if she could take me to Kylene's house so I could drop off her gift. I also asked her if she could take it to the door for me because I wasn't sure how her parents would react. I was just a kid and I simply forgot what Kylene often told me, *I don't want my parents to see us together.*

When I returned to school, I was excited to hear from Kylene. I was at my locker when she came and tapped me on the shoulder. She handed me the wrapped gift.

"I'm really sorry David, my parents said I have to give this back to you and also that I can't see you anymore."

"I don't understand, this is your gift." I looked at her in a little bit of a shock.

She apologized one more time and I could tell that it was very difficult for her. It was her parents that insisted on her not getting involved. I guess I blamed myself for this disruption – taking that Christmas present to her at her house. That day I was crushed, and I could not function very well.

My first ever experience at love was a frustrating one. Here was a girl that had a mad crush on me and then in just a couple of months it was over. The next letter I received from her was not one I looked forward to reading. She apologized one more time and then wrote that she wanted to break up with me due to circumstances. She also wrote that a song called, "Time in a Bottle," by Jim Croce reminded her of me.

I didn't write back to her, and I did honor her request. I was heartbroken and struggled a bit, but somehow regained my self-esteem and composure through keeping my mind on my grades and basketball. I didn't want to think about girls ever again. I didn't want to go through this again. I had some great times with Kylene, even if it was just holding hands at games or talking in-between classes.

Kylene, if you ever read this book, I want to say thank you so much for being my first girlfriend. I never thought any girl would be interested in me. You helped open a door that I never thought I'd find the key for. Thank you for reaching out to me and boosting my self-esteem and confidence – it meant so much.

Despite the break-up I had gone through, that year was still full of encouragement for me. I don't know what I would have done without sports. During the basketball season I was averaging at least 20 points, and 15 rebounds per game. Leon was no longer playing basketball with us, so that opened up more green lights for Thompson and myself.

I remember scoring 31 points in one game. I was in a zone and could not miss a shot. This was the first time I experienced being "unconscious", a term used in basketball where a player cannot miss a shot. The rim felt like it was the ocean – I was on fire! My coach pulled me out of the game after the third quarter. I asked, "Coach, why did you pull me out ... what did I do wrong?" He didn't answer me and I went to the bench to join the rest of the team. I was mad, because I knew I had a lot of points – that was my night, I could have scored more. I was displacing my aggressions after the breakup with Kylene.

This I know God would not like. I was thinking about me and no one else. I was just plain selfish and as a kid I was still learning many things. I sat there and pouted on the bench the entire fourth quarter. We were leading by 25 points.

After the game I didn't say one word. I was angry at the coach and I had tears running down my face. The coach came up to me and explained a few things as I was changing in the dressing room.

David, there are kids on this team that hardly get to play, I want to give them that opportunity when I can. You play a lot all season, I just thought it would be okay to pull you out when we had such a big lead. I'm sorry you feel bad about this. Please keep your head up, okay?

I just shook my head up and down and I started to understand. I guess I never thought about how hard my teammates practiced all week and then not play very much at games. The coach had a valid point and as difficult as it was to understand, I finally did.

I have to be honest that it wasn't easy to get over Kylene and move on, but I think because I had so much going on, the distraction helped. Church on Tuesdays and Sundays, homework, basketball practice, and spending time with my friend Ralph kept me busy. We would play basketball outside and my sisters would come out there often to play with us. They went inside before the boys did, I think we were too much for the girls. Diana was much shorter but still enjoyed trying.

We were heading to the Olton tournament in Olton, Texas. I relished basketball tournaments, they were so much fun because of the many teams that showed up. I met so many players from different towns. I saw so many different designs and colors of uniforms, and I lit up when I heard the crowds cheering – it was my place to be that brought me so much joy. I thank the Lord for those times in my life.

After a difficult break up with Kylene, the last thing I was expecting was to see a smiling cheerleader from Friona, Texas. Friona was playing in the game before us, they had just started their game as our team walked in the gym to sit up in the stadium seats. I walked in behind Thompson and Rocky and noticed this brunette cheering for her team with her red and white cheerleading uniform and her squad next to her. She gave me the biggest smile and looked at me as I tipped my head and smiled back. She had braces and her brown eyes had this touch of green sparkle that caught my attention. I had no clue who she was, and I wanted to somehow make a connection with her.

I knew some of the Hispanic kids that played for Friona just from the past year. After we played our game I was going to ask one of them who she was. We won our game pretty easily and our team was going to hang around to watch the next game.

I was informed by Edward from Friona, that her name was Karen Stevick. Her black wavy hair looked nice and her snow-white skin was flawless. She had a few attractive freckles that blended nicely with her face. I was a little nervous after what happened with Kylene. I decided to wait on talking to her until Friona's varsity team played in Dimmitt, which was coming up the following week.

Friona's varsity team was tough that year. I can't remember who won when they played us in Dimmitt, but I know we lost to them when we played them in Friona. I remember them having a kid that was 6' 7" and could shoot the ball very well. Our tallest player was Bill Gregory at 6' 4". Bill was the brother of my friend, David Gregory.

I didn't expect to see Karen in Dimmitt, but I was hoping she would show up. Sometimes friends ride with friends to away games, or maybe her parents would bring her to the game. I never missed varsity home games, those games were my Friday-night priority. This time though, there would be no Kylene, I would join my friends at the top of the home section. We normally stood up and cheered most of the game. I was so poor that we often watched the rich kids buy food at the concession stand. I was always so hungry. They had mixed chili and Fritos that smelled heavenly. I enjoyed that dish vicariously through some of the kids that had money.

The varsity home games were always packed in Dimmitt. Back in the 1970s there was no iPhone or computer games. In a small town like Dimmitt there was only one sport during the current season, and that was basketball. The town also had the spirit to support their local team – it was amazing!

After the game I made my way through the crowd and I hung around with a friend just outside the front doors. It was what most of the kids did after the games. Sometimes we did it just to watch the visiting team exit the premises. It was then that I saw Karen on the steps talking to one of her friends, Barbara Rhodes. I don't know what came over me, I simply could not pass up this opportunity. I walked over and introduced myself, "Hi I'm David Espinoza, I play for the eighth grade team." She said hi to me and smiled. I remember talking for a while, but not too long. That was the night that we exchanged addresses and we agreed to write each other.

My thoughts were, *wow! there's another girl that might like me, it sure sounded that way when she looked at me.* I was probably about 5' 10" in the eighth grade and eventually grew to be 6' 0". I normally wore cowboy boots, but in the 1970s the shoe styles were platform shoes and the jeans were bell bottoms. I wasn't wearing my platform shoes, they would have made me look 6' 3". Karen must have been 5' 2" or so. I remember she was wearing western jeans, but I'm a little foggy on the shirt – too long ago to remember.

In a few days I received a letter in the mail from Karen. It was exciting to know that this girl from Friona showed interest in me, unfortunately she lived far away from Dimmitt. I immediately mailed her a letter and the pen-pal writing started. I loved writing and it was a pleasure connecting with this brunette from Friona.

I received a letter from her every week and she would get one from me the week after. We planned to sit together at the game between Dimmitt and Friona and this time it would be in Friona. I was stuck because I didn't have a ride to the game. My parents never took us to any away games. The last away game my parents took us to was when Dimmitt played in the regional tournament in Lubbock, Texas, I was in the sixth grade at the time – what a fun experience that was.

My friend David G. was going for sure, so I asked him if I could ride along. He was generous and welcomed me. They had a luxury car and it was his mom and dad taking us to Friona. I told David about Karen, who would be at the game.

When we arrived I looked and looked until I finally found her sitting across from the Dimmitt section. There were so many people there, it was an important game for both teams and toward the end of the season.

I remember Karen being so excited to see me. I had no idea what our relationship was at the time. I knew we were writing each other and we always ended our letters insinuating that we could possibly be boyfriend-girlfriend status, but I never asked her. I was too nervous that night. Just being close to her made me feel good. She was funny and seemed to be laughing most of the night as we held hands.

After that night, we continued writing for a few more weeks and then we just stopped writing. The basketball season was over and the track and field season started. I remember looking for Karen during invitational track meets. Every time Friona was at the same invitational meets we were at, I kept thinking, *maybe I'll see Karen there*. I never saw her again until the Dimmitt Freshman Tournament the following year. We had not communicated in so long that I just assumed she didn't want to talk to me, so I didn't make an attempt to connect with her at the tournament. I never saw her again after that tournament.

Much later I found out from Karen what her thoughts and feelings were the night we met after the varsity game. I didn't know what her thoughts were at the time. I would like to share her quote.

I had traveled to Dimmitt with my friend Barbara Rhodes and her family to watch the varsity game. I remember you approaching me and saying something like, "Hi, my name is David." There was another guy with you, but my attention was set on those dark eyes looking down on me. I guess I was able to squeak my name out. Then we visited about the Olton Tournament, where I first laid eyes on you. On the ride back home that night, my heart was pounding in my chest, something I had never felt before. There were all kinds of feelings hitting this small-town-Texas girl like a whirlwind. I always thought you were a Caucasian kid, it was during one of the later games that I discovered you were Hispanic, and of course my heart started pounding again. It's so fun to recall what I would call my first hand-holding, Mr. Dimmitt Sports man. My parents never spoke a bad word about me getting mail from a boy with the last name, Espinoza. The Friona boys were very jealous that I had a connection with you, all of them but Jeff Whiteside, he thought it was cool.

Signed, Karen Stevick.

Karen Stevick, if you're reading this book, thank you so much for being such a great friend from Friona, Texas. You made me feel great about myself in what I had accomplished athletically and in how you wrote those heart-warming letters.

Track season was in the air and I practiced hard at running the hurdles. I wasn't fast enough to be part of the 4 X 100 relay team so I focused on the hurdles and the high jump. I also threw the discus now and then, but definitely the one field event I didn't work very hard at. I loved watching the events at invitational meets. On the average there were seven or eight teams at these meets.

While I waited for my events to be called, I laid around on the grass area with my friends. There was always music coming from some athlete's radio. So many 1970's songs remind me of certain times in my life. In the high jump as an eighth grader my personal best was 5' 3". I don't remember my time in the 120-yard hurdles or the 330-yard hurdles. What I do remember is how tough the 330-yard hurdles were, oh my gosh, especially the last curve down the stretch.

I remember in one invitational, I had first place wrapped up and I was coming down the stretch, it was a great feeling and I had a ten-yard lead on everyone else. I started getting a little cocky thinking I was good and no one could beat me in the 330-yard hurdles. Before running over the last hurdle I started raising my arms in the air and looking at the crowd while they cheered me on. Wow I was in dreamland, could this be happening? I was about to get a blue ribbon in the hurdles! As I lifted my lead leg over the final hurdle I caught a piece of it with my toe and I hit the asphalt.

As much as that hurt physically and emotionally, I quickly got up and finished the race capturing the white-third-place ribbon. Never again did I celebrate like that until the actual race was over.

Track and field seasons always flew by so fast, it was the last sport of the year for me. The African-American kids on my track team were amazing. They were fast and a majority of them would often win first place in the running events, mostly the 100-yard dash, the 220-yard dash, the 440-yard dash, and the relays. The fastest kids I remember were Thompson, Leon, Eddie, Reggie, and a few others. Some of the African-American kids would not accept third-place ribbons or anything worse. They would throw them on the bus floor as the coach handed them out. First and second seemed to be okay with them. All I could think was, *I would be so happy if I was fast enough to be on a relay team*. I was fast, but just not as fast as kids like Thompson, who also had a brother, Robert, an all-state running back and a track star in Dimmitt.

Summer baseball was something I would have played if my parents would have allowed me to. I think the financial strain was one reason and my eye was the other reason. It was difficult for me to watch my friends playing baseball in the summer. I knew I could be a great baseball player. Every time we got together with the Torres family, we'd play baseball. My cousins, Jimmy and Paul, played baseball and they were very good at it. I could tell just by watching them. Jimmy was normally the catcher and Paul was the pitcher. Sometimes they would get into these arguments during a game in a pasture close to their house. It reminded me of the arguments I would get into with my brothers in basketball. Anyway, Jimmy would get mad at Paul for something and he would throw the baseball as fast as he could to hit Paul. Most of you probably know what a hard baseball feels like. Paul would turn around and catch it, look at Jimmy, and say, "You better make sure you hit me next time."

Paul was one of my favorite cousins and still is after all these years. I guess because of his work ethic in sports – it was a lot like ours in my family. We also joked around a lot and told funny stories to each other. He asked me if I played for a baseball team when our families would visit, and they were rare visits because of the geographical distance. I was never brave enough to tell him why I didn't play baseball. I guess I could have worn an eye-patch shield over my left eye, but then people would have asked me about it and attention would be drawn to that. It just worked out better for me to continue with track and field. I think God was giving me all kinds of hints.

Eighth-grade graduation was a pretty big deal at Dimmitt Junior High. We were all advised that it would be okay to have a date for the dance in the evening, there would be chaperones there. I was a little foggy on who to ask. Would any girl go with me to the dance and then to the movies afterward? It was cool because the Dimmitt Theater was reserved for us that night. I didn't have much time to think of who to ask so I had to move quick on this. I didn't want to be one of those guys without a date.

Earlene was a girl that was in several of my classes and we seemed to get along pretty good. She was blonde and her eyes were green. I don't know what got into me, I just walked up to her in class the day before graduation and I asked her, "Would you like to be my date for the dance and movie?" She said, "Yeah, I'd love to." I about fell backwards, I thought she was going to say, no. The agenda for graduation day was, a swimming party first, go home and get dressed for commencement, and then go home and get dressed for the dinner and dance. After the dance, every-one would meet at the Dimmitt Theater with their dates. There would also be chaperones at the theater.

The swimming party was so much fun, there were all kinds of food set up on large tables. We swam and feasted for a few hours. Everyone was nice to everyone, we would all be in high school the following year. I had the chance to talk to Earlene and plan on how she was going to get to the movie. I was going to walk over with some of my Hispanic friends from my old neighborhood. Rudy was one of them. I can't remember who all was in the group, but I know there was at least four of us. Earlene was going to get a ride with her older brother. We agreed to meet there after the dance was over.

When the commencement began, I couldn't help but reflect in my mind what a great two years it had turned out to be despite my challenges. I had learned so much, and I thank the good Lord to this day for being there with me even when I didn't know it. All of my hard work studying and trying my best to be nice to everyone at my school, earned me the Eighth Grade Class Citizenship Award. I was shocked, because I never won anything so prestigious as this award. Some of my wealthy friends always won things like this. It was such an honor for me to walk up and accept this award. It meant so much to me after all I had been through and what I had survived. And then a few minutes later I was called up again. I won a math award, and an athletic award.

The dance that evening was fun. I danced with several girls from my grade, and we drank punch. I even danced with Sheryn Roberts and Darenda Moore – how cool was that? Darenda was probably the prettiest girl in our class. The dance finally came to an end and most of us were preparing for the movie date at the theater. We had an hour or so to get there and it was maybe about ten blocks from the school.

My friend Rudy and several of us Hispanic kids started walking to the dance, mostly reminiscing about the school year and also asking each other who our dates were. We were within three blocks of the theater and walking across the street, when a nice truck sped up and tried to run us over on purpose. We all started yelling at this jerk. What are the odds that on graduation night, something like this would happen and spoil the mood.

The truck or pickup, spun around and came back to where we were. A high-school kid jumped out of the truck.

"Come on, I'll take on all of you losers!"

Naturally this rich-Caucasian boy was trying to start something. I was splat in the middle of all this. I was hoping we would just keep going and not look back. He was much older and stronger than most of us, at least that's what I assumed. My friend Rudy said something to him referring to his reckless driving and almost running us over. This kid's name was Steve S. I remember his small-afro head and Caucasian face. Some of the Caucasian kids would curl their hair into an afro back then – it was the style for some. Rudy was about to get into a fight with Steve.

I kept thinking, *are you crazy, Rudy?* I didn't say anything, I just stood there and hoped Steve wouldn't come at me. While Rudy and Steve were staring each other down and waiting for that first punch, here comes a group of African-American kids from my old neighborhood. We were all decent kids, we had all graduated. R. Ewing was among that group approaching our location. The African-Americans did not like some of the Caucasian kids in Dimmitt. R. Ewing was one of our running backs in football and he was also a linebacker.

Ewing walked up and said, "You wanna fight someone, take me on I'm ready for you!" So Steve turned around and started to say something to Ewing, but he didn't realize this African-American kid was not about words. Ewing threw a fist right in his mouth and they both started punching like crazing. They started fighting on the ground and wrestling to defend and to punch. Ewing was definitely winning this fight.

All of a sudden a Caucasian-lady teacher pulls up with her car and yells out, "Okay break it up! What's going on here?" Steve and Ewing broke it up and stood there for a moment. Steve had blood running down his mouth and nose. I knew there were teachers that were discriminatory, my brother Loop would tell me about how they would not support him on a dispute with a rich-Caucasian kid. That's one of the reasons he left Dimmitt to graduate early. That night, I knew what Loop was talking about.

What this teacher said to Steve S. was a little troubling to me. She saw a group of Hispanic kids and a group of African-American kids and made her own assumption of what happened. I'll never forget that night – it just affirmed discrimination and stereotyping in one sentence.

She started lecturing us and went on a rant making assumptions. The quotes may not be exact, but I'll lay them out pretty close.

"Break it up and move on! Steve, you know better than they do, I know it's not your fault, please Steve, just get in your truck and go home!"

"Hey, we didn't start anything, he's the one that tried to run us over!" I yelled.

She gave me a dirty look and said, move on. She consoled Steve and walked him to his truck. I just shook my head and said, *let's go watch a movie y'all.*

It was a normal thing to have incidents like this in Dimmitt, it seemed like there was always some altercations at one time or another. I just tried to avoid them whenever I could. People had tempers and they were always trying to prove how tough they were. I often wondered if it was just for them to get the attention that they were tough.

I remember once, my old neighbor, Freddy, who I had beaten at boxing during my grade school days in our backyard, he came calling to fight me. I was walking through the city park. He had grown to be a little taller since he was in high school, but he was still very skinny. It shocked me when he approached me with his friend following him. Someone told him that I said I could whip him. I didn't know how to respond as he kept looking at me with his three-inch-heel boots on. I had my flat Converse on that had a hole in them. This was my friend back in the days, and his brother, Ralph Junior, was a good friend of mine. I was totally not expecting this. His parents were some of the nicest people I met in Dimmitt.

I had been lifting weights and with all of the fixing tires during my gas station years, I had developed into a pretty strong eighth grader. I was hoping Freddy would make the first move. I didn't appreciate him making such a false accusation on me. He knew that my older brothers weren't around to protect me. We looked at each other for five minutes before he decided to make a negative comment, which I won't repeat and then he just walked away with his friend.

I think Freddy might have had second thoughts about making that first move. I was definitely stronger than ever. When I got into that fight with Leon, I gained confidence in defending myself and Leon was four times stronger than Freddy. Again, I would do anything to avoid fighting, I was at a disadvantage with my left eye. I certainly didn't need to return to the hospital. I was thankful that Freddy didn't make the first move. And with one of his friends behind him, I didn't know if they would team up against me.

That incident bothered me, not only because some kid told Freddy a false statement about me, but also because Freddy believed that kid despite knowing our family for so many years. I kept telling myself, maybe I should have just given him a beating. At that age I was angry at him because of what he did to me – there was no real reason other than him trying to prove he was a tough kid around his friend.

Now let's get back to the movie date. The movie was next and Earlene was waiting for me, I apologized and told her about the whole incident with Steve S. The rest of the night was amazing and I made sure Earlene and I had a great time the rest of the evening.

My junior-high days were so memorable, I'll never forget them, I still remember most of my teachers and most of the kids that had a great impact on my life. God blessed me with overcoming something I never thought I would. He was there for me throwing all kinds of adventures; lessons; pain; laughter; romance; sports; friendships, and more. It was only the beginning, because I was about to face more challenges in high school.

12.

Summer Before High School

During the summer before my freshman year of high school I wanted to avoid the hot-summer field work. I started asking questions at the high school. How can I get a job working for the school this summer? I remember talking to, Edward Nino, a friend of my brother, Loop. Edward knew who I was, and he thought highly of me. He was one of the varsity basketball players. Edward was the first person I saw in the office. He gave me some compliments right away on how I kicked the football and on how great of a basketball player I was. I had no clue he was paying attention to an underclassman like me.

I asked Edward how I could get a job for the school. He explained to me that all I had to do was apply for a job and they would call me if there was an opening. So I did just that and in a few days I received a call from the school district. I was so overjoyed, no field work for me this summer. I was assigned to clean student desks and chairs. Some needed painting too.

Throughout the years I had been harassed by several Hispanic girls about me being around Caucasian girls only. They gave me an occasional, *why don't you go out with a Chicana? They are your own kind.* I didn't know how to respond to that. And I guess I didn't know the answer to that. I personally thought there were a lot of nice looking Hispanic girls at Dimmitt.

Working for the school I met a Hispanic girl that worked with me and a few other Hispanics that worked in other sections of the school. We carried chairs outside to wash and dry and then we took the chairs back inside. This went on all week before moving on to the next task. I made her laugh now and then. She had dark hair, dark eyelashes and long stringy hair. Her name was Christina. I eventually asked her if she wanted to go watch a movie with me at the Dimmitt Cinema. We only had one movie theater in town. It was one of those places that you would sometimes stick to the floor – ha-ha!

Okay, she was Hispanic and the first time I made an attempt to ask my own race on a date at the movie theater. We met there and I can't even remember what movie we watched, but this mishap will always stay in my memory. It was a Saturday night and a beautiful evening, I remember I walked there. I told my parents I was going to the movies, I did not mention that I had a date.

Once Christina and I made it there we talked a little bit about work and the past school year while we were waiting for the movie to start. It was nerve-racking for both of us, I think, at least it was for me. She had a soda placed in the holder between us adjacent to our knees – a large-size drink. We had just been paid and we had money. Halfway through the movie, being a teenage boy and all, I decided to turn to her and try to kiss her. I didn't know if she would slap me or if she would be okay with it. As I got closer to her lips, I saw her face and finally touched her lips with mine in the dark theater. She jumped and I moved back quickly! She grabbed some napkins and started wiping her pants off. Oh great! I had knocked down her soda and it spilt all over her white pants.

That was so embarrassing and I kept apologizing the rest of the night. I felt so bad. She went to the girls' bathroom to clean up and then came back and we finished the movie. With half my peripheral vision gone I often knocked things over. This time it wasn't a stack of cans at the grocery store, or a desk at school, it was a soda that soaked my movie date.

After that weekend we were placed in different areas of the school. I never talked to Christina again that summer but I wanted to say hi and still be friends with her. She didn't get angry with me. What I remember about Christina is that she was polite and kind.

While working for the school I looked into a job that looked a lot more fun than what I was doing. The head-football coach was managing the public pool, which was located right next to the junior-high building – that's where we had our graduation swimming party. I asked Coach Smith how I could get a job as a lifeguard. I told him I was a good swimmer and that I could even do a one-and-a-half off of the fifteen-foot board. He wanted to see me do that. Coach Smith knew about me and how far I kicked the football, I think that helped me make a connection with him.

Coach Smith taught me how to save a life, he said that was required. I also had to take a written test on the swimming pool rules. There were guidelines swimmers had to follow as kids and adults. Swimmers came from all over town and would pay fifty cents to swim all day. The fee had gone up twenty-five cents. I had never studied as hard as I did for this test. I passed it with flying colors. The coach then had me take a live test saving a life. I actually saved a little girl's life and then I actually saved my coach's life when he threw himself in the pool and asked me to save him. I was unsure of myself because he was about 6' 5" and 250 lbs. He assured me I could do it. I remembered his words, *just remember what I taught you, David, let the water be your friend, all you have to do is pull me to the side of the pool.* I managed to do that successfully.

He immediately hired me to be one of the lifeguards. I couldn't start until the last half of the summer. He had me fill out all of the necessary paperwork and I was all set. I informed my supervisor who was having me move desks out of classrooms at the Dimmitt North Grade. He was the year-round janitor there and he was happy for me to have landed a job as a lifeguard. I remember he was always trying to set me up with his daughter, he would joke around with me all the time. He was a nice and funny Mexican man.

Being a lifeguard at the Dimmitt Public Pool was challenging, fun, and rewarding. I had to instruct people on where to wait and keep them updated as to when the pool would open, because obviously no one could read the sign that said, OPEN at 1:00 p.m. Normally there would be a lot of kids of all ages excited to jump in the pool on a hot-summer day.

At this swimming pool a lifeguard didn't just watch people and save lives. There were three of us employed there, Roman, myself, and L.V. We all had to work as a team every morning to prepare the pool for business. L.V. was a jokester and he would always punch on our arms as we were trying to do our work. I would punch him back but he was a lot stronger and taller than I was. He was going to play on the varsity football team as a sophomore, I was going to be a freshman.

Our routine as lifeguards was to show up early at 6:00 a.m., hose down the concrete dressing rooms, vacuum the entire pool, and check the chlorine levels. We would then put all of the equipment away and go home for lunch before opening the place up for business. We never worried about taking in the money for the concessions. They normally hired a high school girl to take care of that and Coach Smith would often come around to check on things.

Up to this point I had been a pretty good kid other than a few times that I got into trouble with teachers, or like that time I got into a fight with Leon. There was one other time that I was asked to go out into the hall. I was simply talking about a neighborhood dog and how fat this dog was because my friend would feed him a lot of beans and tortillas. My math teacher walks in while I was saying that and he made a bad assumption. He thought I was talking about him. I tried my best to explain that it wasn't him I was talking about, but he had his mind made up already. He took me out to the hallway and hit me with the board three times – painful and unfair – nothing I could do about it.

Like I said, I was a pretty good kid. I always tried to do what was right. Oh sure I'm not going to say I never tried puffing on a cigarette. I tried that once in an alley with my neighborhood friends – yuck! Not for me, that was horrible and I stayed away from smoking. Drinking beer? Oh, well my dad and my Uncle Jessie used to drink just about every weekend while playing music. What young kid on earth would not want to taste this drink that was popular among adults. Okay, please don't crucify me, I was only a kid, but yes, I David Espinoza did steal a couple of drinks from my dad's can of Coors beer. It tasted okay, but nothing I wanted to continue. I knew it was wrong, and my parents told me to stay away from alcohol.

I think those were the only times I tried smoking a cigarette or tasting a beer. I was an athlete and it just wasn't for me. I learned in school about the negative affects of alcohol and smoking. After those two experiences I went to confession and confessed those sins. I had to say ten Our Fathers and ten Hail Marys – a Catholic thing for some of you that might not understand. I also prayed to God and asked for his forgiveness. I remember feeling so guilty about these mistakes as a young kid.

Another time at the pool, we were all very hungry, L.V. and Roman saw that there was a crack in the thin and silver-metal door that was locked. This is where all of the snacks were kept overnight. These were sold to the swimmers that were customers. Well, one thing led to another and we all reached in there and grabbed some candy bars. I think we must have eaten about three or four each. I felt guilty about stealing those candy bars. I knew what was on my list to confess for Friday. Our coach figured it out once he counted the inventory verses the sales.

He brought us all together and asked us if we took those candy bars. I told him that I took them and I would pay for them out of my check. Roman and L.V. looked at me. The coach asked the other two, *is that true?* And then they responded, *no we did too*. The coach was furious and I remember his words to us, "If y'all wanted candy, why didn't y'all just ask?" Again, I noted that on my tablet at home – confession time at church on Friday was at 7:00 p.m.

In junior high, we studied about the different kinds of drugs and how dangerous they were to our health and mind. The teacher taught us about L.S.D., marijuana, amphetamines, downers, and more. One time our teacher brought these items to the class for us to see what they looked like. To me, I didn't understand why people wanted to do such a thing to their bodies. Never did I expect one of my friends to be a drug user.

L.V. was such a talented football player. I thought, going into my freshman year, that I was the best punter and kicker in Dimmitt – without a doubt. The coach wanted L.V. and I to do some punting-the-football after work. So we did just that. Roman wasn't a special-teams football player so he wasn't asked to do that.

Roman would often fall asleep while he was vacuuming the pool. L.V. would pull him by his legs and throw him in the water. The shock from Roman was a funny sight. I knew L.V. and the prankster he was. That was a mean thing to do, but at the time I was a young kid and I laughed at things like that.

The first time I went to punt the football with L.V. I thought to myself, *okay, so this guy is 6' 1" and I'm 5' 11"*. The coach had some receivers from the varsity team show up to catch the footballs and throw them back to us. I watched L.V. take the first punt – holy macro! He connected on a clean spiral and the distance was beyond what I could match. He punted the ball fifty-yards in the air. When my turn came up, my punt went forty-five yards in the air. I never could beat L.V., and it drove me crazy, however, that encouraged me to practice even more.

We also started lifting weights, I focused on getting stronger, legs and arms. L.V. and I would walk over to the weight room, the coach had given him the key to the field house, where all the weights were. I looked up to L.V. and had much respect for him. He was one of the most talented and athletic Hispanic kids I knew in Dimmitt. He also ran races like the 880-yard run and the 4 X 440 relay. He lived three blocks away from us when we lived in the old-poverty neighborhood.

I was becoming a good friend of L.V. and we practiced together at the football field next to the field house. I remember him telling me to punt the football low if there was a strong wind coming at us. The ball would go much farther, otherwise the football would fly backward. It worked for me and for him.

As many friends that I enjoyed making in Texas, I also lost just as many. One morning, we had just completed our work at the pool. I walked over to the field house with L.V. to lift weights. As I'm starting to do some bench pressing, I looked over to where L.V. was. He pulled out a bag of marijuana and started rolling a joint. I took a big swallow, I was startled because I knew what drugs did to the human mind from the class at school.

"What the heck are you doing!" I asked.

He just laughed and lit up the joint.

"L.V. why are you doing this, man, you can get into big trouble."

"Don't be such a square, man," L.V. said.

I was very alarmed. I told him I was getting out of there. The first time I ever heard, *don't be such a square man, come on, try it with me*, was when L.V. said that to me that depressing day. I started to walk out of the weight room.

"Don't tell anyone, okay?"

"I won't tell anyone, but please think about what you're doing, you could get kicked off the team." I turned around and never looked back.

That was the last time I hung around L.V. I am so thankful to God for being there for me and guiding me in making good decisions.

I was torn, not only because I had made a good friend that had so much talent, but also because I was confused on what to do. Should I tell the coach, or should I just stay out of it? I told L.V. that I would not say anything. I did keep my word, I didn't want to be the reason why he would get kicked off the team. At that age I didn't even think about God and I didn't even think about praying for this teenage kid that was making a huge mistake. I didn't know anything about Jesus, I just knew that there was a God and that I had to do all the things that the Catholic Church was teaching me.

This incident woke me up. That's when I realized the teacher was telling the truth, people actually do drugs and get high for thrills. I didn't want to believe it, I was naive. The truth hurts sometimes, especially when it's someone you know.

L.V. went on to play sports that year, and later on I found out he got kicked off the team. I hope that he learned and that he changed his ways. I never saw L.V. again and I never knew what happened to him.

God was with me even when I didn't know it. He allowed those negative things to come into my life and he gave me the choice on how to react. I knew there was a God and I knew it was a sin to disobey my parents and to also do something that would damage his creation. I thank Jesus for being there with me and how He protected me.

While I was a lifeguard that summer I would run into teenage kids that carried a bag of marijuana with them. They would try to sell it outside the pool fence. I would always walk over to them and tell them to get off the premises before I called the police. They would walk away quickly, with no questions asked. It only happened a few times that summer, but it did happen. I informed Coach Smith and he said I did the right thing.

It was a confusing time in my life. I didn't understand why so many kids were getting into smoking marijuana. It was mostly African-American and Hispanic kids that I knew of doing these things. I'm sure there were a few Caucasian kids that got involved with drugs as well, I wasn't around them off school hours like I was with most minorities.

Satan tries to steer us away from Jesus during our early age, I was so glad that I had been brought up attending church and learning about God and His commandments. I certainly can now see why it's so important to spread the Word, some people may have never heard of Jesus Christ.

Mark 16:15-16 And He said to them, "Go into all the world and proclaim the Gospel to the whole creation. Whoever believes and is baptized will be saved, but whoever does not believe will be condemned."

Coach Smith kept asking me why I wasn't going to two-a-days, a summer program that prepared the incoming football players. If you were going to be a freshman and you wanted to be on the varsity team, it was required that you go to this daily-doubles training, which meant 5:30 a.m. workouts and 5:30 p.m. workouts. I told Coach Smith that I was too tired and exhausted early in the mornings and in the evenings. I had to help my dad around the house. We were doing a lot of backyard work at the place we moved into, which was next to the city park. My dad was planting peach trees and he wanted me to help dig the holes and clean up the backyard. After giving me the green light to play three sports at school, I wasn't about to push my luck with asking him if I could attend two-a-days.

The reason I wasn't on the varsity football team my freshman year, was because of me. I didn't want to let my dad down. He had put in so much sacrifice for our family. I had my disagreements with him about sports, unfortunately I felt in my heart that it was the right thing to do. Loop was working to help out the family. He had received his GED and could now work full time as a young kid. My dad helped get him a job working for Killingsworth Ready-mix. I could tell he enjoyed working with my dad. Next, they helped get my brother Gilberto hired.

I always enjoyed hearing about the jobs they did, whether it was pouring cement for a feedlot or pouring a driveway. My dad was smart, he built us a little driveway with the leftover cement from his job. Little by little the driveway would be completed. We had the boards all set up and I helped him when he poured the cement. So as you see, I would feel awful guilty if I started going to two-a-days and not help my dad at home.

When the summer was coming to an end, I reflected on what I had accomplished that crucial summer of lessons learned and my junior-high education completed. Wow! I mean, to be an official lifeguard before my freshman year of high school, I just couldn't believe it. It was amazing to tell people that I was a lifeguard when they asked me. The respect and admiration was beyond honor. It sure sounded better than *farmhand*.

I planned on connecting with Christina again, I hadn't seen her since that movie date where I spilled Coke all over her. We were watching the news late one night on one of the local Amarillo TV stations. The news broadcaster started talking about a serious head-on collision halfway between Friona and Dimmitt – about fifteen miles out of town. I heard the reporter say that it was Christina's family. They showed the video of her station wagon – the entire front part of her car was smashed. They mentioned a few members of her family and then they mentioned Christina. She was in critical condition at an Amarillo hospital. It was hot that night, and I walked outside for a few minutes. I didn't know what to think, and I didn't know if she was going to make it. I was worried and I didn't even know her that well. My summer ended on a sad note.

13.

Freshman at Dimmitt High School

I finally started my adventure at Dimmitt High School on 1405 Western Circle Drive. During the beginning of my young adult years, I remember going to several checkups at my ophthalmologist in Amarillo. These appointments were normally during the summer. My eye doctor made a new eye for me, it was the second eye made for me that I can recall. Maybe one was made when I was younger, but truly I can't remember. It was like a nightmare going through those procedures – it was difficult. It always took me about a week to recover from the swelling around my eye area.

I had new boots, new bell-bottom jeans, and new shirts. I was ready for another year of challenges and lessons. During my teenage years I always had money at the beginning of the school year, but ran out soon. Coach Smith came out to our first freshman football practice. When he watched me punt the football and then kick the football, I heard him telling the other coaches, *I sure wish he would have gone to two-a-days.*

When practice was over I was walking by the coaches into the field house where we dressed down. My coach grabbed my arm and looked at me.

"Espinoza, you'd a gone to two-a-days you'd be on varsity."

"I know, coach," I just looked down and shook my head up and down.

I heard a few of the players talking and saying that Thompson made the varsity team. He would be playing with his talented brother, I still remember Robert's number, 22. I was always competitive with Thompson and it didn't go well with me, he was on varsity and I wasn't.

For me not to be on varsity was a blessing in disguise, because I became the halfback running out of the "I" formation – it was an unbelievable season. Tommy was the quarterback and I can't remember who the fullback was. A fun year and we had a winning record. I think we only lost two or three games all year. When I kicked off to start games I was putting the ball in the end zone consistently. I never saw our varsity kicker do that on Friday nights, which made me feel good. He was a good kicker though and was pretty consistent at making field goals. I would have loved to compete with him for that spot, it just didn't happen.

I loved art class and English. I took shop class just because of my dad who often had me under the car working with him. I wanted to learn more about car engines and stuff. I didn't have much fun in that class. The excitement was watching a fight between Reggie and one of my teammates, Eddie. I don't know how it started, but I remember it lasting a very long time and we were all just watching it. My shop teacher walked in and tried to break it up, but they were held up in a locking position. Eddie had Reggie's head locked up and wouldn't let go. The teacher decided to just let them keep fighting so they'd learn a lesson and tire out. I was actually surprised about that. Later on the teacher was questioned about the handling of that situation.

Dimmitt High School was more calm than junior high about fights after school, but it was still a little scary at times. Some kids were just out to cause problems. Again, this school was diverse – a mixture of Caucasians, Hispanics, and African-Americans.

Math class was great, not my favorite subject but definitely in the top three. We were studying pre-algebra. My teacher was Coach Cleveland's wife, Libby Cleveland. One time I was in a real hurry and I was running a little late coming all the way from the opposite side of the building. I walked inside the classroom just barely beating the second and final bell. I couldn't see the corner of a first-aisle desk due to being blind on my entire left side. I rushed toward my desk – *bam!* I knocked the desk over and fell to the ground. I just lied there and everyone started laughing at me. Those kinds of laughs didn't bother me because they weren't directed at my eye.

"David, are you okay ... didn't you see that desk?" Mrs. Cleveland asked.

"I'm sorry Mrs. Cleveland."

My challenges were daily, with only half of my peripheral vision I had to make that adjustment of turning my head more and being more careful. I always wanted to play quarterback and it drove me crazy when coaches knew about me not being able to see out of my left eye. I asked them if I could play quarterback, I could throw the football very well. In the playgrounds kids would always want me to play quarterback because I threw the ball well. I could never convince my coaches. One coach made me feel bad the rest of the school day, "David, we don't allow one-eyed players to play quarterback." That disappointed me, and I had to accept the fact that it was not going to happen.

Close to the end of football season I found myself sitting alone eating my free lunch. I tried sitting with the Caucasian kids, but I was not fitting in with their little group and I felt uncomfortable with the way they looked at me and then whispered at each other while they laughed. Word was getting out that I had a funny eye and I could not see out of it. That question kept coming out, *what's wrong with your eye?* My answer was, *I was born like this, I have lazy eye.* Even after that I could tell that I was going to be ignored so I left their table and went to sit at another table far away. I just wanted to eat my lunch and get out of there.

I often sat by myself in the lunchroom. It was a lonely feeling that I wouldn't wish on anyone. I sometimes got the feeling that no one wanted to be around a unique kid like me.

It was nice that the school had installed a juke box. Kids would put their nickel in and their song would start playing. I remember one song in particular that kids started hating because it was selected all the time. It was "Kung Fu Fighting" by Carl Douglas. It had a good beat to it, but the students just wore it out.

I started feeling not so normal again, and then when it was time for football practice, I felt normal again. My teammates looked up to me, I was one of the top players on the team and I was also the punter and kicker for the team. The sport I played was my counseling. I know God had to put sports on earth for people like me. God was there for me even when I didn't know it.

I'll never forget what happened to me at the high school cafeteria my freshman year. I saw a girl with long-dark-stringy hair limping along in the lunch line. All the students would grab a tray and the cafeteria workers would scoop the food and place it on the trays. The girl also had an arm that was not stable. She looked very disoriented and I was right behind her. No one was talking to her, she was being ignored by just about every kid in the cafeteria. I saw a few kids making fun of her, curling their arm and limping like she did and then laughing – luckily she didn't see them. I saw them and it angered me.

She had her head down the whole time while standing in line except when she was about to grab a tray. She was struggling because of her arm not functioning very well. I reached over and grabbed the tray and placed it on her hand so she could hold on to it. She turned and looked at me as to say, *thank you*, but didn't express words, instead just a very tiny smile. It was Christina! The girl from my eighth-grade year who I accidentally spilled soda on at the movie theater. I just took a big swallow and did not say one word.

I knew she had been in a big accident at the end of the summer. She pulled through and was obviously recovering from some kind of brain damage she suffered. I didn't know if she even remembered who I was. She never looked at me again, she just kept walking with a limp and very slow.

I started having more compassion for people like Christina. Lord knows what I had gone through and still continue with my challenges, but I couldn't measure to what Christina was going through. When I saw her in the hallway she was always by herself. I tried to say hi to her, but she seemed to always look down. I felt so bad for her, what a nightmare she was going through as a freshman in high school. After that I never saw Christina again. I never knew what happened to her.

The weeks went by and I was doing very well with my grades and homework. School studies were never-ending, especially for someone like me, I had to study hard to do well in school. I also had to study the playbook for our team. I didn't have that natural gift of retaining everything I learned quickly, like my friend Tobin. He was one of the brightest students I knew during my school days in Dimmitt.

At the end of football season, I never thought I'd meet a girl that I could hold hands with again. I often saw my friends with their girlfriends and I hoped that maybe someday I could possibly attract another female. I completely started ignoring the Hispanics that suggested I stay with my own kind of race.

There was this tall-thin-blonde girl that I had never seen before. She was a sophomore, a grade ahead of me and she seemed a little distant from everyone else. To me she was very pretty. She must have been at least 5' 10" and her blonde hair came down to her shoulders. Her name was Joy Slaughter. Some of the students joked around about her last name. I didn't care what her last name was, but wow, she was nice looking. She was like a model on TV – I didn't overlook that.

So Joy eventually became my girlfriend. We had a lot of fun together and she never once brought up anything about my eye, of course I was pretty careful about positioning myself when I talked to her so my eyes looked close to the same. I had crazy-mixed feelings that I didn't understand. Why were kids so rude and mean to me because of the way I looked, and then why did this beautiful girl like me so much? I was totally confused, she made me feel accepted and wanted. I was lucky to have been her boyfriend my freshman year.

I remember once, Joy came to my house. She said she couldn't stop thinking about me, so she decided to walk over to my house. I didn't know that she lived a few blocks from us and that her dad was a policeman. When she knocked on our door, my mom answered and she ran her off. Mom told Joy that I was too young to be hanging around girls.

When Joy told me this, I just laughed, "That's my mom. I normally don't tell her if I'm around a girl. She's overprotective of us, especially my sisters." Joy understood that and agreed to just meet at the park or at the movie theater if we went out on a date.

I was often found in the gym during basketball season along with my brother Richard and some of our friends from the neighborhood. My brother did not believe that I kissed a nice looking girl like Joy. He and his friend would often make fun of her last name in front of me just to tease me ... it didn't work though. That night at the gym she came by to say hello and to see what my world of sports was like, because trust me, she was not into sports.

"Okay you don't believe me huh?" I told my brother.

I walked over to Joy.

"My brother doesn't believe that I've kissed you."

Joy started laughing.

"Let's show him," Joy said as she put her arms around me and kissed me for a few seconds.

"I guess we answered his question," Joy said as we laughed together.

She filled me in on the reason she stopped by. I guess she missed me so much and had to stop by to say, hi. That made me feel good.

I liked Joy, but our relationship came to an end when I couldn't invest the kind of time, with her, that she wanted me to. I was heavy into sports and I was practicing every day and studying in preparation to someday have a decent job. After landing that lifeguard position, I gained so much confidence, and I wanted to be successful in whatever I ended up doing. An NFL career, or a professional-job career would provide for me in the future.

Joy was a pretty girl and I was lucky to have been her boyfriend. I want her to know that she bounced my self-esteem up to where Kylene and Karen did in my early years of school. I had some great times with Joy, I'll never forget what she told my sister, Louise, *David and I are someday going to get married and have one hundred kids!*

I started feeling pretty good about myself despite half of my peripheral vision gone. I was still insecure about my looks even though I had proved not only to myself, but to my friends and family that I could have a nice-looking girlfriend. To me that was a huge challenge that I overcame.

I decided that I was done with girls for awhile and I was going to focus on my athletic career. I wanted to be on the varsity team the following year and that's what I would focus on.

The football coaches in Dimmitt started this 200 lbs. club. This meant that anyone on the football team that could bench press 200 lbs. would earn a T-shirt with that label on it. That put fuel on my flame, because I wanted one of those T-shirts. I saw some of the varsity linemen and linebackers wearing them in the hallways. At Dimmitt High School the hallways were connected in a shape of a large rectangle. This meant that in the mornings all the students would walk around until school started. It was also the time when couples would hold hands walking around the hallways. I did that many times with Joy. We continued to say hi to each other and to catch up on how things were going in school and outside school. She also managed to come to one of my football games.

During football season we had weight training three days a week and we always tried the T-shirt challenge once a week. A coach had to watch us lift 200 lbs. one time on the bench press. It took me a few weeks to reach that goal, but I finally did and joined the 200 lbs. club. I was starting to look pretty fit and several girls started talking about me and how they liked me.

One day at the cafeteria I was sitting at the table with several Hispanics. One of the girls was talking about Rosa and Estella getting into a fight. I asked her what they were fighting about. She said, "You." They were fighting over me? I had no idea they both liked me. I remembered spending time with both of those girls on separate occasions, but never knew that they liked me that much. Again, I was so confused my freshman year.

When basketball season started, I wanted to try out for the varsity team, but I never heard when the tryouts were. I missed them and was very disappointed. I don't know if I would have made the varsity team, but I would have loved the try-out opportunity. It was okay because I had a blast playing freshman basketball.

My life began to revolve around sports. With basketball season getting ready to start, I would find myself spending hours at the high-school gym working on skills needed and playing pick-up games with friends and teammates. This was a time in my life where our family continued to struggle financially. It was the norm to listen to my mom talk to bill collectors. My parents would often have to charge our Christmas presents, furniture, or clothes.

Coach Cleveland was good to my brother, Gilberto, he'd always let him borrow the key to the gym and when we were done practicing, Gilberto would bring the key right back to Coach Cleveland. The gym was isolated from the school so it was just the gym that we would get access to. We would spend hours at the gym. I remember one time I played basketball from 10:00 a.m. in the morning to midnight. Talk about an exhausting day of fun. We drank water throughout and sometimes we would bring our lunch.

They had this soda machine in one of the rooms where players would get treatment for aches and pains, or ankles taped, that sort of thing. Now and then when I had 25 cents, I bought a soda. I liked Coke and Dr. Pepper. They also had Orange Crush and Sprite. Talk about a refreshing drink after playing basketball for hours.

One time I was in the gym with my brother. He was working on free throws a long time and wasn't ready to go home yet. I was wanting a soda but I didn't have a penny on me. I had exhausted my funds from my summer job and I was plain broke.

I didn't think about church or what God would say about the sin I was about to commit. All I could think about was how those soda cans would drop down when one was purchased. I started analyzing the possibility of lying on my back and reaching up with my arm in hopes that I would figure out how to get a soda at no cost to me.

As I reached up with my arm slowly, I made it all the way up to where there were levers lined up across. My shoulder was snug against the bottom area where the sodas dropped down. I could hear my brother bouncing the basketball and taking shot after shot while I was trying to borrow a soda from the school. I'd like to think it was borrowing, but it was actually stealing a soda. I pressed the levers different ways until finally the lever gave and down came a can of soda and landed on the top part of my hand. I turned my hand around, grabbed the can, and pulled my arm out. I knew now that the timing had to be just right to catch the soda as it came down rapidly. I could only get Coke or Dr. Pepper. The other levers were too far to reach. I couldn't believe what I had just done and how easy it was for me to figure it out.

I brought my brother a soda and he said, "Thanks!" We drank our sodas and played a game of one-on-one. I can't describe to you how tasty and refreshing those drinks were – ice cold and very thirst-quenching. I knew in my heart that it was wrong and that it was stealing, but I didn't tell anyone. The only one I told was my brother, Richard. It was our secret and I was a very popular brother. He couldn't do it when he tried. On another day, our friend Ralph saw me taking one out. He wanted to try and see if he could get a free soda. It was not an easy thing to do, and I was the only one that mastered that skill.

Ralph got his arm stuck trying and could not get it out. We were all yelling, "Here comes the coach!" Ralph was panicking and under a lot of stress thinking he was going to get caught. He didn't know we were all just joking. We finally saw how emotionally stressed he was and told him we were just kidding. Ralph finally got his arm out.

Over a period of time I probably took about eight sodas for me, five for my brother, two for my brother Gilberto, six for Ralph, and two for my teammate, Eddie. I told Eddie that if he stopped making fun of kids on our team, I'd get him a soda for an away basketball game. He definitely slowed down on bugging kids. We were the two top athletes of the freshman team that year.

I had taken twenty three sodas from the vending machine before I started feeling guilty. I went to confession on that Friday during basketball season and I told the priest that I stole twenty three sodas at the gym. The priest said that I was forgiven and not to sin anymore. For penance, he told me to say twenty Our Fathers and twenty Hail Marys – prayers that the Catholic Church had us memorize. I didn't feel like that was enough punishment for what I had done. After I said the prayers as penance, I asked God myself for forgiveness. I never felt comfortable doing the many rules the Catholic Church required, but I did them because my mom asked me to and I knew it was a sin to not honor my mom.

My brother, Gilberto, was not happy when I told him what I had done. He kept telling me that he was going to report this to

Coach Cleveland. I begged him not to and I told him I would never do that again. He took my word on it and did not go to the coach.

What I ended up doing was sweeping the gym for several days to pay for what I had stolen. No one knew about this, but me. I asked Coach Cleveland if it was okay for me to sweep the gym before we played on it. He said I didn't have to do that but if I wanted to, it was fine. I swept the gym every time I went there before we practiced or shot baskets. I swept it more times than you can count. I learned a valuable lesson and I felt at peace with how I resolved my guilt. My basketball friends kept asking me if I could get them a Coke, I finally said that I couldn't do that any- more, they had rigged the machine and it was impossible. They all left me alone after that. That was the last time that I stole anything. I felt restitution for what I had done.

We were often in the gym working on our shooting or just playing two-on-two or one-on-one. It was fun and several of us were trying to get better. Coach Cleveland stepped into the gym and began to walk to his office which was in the gym. He had a big glass window which allowed him to see the entire floor. I was the only one left in the evening shooting baskets. He stopped and watched me shoot a few shots.

"Hey David, I was talking to one of the football coaches and he was telling me that you could only see out of one eye ... is that true?"

"Yes sir, that's true."

I went on to tell him what happened to me when I was five years old. He said he was sorry and he also said that I could hit the basket pretty darn good. He was looking forward to me playing for him on the varsity team in the future. That made me feel good, all of my hard work practicing had paid off.

Coach Cleveland was a big deal in Dimmitt – a great coach. This coach had the ability to develop players, create a relationship with them, and coach them to play one of the best zone defenses I had ever seen. I watched the varsity practices just to learn from Coach Cleveland. On Sundays after church, I would go to the gym to shoot on the side baskets while the varsity team played half-court five-on-five. Coach Cleveland and some of the other coaches and friends would sit against the wall behind the baseline and socialize while they watched the players. Playing in front of coaches made the players better because they were all fighting for a spot and playing time.

There were times where they needed one more player if they didn't have enough players that showed up on Sundays. Coach Cleveland would always ask me if I wanted to play. My answer was an exciting, *yes!* I waited for those opportunities to get a chance to play with kids like, Jim Birdwell, Johnny Hampton, and Keith Crum. I remember Jim Birdwell so well, this kid was about 6' 3" and one of the reasons the Dimmitt Bobcats were state champions my freshman year. I wanted to go to that game so bad, but I had to settle for listening to it on a transistor radio while I was practicing the high jump out on the new track that was under construction. Dimmitt would have a new track and football stadium next season. Listening to the state championship game taking place in Austin, Texas, was like being there because of the play-by-play calls. It was a memorable year for the Dimmitt Bobcats' Basketball Team.

Track and field season was in the air. The coaches were looking at everyone to split up into freshman, JV, and Varsity teams. During practice I was clearing 5' 4" in the high jump and I could three-step the 120-yard hurdles most of the way. When we started traveling to invitational meets my hurdle time was 16.3 seconds and my high jump clearance was 5' 6". It was enough to compete, but certainly not enough to place in the top four. Again, our track meets in Texas were just invitational meets with at least 8 schools from everywhere.

I was under pressure every meet, because we had several talented African-American kids that were some of the fastest sprinters in the state of Texas. In the hurdles we had Kenny who was a senior. He was a Caucasian kid that was tall and won just about every hurdle race. Kenny usually came in first place. I normally came in fifth or sixth place out of eight runners. He would often give me tips on technique and stretching out. I learned from him to stretch out at least fifteen minutes before warming up on hurdles. I would usually make the finals but I never placed in the top four. I kept forgetting that I was only a freshman on the varsity team. I was able to earn my letter as a freshman that year.

While waiting for my events to be called I remember lying on the grass, a waiting area for all teams. There was this song playing called, "Wildfire," by Michael Murphy. Throughout my lifetime, for some reason, 1970's songs brought back memories for me.

Track and field was so much fun during practices and at meets, but I never looked forward to the bus rides back home. My teammates were all a lot older than I was. Half of them were African-American and very competitive. They did not like third-place ribbons or anything below that. They pushed me to get better as the season progressed. I never had their respect until the Odessa Invitational at Permian High School.

I felt blessed that the Lord gave me the talent to achieve what I did in track and field at such a young age. At the time I didn't think very much about God or the gifts He blessed me with. It wasn't until much later in my life that I realized all of this. God was with me even when I didn't realize it.

The varsity track team was leaving early in the morning at 4:00 a.m. on a Saturday. Odessa was 201 miles away from Dimmitt – a 3 1/2-hour drive. That was the longest away-trip I ever experienced as an athlete in Dimmitt, Texas. I could never forget that long paved road with many dips along the way and a lot of cowboy country.

Everyone was asleep except for a few including me. I couldn't sleep in a moving bus and with such an exciting adventure ahead that I had never experienced, it was even tougher. Everything was paid for, my track spikes, my nice purple and white warm-ups, and our meals. We were treated like an elite team, even a charter bus was provided at times. I took it all in, this is what I worked so hard for, to be one of these talented guys. The best part was the distraction of my talent in high jump. My teammates never made fun of me or asked about my eye, even when it was swollen from me rubbing it so much because of the dry-spring weather.

Sometimes it was windy and I couldn't afford lubricant eye drops. I would run over to a water fountain and put water on my eye. I would often try to yawn to generate tears for moisture. My last resort, if there was no water around, I would spit on my fingers and gently rub the spit in my eye to moisturize it. I know it sounds gross and unsanitary, but that was in desperation mode. I would do whatever it took to get moisture to my eye in this dry Texas weather. It was not fun and I felt so alone because I didn't want people to see the bizarre habits I created due to my eye. When the wind slowed down and sweat actually stayed around my face, it was like paradise in heaven to me – my eye was moisturized.

At Odessa, I made it to the finals in the hurdles, I survived the prelims and the semi-finals. Some of my teammates would yell out at me, "Nice work Espinoza, you're a stud!" It made me feel good and motivated me to do my best. I couldn't believe how many fast hurdlers were at this invitational.

The times were a lot faster than mine. In the finals I don't think Kenny won, but he placed pretty high. I did the best I could but could not match the talented upperclassmen I was running against. I placed eighth out of eight finalist. That was the bad news and I didn't feel bad because I made it to the finals in Odessa, Texas, wow! I not only got a PR (Personal Record) with a time of 16.0, I also three-stepped the entire ten hurdles. To me that was such a huge improvement and my goal for the year.

In the high jump, Eddie, my teammate, would always beat me in every invitational track meet. There were ten athletes left and the bar was at 5' 8". Eddie and I were the only two left from our team. There were high jumpers there that were a lot taller than I was. When my turn came up, I felt good, my steps were marked and I focused on everything I had learned. I planted my left leg and threw my right knee up while swinging my arms for that extra help. I was surprised when I cleared 5' 8" and landed on a nice high jump mat. My teammates cheered loud for me. That was my best jump, and another PR. Eddie missed twice and just quit and walked off frustrated. He looked at the judges and said, "Scratch me, I'm done." He was frustrated and not happy.

I went on to clear 5' 9" and then 5' 10" before being elim-inated. I had jumped an all-time-best height and I had earned the respect of all the African-American kids on my team. It was one of the best rides home I had experienced. There's no way I was throwing my fifth-place ribbon away. I worked too hard for that ribbon. The winner of the high jump went on to clear 6' 4" and he was a senior in high school.

That season was also when I first saw myself on TV. We were traveling to the Amarillo Relays – a huge invitational track meet. This was the first time I had been away from home overnight. What an experience that was and I couldn't believe how much I missed my mom and dad and family just being away for two days. I had never stayed in a nice hotel before. I still remember my roommate, Trevino, he ran the mile. We ate dinner at this nice buffet restaurant. Having all expenses paid was one of the many benefits of being on the varsity team.

I was expecting to do well again, but what I wasn't expecting was running the hurdles in thirty-five-degree weather with sleet coming down and a strong headwind during my race. I was so cold, I couldn't even warm up properly before any event. My coach kept telling me, "Espinoza, just do the best you can, the weather is pretty rough and they are on a tight deadline with a scheduled time." I just shook my head and didn't say anything while I shivered frantically. There were so many teams there, this was a real big deal and one of the largest invitational meets around.

I ran in the third heat of five. I remember being at the starting blocks. All of the competitors were wearing tights under their track shorts. I had purple tights and purple track shorts. We look-ed at each other as we were freezing and shaking before we heard the official yell out, *Go to your marks! ... Set!* ... and the gun went off! I tried my hardest to sprint but I couldn't feel my legs so I just kept going, made it over the first hurdle and was keeping up with the pack for about six hurdles. When I came to the seventh hurdle I was in third place, but then I hit the hurdle with my lead leg and I fell straight down. The runner on my left grazed my head a little with his shoe. I just stayed down for a few minutes on the track filled with wet sleet everywhere. I was disappointed that this weekend had turned into a cold nightmare.

The high jump wasn't any better, it was raining and I man-aged to get over 5' 8". The Amarillo news was filming while I high jumped in the rain. Later that night at the hotel, Trevino and I watched the track competition on TV. That was pretty cool despite a frustrating meet.

When I returned on Sunday, I was glad to be home. As I walked in I didn't see anyone there. It was a quiet house, so I threw myself on the couch and fell asleep thinking about the coldest meet I had ever participated in. A little later my parents came home. I remember feeling loved so much.

"Awe, there's my David. It's so good to see him," Mom said.

I could tell she missed me and it was only two days. I felt the same and I was glad to be home.

During the final track meet of the year, I managed to do pretty well, but the surprise I got was unbelievable and unexpected. I ran into Baldomero, my first-grade friend. I hadn't seen him in ages! We talked for a long time and I found out his older brother ran with the Springlake-Earth 4 X 100 relay team. I also saw Isabel's older sisters, they were some of the most attractive Hispanic girls I had ever seen. I talked to the oldest sister and asked her about Isabel. She informed me that Isabel didn't run track and she stayed home that day. I mentioned to her that I would love to see her again. She said that they went to the Dimmitt city park on Sundays now and then, I should go there to talk to her. That worked since I lived right next to the park. I looked forward to that.

I stopped thinking about having a girlfriend after my experience with Joy Slaughter – I just wasn't at that place yet in my life. I was definitely open for friendship with someone like, Isabel, my first-grade friend. The first time I ever got into trouble was with her. We kept playing with the puzzles when the teacher instructed us that it was time to put the puzzles away. I guess we were having so much fun together that we ignored the teacher.

My freshman year of school came to an end. My favorite classes were, English, art, and math. I wanted to take band because I loved music, but my parents could not afford the instrument and they didn't have guitar as one of the instruments in the band, so I guess it just didn't work out for me.

I was maxing over 200 lbs. on the bench press and I felt stronger than ever when I completed the weight training program.

I became an all-around better athlete ... and, I was told by several girls that my body was to kill for. I never looked at myself in that way, but I was flattered and once again, that information was a confidence boost.

14.

Sophomore Year Bittersweet in Dimmitt

I finally received my driver's license. Thanks to that free driver's education class that was offered to low-income kids like me. The previous year I took the class and that summer I went out on the highway with my instructor to train. His compliments to me were extremely positive. He didn't know that I started driving when I was thirteen-years old.

I was driving the student car toward Hereford, Texas, with my instructor on the passenger side. I explained to him that I could not see out of my left eye and I was worried that I might not be able to get my license. He looked at me, "So?" He went on to explain to me that our bodies allow our heads to turn for a reason. I just had to turn more than most people for blindsides and awareness of other vehicles or pedestrians.

I felt great and relaxed after his answer, because he never brought that up again. I found out that I needed glasses. I was nearsighted, I couldn't see things clear from a far distance, but I could see clear from a short distance. God put something in front of me that I could go after. So, I did, I had my eyes checked. It was funny because my eye doctor kept checking my prosthetic eye even though I had already explained to him that I could not see out of it.

Glasses, or spectacles as some might call them, were heaven to me for so many reasons. I could actually sit at the back of the class and see the chalkboard. Before I had my glasses I would squint and eventually move to the front of the class. My sophomore year was going to be amazing! One of the best reasons for me to wear glasses was the comfort I gained because of how the glare would hide my eyes a little. I felt like a normal person that had two eyes. I didn't wear them when I practiced or played games, but I wore them everywhere else. Oh, how I loved it, when kids would call me, four eyes.

During the summer I was working a lot and my time at home was minimal. Late nights I would hang out with my friends listening to music and playing basketball at the city park next to our house. I would also punt the football with my brother and best friend, Richard. He always had close friends during and off school hours. He would go shoot fish with a bow and arrow with his friends and hang out with them at their house.

My friends were kids that played basketball at the park, or kids that were smart and could discuss things like math equations, writing styles from our English class, or current events with the economy. My friends knew what recording artists sang the popular songs that we heard on the radio. Sometimes we would talk about colleges and what it would mean to earn a college degree.

My brother was always there for me at home, he helped me become a great athlete in whatever sport we played. Our one-on-one battles never stopped. Despite our age difference our skill level was close to evenly matched. I was a little better than him at certain skill sets and he was a little better at other skill sets. We both didn't like to lose and we both had our moments that we displayed bad sportsmanship. To this day, I love my brother despite the fact that we are different in so many ways. It was so cool to see how we had both become so successful playing for our teams and it didn't matter what sport it was.

It always drove me crazy when I could never beat my brother in a running race, he was always just a step faster than I was. In basketball, I was a pretty good outside shooter, but never as consistent as Richard. In any relay team that I ran, it was always the third leg or the second leg. Richard always ran the first leg, second leg, or the anchor leg. I was the better punter and kicker in football, but as we grew older, Richard became the better punter and I became the better kicker.

I couldn't have made it through high school without my brother there with me. There were times where I felt so alone in life because of my eye. My older brothers were not around, but my brother Richard was always there. He never saw me as some-one with a handicap, he never went easy on me, he never made fun of me, he just encouraged me in his own way. I thank the good Lord for my brother, Richard.

The entire time I played sports, there were two incidents that scared me. In a football game, when I was in junior high, I block-ed a punt. I was on defense and I broke through the line holding my hands up high while running straight to the punter. The foot-ball hit my faceguard and my good eye at the same time! I started yelling and fell down to the ground. The official called a time out and my coach came out to look at me. I had my eye covered with my right hand and I was in a full state of shock. My mind was full of thoughts, *what if I won't be able to see anymore?* My coach ran out to the field.

"Is my eye okay ... is it bleeding?" I asked.

My entire body was shaking and I was in full-mode fright. The coach's words were, *David ... it looks okay, but it's really red.* A big sigh of relief came from me and my emotional state. I thanked God for saving my only eye. It took me a week to recover from this horrible accident. We did score a safety with my block, but I paid the painful price. I couldn't understand how all of the many places the football could have hit me, it had to be on my good eye.

The second time was during a pickup basketball game at the high school. I was dribbling the ball past Paul Langford, one of the best point guards Dimmitt ever had. He reached to steal the ball and his thumb went straight into my good eye. It was a painful moment, I started crying and ran straight to the dressing room to make sure it was okay. I heard my brother, Gilberto, explain why I freaked out like that. Paul understood and apolo-gized repeatedly to me. Paul was a kid that I thought hated me, or Hispanics in general. He would never talk to me, and he never wanted to play me one-on-one. That day, things changed for us, he always said hi to me and showed true respect acknowledging my play and presence. He even started playing me one-on-one – I could never beat him, he was tough and four years older.

I walked around school with a red eye for days before it recovered. Many kids joked around about my red eye, I was thankful the jokes weren't directed at my other eye. I remember both times thanking God for keeping me safe in scary situations. I would always say to Him, *please Lord, help me,* minutes after things like this happened to me.

During the summer I was able to attend daily-doubles, back then we called them two-a-days. I was working as a lifeguard and also painting the football-stadium bleachers – my school-district job. By the end of the summer I was able to climb the rope to the top of the gym consistently. The ceiling was roughly thirty-five feet high. I had to use two hands and my feet, there's no way I could have done that with just my arms. A few kids did it, but not many. We had a couple of linemen that weighed at least 280 lbs. They would make it up one-third of the way to the ceiling. The secret for me was to not look down the entire time. I just climbed up and touched the ceiling and then made my way down.

We also ran all kinds of agility drills, pass patterns, and I kicked the football as well as punted to receivers. I had a good feeling about making the varsity football team as a sophomore. No one could kick or punt the football as far as I could and with the hang time I had, my chances were even better. Jim, who was once my teammate during grade-school Little Dribblers, was my competition, but his distance was twenty yards shorter than mine. The coaches still had us try out for the spot. Jim's wealthy friends were all hoping he would get the spot. I was glad it was up to the coaches to make that decision. Jim became my backup on the varsity team.

My sophomore year I wanted to take typing class, but it was already full. Johnny Hampton, who became a major contributor on the varsity basketball team was taking typing. I remember talking to him in the mornings before school started. He would normally stand outside his class and watch everyone walk by. The class looked like fun and I wanted to learn that skill for my future. I would have to wait until next year to try and get into that class.

I loved English class once again, my teachers were always giving me compliments on the stories I wrote. I paid attention to the corrections they made, or the suggestions they made on my writing. I remember learning about verbs, adverbs, conjunctions, and all sorts of grammar stuff. It was hard work, but once I got past all of the technical grammar, the creative writing part was fun. I never advertised that I loved English class to my teammates or friends.

I also enjoyed math and biology class that year. High school was a time where my identity started being *one of the best kickers in football* the school had seen in a long while. I felt popular for the first time in my life, and I was adjusting from a nobody to a somebody as an underclassman.

When the practices started I discovered how brutal they were. Everyone was a little bit bigger than I was and my thoughts were, *what did I get myself into?* I felt that I was strong enough to hold my own ground, after all, I had been lifting weights and had increased my bench-press-maximum lift to 240 lbs. I was benching 60 lbs. over my weight of 180 lbs.

The coaches were firm and they yelled a lot. They were motivators and took winning very serious. They placed me as the backup tight end, backup defensive end, and starting punter-kicker. We would practice for over two hours a day right after school. We had a couple weeks to prepare for our first game.

During practice we would run short slants, where the tight ends ran past the defensive backs toward the middle. Senior Ronnie Lawson was the quarterback. He yelled out the signal and I sprinted cutting inside as fast as I could go. We were in full gear, helmets and pads. In football, when a receiver is running and waiting for the football to get to him, no defender can touch him until he touches the football. If the defender touches the receiver before the ball gets there, it is a penalty.

I was watching for Ronnie's pass to me. I saw him release the football, and I had no peripheral vision to my entire left side. I just heard this loud sound – *crack!* One of the players on defense took a cheap shot at me while the football was in the air and not even close to me. In the NFL, players now get fined for cheap shots – defenseless.

I was knocked out and went unconscious for a few minutes. It felt like I was in a dark, but yet bright dream, while this pendulum was bouncing on my head making a loud noise each time. It was very strange, I had never experienced anything so scary.

The coaches were trying to wake me up by waving some ammonia in front of my nose. I finally came to, I heard my coaches calling out my name, *Espinoza ... Espinoza ... you okay?* I got up and tried running to the back of the line where the receivers were waiting for the next play. I was disoriented and could not keep my balance very well. Head Coach King followed me and asked me a few questions, but I just stared and could not answer any of them. They had me sit out the rest of the practice.

I received a pretty serious concussion. I couldn't even remember where I lived. Slowly, as practice came to an end, my memory started coming back. I had such a headache the rest of the day. I was so mad at my teammate, he wasn't a big guy either. He was someone that I could take easily. He apologized for the cheap shot several times. I said, "It's okay ... it's already happened ... I just wished I could have seen you." That was one of many times that I missed seeing out of my left eye.

It took me a few days to recover, but I finally did, thank God for the strength and comfort he gave me. I learned to be more cautious on those routes in practice and in a game. Playing on a varsity football team was tough. There were a lot of banged-up players during practices. We hit a lot and we hit hard, whether with tackling drills, or during scrimmages. We ran plays over and over until we got them right. The coaches would make us run with full pads for conditioning. In early September the weather was hot, sometimes 110 degrees. Water breaks were required every fifteen minutes. It was tiring and my muscles were so sore after every practice.

Varsity players were treated so good in Dimmitt, we had such an amazing booster club and support system. The town businesses would display one varsity player on their front window. When I was in grade school I remembered seeing 11 X 17 posters of varsity players at each store. And now, here I was a Dimmitt Bobcat and soon I would see my poster-size photo displayed in front of some store. There was a day that we had a photo shoot with a professional photographer. We were like celebrities in Dimmitt, the town took it that seriously.

My mom found my poster at a car dealership on the front window. She asked me to walk down there and ask them what they were going to do with the poster when football season was over. So I went there and asked them what she requested. The owner happened to be there and saw that it was me on the poster. He said, "Hey, that's you!" He was kind and encouraged me to come pick it up when the season was over. That's how I got the poster and I still have it today. It's a memory that is so special to me – a lot of subtext anytime I look at that poster.

The Thursday before our first game, it was tradition for an evening bonfire and the introduction for the new team. They had us all sitting on chairs that were staged on top of a flat trailer. I remember burning up, that flame was so hot! I think all of us players were hoping it was over soon. When my name was called I stood up and raised my hand. Just hearing all of the cheers and claps was the beginning of my glory days at Dimmitt High School. I can't describe how good it felt to achieve something that I had dreamed of since watching the Bobcats practice through that metal fence in grade school. It was real and I was receiving guidance from God when I didn't even know it. He placed opportunities in front of me and I made decisions to go after them. I overcame obstacle after obstacle and never gave up despite my disability, which I turned into a huge possibility.

The following day we had a large pep rally and soon after we were on a luxury charter bus headed to Muleshoe, Texas, to play our first game of the season. When we arrived there, we walked in with all of our equipment. We had our silver, purple, and white game jerseys on. We carried our helmets, cleats, and pads.

In the dressing room the coaches would always play Hank Williams' songs. I wasn't much into his music, but it kind of grew on me as the season went on. Whenever I hear Hank Williams' songs, I revert to the good old days of Dimmitt Bobcat football.

When we ran out to the field for warm-ups I felt so ready. The sold-out crowd gave me so much energy. The football-stadium lights were pretty high, and when I started taking some long snaps from our center, I went to work. My punts were hanging high above the shining stadium lights.

I remember looking up at the stands and watching the young kids sitting together, some were pointing at me. I knew exactly what they were thinking. I was once one of those kids with my brother sitting up on the bleachers. I could hear the announcer in the press box. I felt like it was a dream come true. I took another snap from the center and punted another high spiral, this one about fifty-five yards in the air. I heard the *awes* and *oohs* from many of the fans.

None of my family members were at that game, but they knew where I was that night and they were thinking of me. Travel for my dad was always tough, with the money situation and the late hours at work, there was no way my mom and dad would be there. My two older brothers were out of town that year. Gilberto was at Cisco College playing football himself. Loop had moved to Amarillo with a friend and was working there. I'm sure my brother and sisters wanted to be there, but they had no way of getting there. I thought about my brother Richard. Before I took the next warm-up punt, I thought to myself, *this one's for you Rich, thanks for helping me get here practicing so much on Dulin Street and at the city park.*

When I kicked off for the first time as a varsity player, I booted the kick all the way into the end zone. The receivers were waiting at the twenty-yard line, they saw my kick go flying over them for the touchback. Then later in the game, I punted the football for the first time in a real game as a varsity player, it was a miraculous feeling.

Let me give you more details on my first punt. When our offense didn't make the third-down conversion, my coach yelled, "Espinoza ... let's punt it!" I was so nervous with all the people having their eyes on me as I ran out to call the play. We broke up the huddle and I positioned myself thirteen yards away from the center. I yelled out, "Set!" And then I motioned with two hands for the snap. The defense came rushing in and I could hear my offensive line blocking for me – the helmets banging against the defense. I caught the football and took two steps before pointing my toe down and connecting perfectly to create a beautiful spiral.

I booted the football as hard as I could. All I could hear was the Dimmitt crowd going crazy! The announcer said some positive words about the punt. I couldn't see my own punt because I had guys that were 6' 6" coming at me. I didn't know where the football was because it had vanished above the lights for a second.

When I hustled back to the sidelines, all of my coaches came to me and said some encouraging words. I had not seen them this excited about something I did, and I punted the ball in practice many times. We won the game and I became an instant hit in Dimmitt. The bus ride was so much fun and my teammates were all complimenting me on my kicking and punting.

It was the first time that I heard my name on the radio the next morning. The games were all recorded and then played on the radio on Saturday morning. There was no livestream of any kind back then. That day I learned about my first punt going sixty yards in the air – wow, I couldn't believe it! Those positive endorphins that shattered any kind of blues I had, made me feel like I was above cloud nine.

I didn't have all the knowledge I needed about Jesus Christ, but I prayed the *Our Father* regularly and every Sunday at church. Could He have somehow given me a lift through sports? It sure felt that way. And was it with His own timing? As a sophomore, to be honest, this didn't cross my mind. But later in life, it sure crossed my mind.

The next Monday after our first game of the season, I drove to school in an old-light-blue 1963 Chevy Impala, a used car my dad purchased for the purpose of driving myself and my brother to school. I spent a great deal of my life with my brother Richard, I couldn't name a tougher kid than him in his grade at Dimmitt – he beat up a few kids in fights. In football he once knocked out a player with a devastating blow, helmet to helmet.

We went to the movies together or to TG&Y to look at toys. Sometimes we'd go fishing at the small ponds just outside of town. We would ride our bikes together just about everywhere. We didn't always see eye-to-eye in everything, but we got along pretty well.

That morning I remember my brother not making a big deal about my game, which he didn't see and probably didn't hear it on the radio. I think he was proud of me for making the varsity team as a sophomore. When I walked into the school I headed straight to my locker to get my first-class-of-the-day book and notebook. I did not expect what happened next.

There were so many students that knew who I was all of a sudden. "Great game Espinoza!" There was another kid that said, "You really put the boot to that football, sixty yards!" One of the senior cheerleaders, who never looked at me much less talked to me, walked by and said, "Espinoza, I'm so impressed, you played big last Friday." If you can picture these comments in a southern-Texas accent, then you will get the full affect. I myself had a southern accent the whole time I was in Texas. We would use phrases like, *I'm fix'n to* and *how y'all doing?* Or, *Mondee, Tuesdee, Wednesdee, Thursdee, Fridee,* I think you get my drift. The southern drawl, too me, is a cool-sounding accent, but maybe because I was raised in it.

It was a milestone I thought I would never reach. I was taking in the fun and passion I had for football. In addition, instead of kids making fun of me, they were acknowledging me and giving me so many compliments. I was overjoyed and relieved. Oh sure, there were kids that were never going to let go of their jokes, but I ignored those kids. A lot of them were envious of my success on the football field.

I remember the bullies that always tried to pick fights in my earlier grade-school years. Some of them continued to exist in high school. When I walked by them I was a head taller than they were and a lot stronger due to the weightlifting programs through football. How I wished they would try to pick a fight with me again. None of them ever said anything to me again. They just looked at me as I walked by and I looked at them tipping my head. I was ready to defend myself and to tell them my thoughts. I'm so thankful it didn't come down to that.

Being an athlete on the varsity team was not just glory and full of positive lessons. I feared several things. Let's start with one coach, and I'll refrain from mentioning his name. He was a very competitive coach that didn't seem to care about what an athlete's concern was.

I can count a few times that I was yelled at and put under so much pressure. I was a talented field-goal kicker, and there was a time when we were playing the number-one-ranked team in the district. Right before halftime we were trailing and we didn't convert on third down. We were within field-goal range and the football was spotted at their thirty-five yard line. I was a young kid playing on the varsity team.

We were trailing, 14 - 16. The coach yelled out, "Espinoza, let's kick it, get out there!" So I hustled out to try and give us a lead going into the half. The center snapped the football to our holder and he quickly placed it on the ground. I made the motion to kick the football, I could see their middle linebacker breaking through the line and come hard at me – he was quick. I put my head down and swung my leg forward. As I punched the ball with my foot, the linebacker cracked me on the side forcing the football to swerve slightly to the right and I missed the target by a foot or so. I was on the ground flat on my back and I could hear our head coach yelling at the referees, "That's roughing the kicker – come on ref!"

During halftime, in the locker room, the special team's coach came straight at me with the evilest eyes I had ever seen in him all season long. He was a pretty big guy, maybe 6' 2" 240 lbs. His fast-pace walk and his pointing-the-finger-at-me was something I wouldn't want any kid to face. He stared at me for a few seconds, his face was about one inch from mine and his veins were about to burst. I didn't say one word, but my heart was pounding and I was in alarm mode. I knew I was in trouble and if I tried to explain to this coach what happened, I was so afraid he was going to slam me against the lockers. He said to me, "Espinoza, there's no excuse for you missing that field goal – an embarrassment to all of our team. We should be leading right now." I didn't say one word, and the coach closed his eyes and walked away in disgust. Several of my teammates heard him and also pointed the finger at me, mainly some of the African-American guys.

This coach not only belittled me by not knowing what happened out there, but he also gave approval for my teammates to hate me and to put the blame on me for not connecting on a forty-five-yard field goal. The head coach knew what happened – roughing the kicker, which the officials missed. I was lucky that the special team's coach didn't shove me against the locker, it was so important to him that we beat the top team in the district.

That anger he developed toward a young kid like me, that was still learning and experiencing the game, was a good example of the type of fear that some athletes go through. That year I was one of the athletes facing that.

Another fear during the 1970s was how upperclassmen would initiate the underclassmen coming in new to the team. This was my first year as a varsity player. My brother Gilberto had mentioned some horrible stories of hazing. Initiations would take place a certain day and all first-time players would be required to attend. Hazing is against policy now, but back then it was allowed – upperclassmen even used school facilities at times. There have been severely injured athletes as a result of hazing. Some schools and colleges have had deaths as a result of hazing.

In Dimmitt I heard from sources that the upperclassmen would have kids take their clothes off, and then they would drop them off out in the country. The players getting initiated would have to make it back on their own. This was humiliating and embarrassing to any boy.

I also heard that they had spread Icy Hot inside the player's jockstrap and then they would have them wear it all day. That didn't sound like something I would ever want to have done to me and I was going to prevent any of those uncomfortable situations that should not have been allowed in the first place.

One of the other things the upperclassmen would do is hit the players with a board several times. There were other embarrassing and painful things, I just wanted to mention a few I heard about. It wasn't all of the seniors and juniors doing this, just the ones that were out to do this because it was done to them in previous years.

It didn't take long for a senior to come talk to me about this horrible event. He threatened me with what could happen if I didn't show up on initiation day at the field house. It was an intense alarm, maybe registering overload-mode on the nervous scale. There is no way on earth that I was going to show up, despite what their threats were.

The weekend after the hazing took place, several lineman and a couple of running backs approached me in the hallway at my locker. I was harassed about not showing up. I always stayed out of their little popular group whether in the locker room, during practices, or off the field. I always kept my distance and just did my job as a teammate.

I explained to them that I had to help my dad, I could not make it. I don't want to repeat the names they called me. At one point I thought they were going to beat me up pretty bad. Instead they just walked off and continued calling me names. I was so relieved after they walked away. They never bothered me again. I avoided that entire hazing garbage and I was never part of that uncivilized hate. I felt sorry for my friends that were involved with that group and felt pressured to attend that waste-of-time event.

When football season was over, I had made a mark at Dimmitt High School. I was remembered for a long time, and still today if I were to visit my old hometown, people would remember me as, *the kid that could boot the football out of the stadium.*

Coaches approached me in the hallway and informed me that West Texas State was interested in me, or University of Texas, or Texas Tech. It was my football career that was going to pay for my school, or at least that's what my plan was.

When basketball season was about to start, I think it was Johnny Hampton and a few other upperclassmen that asked me, *why weren't you at varsity tryouts?* I responded, "What? I didn't hear when they were taking place." I was so disappointed that I missed the tryouts. I had no clue, no one told me and there was nothing posted on the board. I didn't understand why I wasn't informed. The announcement must have been made when I went to Amarillo for an eye-doctor appointment or something.

I played on the JV basketball team and made some new friends. My season was so much fun, because once again, I was one of the starters on the team and I played a lot of minutes. My average wasn't as good as my freshman year, but it was still around fifteen points per game.

Sometimes I would hang around for the varsity practices. Coach Cleveland would ask me to stay and watch in case he needed me, I was there most of the time. Thompson did make the varsity team, he knew when the tryouts were held. I was so mad about that.

During one practice, Coach had me play defense on the press. Thompson was dribbling the basketball and passed it over me, I don't know if he realized I had worked on my leaps a lot. It was easy for me to jump up and time a steal perfectly, and to then continue finishing with a lay-up at the opposite end. Coach Cleveland said, "Nice work, David!" Thompson was not very happy at all, and I knew he wouldn't be. He walked by me to retrieve the basketball and he said, "Espinoza, you got lucky ... that'll never happen again." I just smiled at him and walked off to the baseline.

My track and field season went smooth, and again, I had so much fun at the invitational meets. I improved my high jump PR (Personal Record) to 6' 0". My best time that year in the 120-yard hurdles was 15.9 – I was able to three-step all ten hurdles consistently.

When track and field season ended I was spending more time at home. I crossed my street to the city park to hang out with my old friend Baldomero. We started playing basketball with a few kids that would show up. Some were from my old neighborhood and some were from the housing projects close to where our FINA gas station used to exist.

I finally connected with Isabel, she had grown to be a beautiful Hispanic girl. Her skin color was lighter than most Latina girls and she had very dark hair. Her family would normally stop at the park on Sundays, they were dressed up pretty nice, so I assumed they were at church previous to this. Sometimes the parents would drop them off at the park and then come back later for them.

On a Sunday afternoon, I finally had the courage to walk up and talk to her. It was almost time for them to leave as we had finished playing a few games. She was with one of her sisters at a picnic table. They would normally watch us play basketball and just hang out having fun.

I didn't know if she remembered me from first grade. She said that she did remember me and that her sister had given her a message awhile back from the track-meet day. We talked for a little bit and I felt comfortable with her responses. I still couldn't believe that it was Isabel after all these years, wow.

I asked her if she would take a chance on a guy like me for a movie date sometime. She laughed and her sister smiled and looked at her in a *yahoo!* way. Isabel looked at her and laughed like a girl playing around. Isabel told me that she would love that, but would have to ask her parents if that was okay. She didn't have a way to come back to Dimmitt unless they brought her.

I was so glad and said, "Great, I was worried you might not like me." I'll never forget her response, she replied with a smile, "I'll see you next Sunday, okay?" I shook my head up and down and waved to her. I will never forget that photogenic face with a smile. I was excited about seeing her the following Sunday. Could it have been that I might have had a girlfriend for that summer?

On the last day of school as a sophomore, I stayed awhile at the gym to shoot some baskets while Coach Cleveland was still in the gym. Afterward I drove home and saw our green and white 1969 Ford station wagon loaded up with clothes and all sorts of stuff. I also saw our white 1963 Ford Sudan with a trailer hitched to the back of it. My sister, Louise, had a 1974 Impala and it was loaded up with her stuff.

I walked inside and said, "What's going on?" My dad said we were moving to Oregon early in the morning. Most of the siblings were excited and they remembered what Oregon was like when we visited years ago. Oregon is a beautiful state. I liked Oregon too, but I was a bit disappointed. I guess to me it was a bittersweet moment. I finally connected with Isabel. I also had colleges from everywhere looking at me to play for them – I could have received a scholarship to play football for a major college. I finally gained respect from many of my school friends, everything was going well and I was having fun at Dimmitt High School. Unfortunately, I knew that my dad's decisions were usually final.

My mom had family in Washington State and in Oregon that she had not seen for a very long time. My dad's side was who I grew up with. I'm thinking it was a compromise between my parents to move us all up to Oregon.

15.

Moving to Oregon

Early the next morning we stopped at the local gas station to fill up all three cars. It was such a weird feeling that morning. We were leaving the town that I lived in for so many years. My friends that I worked so hard to make would never know what happened to me. We didn't have iPhones or email back then. All we had was a rotary phone on our house wall that we had just installed. Isabel was going to hate me – I left her wondering what happened to me. My coaches that invested so much time in me would miss one of the best kicker-punters projected to play again on the team next season. I was at a dead silence with many things going through my head.

My sister, Diana, was so excited about moving. I didn't spend much time with her, I think because of our age difference I didn't see her a whole lot. She was mostly around my parents. Diana was the youngest of the family and I always remember her as being cheery about playing games or going on adventures. She also had friends that she got along so well with from her school. She definitely grew up watching us play sports outside, and she would join in a lot of the times. I remember her returning from the store with my parents. She had this huge smile on her face as she got out of the car with a new game in her hands, "Hey, y'all wanna play Hi! Ho! Cherry-o!"

At the gas station my dad encountered a few people he knew. They all asked where we were going, and they got the answer, *we're moving to Oregon.* My dad was always very private and kept anything important in the family. His plan was to rent out our house and to have my grandparents keep an eye on it.

As we drove away toward Clovis, New Mexico, we had the radio on, I was riding with my sister, Louise. She normally loved to listen to music. There was a song that was playing and to this day it has stayed in my memory. A song called, "The Last Song," by Edward Bear. It was definitely the last song I would be singing to all my teachers, friends, relatives, and merchants from Dimmitt, Texas. Thanks for the education and life experiences you enriched me with.

We traveled all day and made it through New Mexico. We stopped in Cortez, Colorado, off of Hwy 491 to eat at a fast-food place. There was a lot of dry country and it was hot in June. My dad was never one to go inside McDonalds. He would always eat his food outside in the car. All of us kids ate inside where it was a lot cooler. I was still a little sleepy, but with the sunshine being so bright I began to wake up a bit. I still had Dimmitt in the back of my mind.

Our next stop was Monticello, Utah, on Hwy 191. I was taken by the red rocks and mountains in Utah, wow, I had never observed scenery like this before. Oh sure we studied all kinds of countries and geographical areas in school, but I had never seen this part of God's beautiful creation. This was a great distraction from my sad feeling of leaving my friends behind and not being able to connect with Isabel. I'll never know what she thought when I didn't show up at the park on Sunday.

Our next stop was Moab, Utah. We were planning on eating some sandwiches. We came to this place called Hole 'N The Rock – an amazing house built inside a huge rock. This was a unique home. It had 5,000 square feet of living space with a trading post and a gift shop that was open year-round. Fourteen rooms and a 65 ft. chimney drilled through solid sandstone. The bathtub and counters were built-in inside the big rock. It was such a miraculous sight for me to see. I think all of us enjoyed something different that we had never seen before. There was something about our family sharing that experience. Loop was the only one that wasn't with us, he was already in the northwest staying with our cousins. It was like taking all of the distractions from

Dimmitt away and spending time together as an escape from our daily routine, we were having fun together.

Albert and Gladys Christensen built this home excavating 50,000 cubic feet of sandstone from the rock using dynamite and other tools. They also used a mule to haul the rocks out. When Albert died in 1957 the home was not complete, so Gladys continued to develop the home for it to become an attraction that would fascinate people today.

This was something beyond what I could imagine anyone doing. I looked at the stuffed mule, it must have been the one they used to haul the rocks out while the construction was taking place. We talked to a clerk that worked there. She said that the temperature remained constant inside the rock at seventy degrees year-round.

It was an experience that I will never forget. On the way out we noticed a sculpture of Franklin D. Roosevelt on the face of the rock – what a cool sight. I wasn't sure what the significance of it was, but it looked amazing.

After an hour of observing the tourist attraction, it was time for all of us to get back into our three-vehicle caravan. We were between two amazing parks, Canyon Lands National Park and Arches National Park. The green trees surrounded by huge red mountains on a clear day was a true blessing to see in a state that was a big contrast to that of Texas.

We made our way to Interstate 70 and drove a few miles before exiting into a two-lane highway that was pointing to Provo, Utah. I was the one that helped my dad with the map in determining the shortest way to arrive at our destination.

Before we reached Provo a couple of things happened. First I'll tell you about the first time I saw something that shocked me. I didn't get a chance to use the restroom on our last stop due to looking at the map with my dad. It was late and we all pulled into this truck stop with a gas station and bar-grill next to it. I was the only one that had to go, so I stepped out of the car and hustled into the gas station. I couldn't find the bathroom. The gentleman working there told me that their bathroom was broken and I would have to use the bar-grill's next door. I ran next door to the bar-grill.

I had never seen a real woman with no clothes on. Well, as I walked in I asked the first person I saw, "Could you please tell me where the restroom is?" The person responded, "Oh sure, it's over there." As I started walking toward the bathroom I looked to where the loud music was coming from. My jaw about dropped, there were two women dancing in the nude on stage.

Now to a normal seventeen-year-old boy, this would have been exciting and a dream come true. I had never experienced that and I knew it was a sin to look at a naked woman. That's one of the things I learned going to church. I was a little embarrassed, so I hurried up to the restroom and took care of business. On my way out, I did look at the females again. The bartender stopped me and asked if he could see some identification. I explained to him that I was told to come here to use the bathroom and now I was leaving. He said, "Okay, see you later." I left and as I was approaching the car, my mom was sitting on the passenger side. She looked at me and said, "David, you look like you just saw a ghost." I didn't know what to tell her, but I had to be honest. When I explained the whole story to her, she busted out laughing – for some reason she thought it was funny. Me, on the other hand, it took me a few miles to erase the image I had in my mind of those two women dancing on stage. We didn't have girls like that back in Dimmitt, Texas, at least not that I knew about.

The long drive was beginning to wear us down. I didn't remember traveling this far any time I lived in Texas. Maybe when I was an eleven-year-old boy, when we traveled to Oregon the first time. That seemed like a very long time ago to me.

It was dark and another day was coming to an end. In the backseat, I was leaning on the door asleep – along with my brother, Richard. It was difficult to sleep with the sound of cars coming from the opposite direction on the two-way highway.

My dad was getting tired of driving. He had driven a lot and decided to stop on the side of the road. All three cars pulled over for a long rest. My mom normally didn't drive, she basically just did whatever was needed in a way of support. She had been a stay-at-home mom for years. She took care of the kids while my dad went to work.

It was pitch black outside and the sound of quiet was evident. Now and then a car would fly by making that tire-road noise. It was 2:00 a.m. and the grounds were unfamiliar. An hour went by and the entire family was asleep on the side of the road with three cars and a trailer carrying a Kawasaki 900 on the back strapped tightly.

All of a sudden – *tap! tap! tap!* The sound came from the driver's side of the car. It was a policeman with a flashlight. He was a middle-age fellow with a dark blue uniform. He had all the police gear around his belt.

"Excuse me sir! Can you roll down the window?"

"Yes sir officer," Dad replied with his eyes red and sleepy-looking.

"Can I see your driver's license?" He shined his flashlight to the backseat while he waited for Dad to pull out his wallet. He observed us while we were stirring to wake up. My dad handed the officer his driver's license.

"We're on our way to Oregon and we pulled over to get some sleep, I didn't want to get in an accident."

"I'm going to run a check on your license, hold on for a minute I'll be right back," the officer said as he walked back to his state vehicle.

"What they get ya for Dad?" I asked.

"I guess sleeping on the side of U.S. Highway 191."

After a few minutes the officer returned. He was a pretty big guy and the gun in the holster was very visible.

"Mr. Espinoza, it's pretty dangerous out here in the middle of nowhere and it's dark. With your lights off you could get hit by a car or a semi-truck. I'm going to let you go with a warning this time. But please don't sleep on the side of the highway again for you and your family's safety."

"Okay officer, thank you so much," Dad replied.

"Have a nice evening and enjoy the rest of your trip. There should be a rest area twenty miles up the road," the officer said.

Dad started up the old station wagon and gave the signal to the others to get back on the highway. He was tired and looked forward to a good sleep at the rest area ahead.

The next morning the old 1963 Ford died on us. We all pulled over and my dad took a look at it. He tried several things to get it started again, but none worked. He narrowed it down to a possible alternator problem. One thing I was always glad about my dad, was his experience in working with cars. That was his passion and he became a great mechanic at a very young age. He saved us so much money on auto repairs.

Dad had tools he carried around with him in the car trunk. He pulled out the toolbox and began to pull off the alternator. Him and my brother Gilberto drove back a few miles in the pickup to a small town we had just passed. We all waited and waited, some of us were complaining about the hot weather and the hunger – we hadn't eaten anything all day. We did have water to drink and a few snacks to tie us over – that kept us going.

After two hours of waiting anxiously, we finally saw my dad and my brother pull up with the pickup. They had a new alternator. My dad installed it and the car started right up. The cheers from all of us were pretty loud as we knew we would get something to eat at the next town.

After our stomachs were full from eating a nice meal at a taco place, we were on the road again, reminds me of that song, "On the Road Again," by Willie Nelson. We made it back to Interstate 70 and passed Salt Lake City, Utah. Cutting through the shortest way wasn't always the easiest drive, especially through Utah. We drove up so many high mountains. I'm glad we did because the scenery was all new to us – an experience that I was lucky to have.

Our next stop was Boise, Idaho. I remember the city was off to the side. We looked for a park to take a break and have a picnic. We managed to find one. We had a football, a basketball, and some Frisbees. Finally a chance to run around and play. We passed the football around and ran a lot – it felt good to get off that car.

My mom was on a swing watching us all. I ran over and sat on the swing next to her. She looked at me with a smile.

"David, you looked sad when we left Dimmitt. Don't worry, you'll meet new kids and you will do well in Oregon."

"Mom, I had everything going for me at Dimmitt, I didn't even get a chance to say goodbye to my friends."

"I'm so proud of you, I still have that mum you got me for homecoming. I was honored to walk with you down the gym floor during that pep rally."

"Yeah, thanks for coming to that, I wasn't sure if you would be there."

She just smiled and then she asked me to imitate some of the high officials in Dimmitt. I used to imitate the way people talked pretty good. My mom would get a kick out of that and then she would laugh a lot.

We continued on and we finally made it to Oregon. We even stopped at the sign that read, *Welcome to Oregon*. We drove passed Ontario, Oregon, and soon arrived at Baker City, Oregon, off of Interstate 84. When we arrived there, we pulled into a gas station. My dad rarely had anyone look under the car hood, he normally did that himself, he didn't trust anyone. Because he felt so tired and exhausted from the trip, he had the attendant check the oil and power-steering fluid.

When the cars and the pickup were serviced, we all started driving through town when the station wagon started showing a red-engine light and it also started making noises. My dad pulled over and walked around to open the hood. I remember his words, "Son of a ..." He wasn't too happy when he found out they had sliced the fan belt. He proved it by saying that if he drove back there they would have the exact size fan belt for the station wagon. Sure enough, when he and Gilberto drove back, they did have the right size. My dad wasn't too happy, but there was nothing he could do about it.

He replaced the fan belt and we were on the road again toward La Grande, Oregon, and then we passed Pendleton, Oregon. We exited off of I-84 towards Umatilla, Oregon, and that evening we reached Tri-Cities (Kennewick, Pasco, and Richland). The freeways were crazy merging everywhere, we had to pay close attention to the signs leading us to Hwy 17 towards Moses Lake, Washington, where my mom's sister, Olivia Torres, lived with her family. We were going to stay with them for a few days which turned into two months before moving to Oregon.

My brother, Loop, had flown there previous to us driving there. I was looking forward to seeing Loop again – it had been a long time. I was also looking forward to seeing my favorite cousin, Paul, who was one of eight kids in that family. He was a great athlete and I always enjoyed playing sports with him whether it was throwing the baseball around or shooting hoops. Their time in Texas was too short before they moved up to the state of Washington. I didn't get to spend as much time as I wanted to with Paul in Texas. I could also relate to Cathy, Jimmy, and Margo as well. I remember Margo being such a great softball player – she could hit some homers in games.

We were getting closer to Moses Lake and the sundown was approaching. I have a great memory of the song playing on the radio. I was riding with my sister, Louise, in her Chevy Impala. She would always listen to the radio, so I always tried to ride with her when I wasn't driving the station wagon. The song was, "Moonlight Feels Right," by Starbuck. We were driving on a long-two-lane Highway 17 and I remember a few dips along the way. As we got closer to Moses Lake there was a huge sigh of relief ... we made it all the way to the northwest part of the U. S. A. It was like a big dream but at the same time a reality that hit me hard. I left pretty much all my life back in Texas. That alone did something emotional to me. I still have my Texas roots planted deep in my heart and I do think about Dimmitt from time to time.

16.

Cousins in Moses Lake, Washington

We were all so overjoyed that we reached the destination. Our first stop in Moses Lake was at a pay phone. My mom called her sister and asked for directions. The last time I saw this place was back in my grade school days. I had grown to be 6' 0" tall and my brothers and sisters had also grown a lot.

My mom was the first one out of the car, I never saw her run as fast as she did that day. Aunt Olivia and my mom were very close when they were growing up in the Rio Grande Valley back in Texas. They both were good singers and often performed on stage during their youth. I never knew this about my mom until much later in life.

Mom was in tears and so was Aunt Olivia. The first time we visited I was a young kid and it didn't make sense. Now that I'm older it makes more sense. I will never know what they went through together living in poverty for so many years as they grew up together. The Torres family had done well for themselves, they had a very nice house. With the extra attic space upstairs, their house was three stories high. It had a long covered porch on the front and on the side. My Uncle Meliton had a good job, he was a supervisor at a potato factory called, Sunspiced.

When everyone greeted each other we went to the backyard where Paul was shooting some baskets on a hoop that was attached to an extra room. The hoop was probably about 9 1/2 feet tall. I was wearing my cowboy boots and walked over to Paul, said hi to him, and we talked a little. I don't remember our opening conversation that well, but I do remember asking him if I could shoot baskets with him. He passed me the ball, I dribbled on the hard dirt, planted my left leg, and went up for a slam dunk – you could hear the rim rattle afterward.

I remember Paul saying something like, *wow ... with boots on too!* I guess I didn't think it was that big of a deal. I just felt like jumping and playing a game after that long trip – I missed playing basketball so much. Paul didn't know that I had cleared 6' 0" in the high jump in my recent track and field season back in Texas.

It was pretty crazing that night, because my cousin, Cathy, had just come back from her graduation night, I could tell she was not happy about a boy situation at school. I only overheard a few details and I don't think she recognized me when I walked in the kitchen to get some water. It was a little awkward, I left the kitchen quickly when I drank a glass of water.

My cousin Jimmy looked a lot older than most of us, he had a dark beard and a mean look on his face, but that was just Jimmy, he was harmless. I walked over to him and said, "Hey Jimmy, it's been a long time, man!" I'll never forget his first words, "Hey, we should all get in the car and go hit a tavern or something!" I'm like, *is he joking?* And yes, he was joking alright. Jimmy was a catcher in baseball, Paul played basketball and baseball in high school.

Our family was in need of money, and my cousin, Meliton Junior, was a foreman who took care of field workers. There were onion fields, potato fields, and other crops that needed weed-cleaning. We definitely had experience in chopping weeds on farm fields.

Within the next few days we had a job. All of our family went out to work in the fields. I just kept telling myself, *I can't believe that I'm working in the fields again, I miss Dimmitt.* My cousin, Cathy, who went by Cat, started hanging around me a lot. We started talking about her boy problems, I was a good listener and learned a lot about her. I enjoyed talking to Cat, we were both the middle child of our families. She gave me so many compliments that it made me feel good. So we became friends right away.

I didn't spend much time with Meliton Jr. I think that he was not comfortable with us staying at their house – can't say I would blame him. I would often go in his room to listen to his Beatles' albums. I never knew who the Beatles were, but I liked some of their songs. Often after a hard day at the fields I would go in and take a nap in Meliton's bedroom. I would fall asleep listening to the Beatles, a popular band from Liverpool in England.

Jimmy and Paul showed my brother Richard and I most of Moses Lake, where they lived since moving from Brownfield, Texas. It had been so long and we all talked about the days back in Texas. We also talked sports, the teams we played on, and how our teams did.

We went to the park to play basketball, or we would play baseball on the pasture across their house. It was fun for us cousins, but as the days went by I knew that the adults were struggling with the entire situation. My parents were staying in the extra room in the backyard – they had privacy. I was caught up in having so much fun with my cousins that I never thought about my parents and what they might have been going through. This family was my favorite to spend time with. I didn't know Rosie very well, she was the youngest. I did get to know most all of the others though. My sister Diana was having fun playing games with Janie and Silvia, the younger girls. Loop and Gilberto were hanging out with Meliton Jr.

Oh my gosh, the debates that Gilberto and Meliton Jr. had late at night were boring. They both wanted to win so bad that they talked for hours about nothing. It was all humorous when you think about it.

Gilberto and Jimmy became friends and they would often visit while chopping weeds out on the farm field. Meliton Jr. was fed up with them talking too much and not doing much work. I still laugh about this today, and every time I see my cousin Paul, we both laugh about this. Meliton Jr. fired his own brother and his cousin. We finished out the field without Jimmy and Gilberto.

We had so much confusion going on during the days we stayed with the Torres family. Our goal was to move to Oregon soon. I think we were out of money and needed to earn some before we could actually load up and drive to Oregon.

I didn't want to go, I was having so much fun. I finally got to spend quality time with my cousins. My Uncle Meliton was able to help get us hired at Sunspiced, the potato factory he was employed at. My brother Richard was the only one that escaped working. He was going through a driver's education program in Moses Lake. I started working the swing shift with Cat, who would carpool with me every day. Everyone else worked the day shift.

Again, Cat and I had fun just talking about all kinds of stuff. I didn't know anyone else during those work hours, so I was so grateful for her showing me the ropes of Moses Lake. The bad part was that I became attached to my cousins, I saw them just like my brothers and sisters – like a family. We even spent the evening at the lake trying to get their truck out of the sand. Jimmy had driven too close to the water where there was a lot of sand and the truck got stuck. Those were some fun times.

I'll never forget the time where Paul was testing Gilberto's strength. We were up in the attic where all the boys slept. It seemed like we always fell asleep past midnight, we just kept talking and laughing a lot of the times. Anyway, Paul had about four pillows in front of his stomach. He said, *no way can you punch me past these pillows.* So sure enough, Gilberto punched him through the pillows and Paul went down saying, "That went through," as he gasped for air. He had knocked the wind out of Paul. After he regained the air to his lungs, we all just started laughing. We were glad he was okay and he never tested Gilberto again.

There were some issues that I don't completely know about and probably never will. I was kind of out of the loop on what was going on. I knew my parents weren't very happy and I knew my Aunt wasn't very happy. The kids were all everywhere going to so many different places and having fun.

I started going to events that Cat and Margo invited me too. I liked the breaks from spending time with Paul and Jimmy to spending time with Cat and Margo. Cat invited me to this Mexican dance. I had an idea how to dance, but had never been to a Mexican dance unless it was one of my aunts' weddings back in Texas. I normally just watched the band at those weddings.

I dressed up in some nice clothes, and I remember Cat giving me some very nice compliments on how I looked. I just said, "Really?" She wanted to hook me up with one of her friends at the dance. I think it was a girl named Naomi. I danced with Naomi one time, the rest of the night I danced with my cousin, Cat. It was fun and I got to learn more about her and what she experienced in high school. She taught me how to dance a little better – a good lesson. It was a fun night and the only night we went to the dance.

Paul and Jimmy took us to a drive-in movie in Moses Lake. That was fun on a warm summer night, we also walked over to a park where they held a large firework display. We were all over the place just having fun, and we never got into any trouble. I do have a memory of our parents telling us where we could go and where we couldn't go.

When two big families get together, there's bound to be some conflicts. We had a few, whether with the parents agreeing on things or some of the kids wanting certain things but couldn't have them. Despite the challenges, I was so thankful that my cousins gave up some of their space for us to move in for two months.

The summer was coming to an end and my brother and I started football practice with the Moses Lake Chiefs. I was going to be the halfback with a kid named, David Cardenas. This kid was fast, maybe a step faster than I was, it was close. Cardenas was a friend of my cousin Jimmy.

It was during our first practice with no pads that one of the coaches at Moses Lake saw me punt the football. He didn't say anything to me, he just opened his eyes and his mouth as wide as it could get. The coach said, "Hold on, let me get the other coaches, I want them to see this." He ran yelling, "Hey coaches, you have to come see this!" When the head coach came to watch me he was impressed and asked, "Can you do that again?" I punted several times and then I kicked off of a tee a few times. They were all glad to have me on the team. At the time I didn't realize I had a gift that the Lord had given me. Not many kids in high school could punt or kick the football the way I could, according to those coaches anyway.

Unfortunately, my parents decided that we were ready to move to Oregon. Things got uncomfortable with the adults and how they wanted their families raised, or at least that was my opinion. My mom, my dad, Louise, and Diana would leave the next day. They would be staying with my grandma in Gervais, Oregon, a tiny town fifteen miles north of Salem, the state capital.

The parents decided that we were not to spend time with the cousins. The only time we could see Paul and Jimmy, was when Gilberto would get off work. Again, we were never told why, it was just a direct order. Gilberto was working at a meat processing plant. He had a girlfriend there so he wanted to stay. My brother Richard and I were told to not leave the small one-bedroom rental. We were bored stiff. We couldn't see Jimmy or Paul. We couldn't go to football practice. We had no idea what the coaches were thinking. They had acquired two football players that had great talent to help the team. I felt bad that we couldn't even inform the coaches about why we couldn't be at practice. We played a lot of checkers and chess and we listened to an album by the group America. I liked some of the songs on that album.

I was so confused and lost. My older brother was the one communicating with my mom and dad. He would take their orders and carry them out. I was thankful for my older brother, he fed us and took us to the Lake Bowl. This bowling alley was a mile or so away from the rental shack where we were staying. We played foosball usually – we were pretty good at that game. It was comforting that we could see Paul and Jimmy at the Lake Bowl.

I'm guessing we were in that small shack for about two weeks before we were transferred to Gervais, Oregon. I can't remember how we got to Gervais. Either my brother drove us there, or my parents came to pick us up. Whatever happened, we ended up in Gervais with my grandma and her family. My Uncle Edward, My Aunt Lydia, and Aunt Delia were all out of the house by then. My Uncle Israel was still living there and had a job at a local grocery store. He had a nice car, a Cougar, and he was normally in his room. Now and then he would come out and visit. It was such an uncomfortable experience moving from place to place at that time in my life, but I was doing what my parents asked of me. Honor thy father and thy mother, one of the ten commandments.

17.

New Beginning at Gervais High School

My mom and dad were looking for work, we were dead broke and our family was struggling. We were close to being homeless. To tell you the truth, I stopped thinking about God. We hadn't gone to church in a long time and my mom suggested we go to the Sacred Heart Church in Gervais. We started attending yet another Catholic Church.

I have a memory of this huge tent that was set up across from my grandma's house. It was some kind of church revival. I knew that we were not supposed to go to any church other than a Catholic Church. I had been told in the past that it was a sin to attend any other church. Well, I decided to sin because this church had a band and was rehearsing for the evening service. I walked over and noticed that no one was on the electric guitar. Wow, it was a nice blue Fender guitar. I missed my cousins so much and I wanted to do something to distract my mind from thinking about all the fun we had in Moses Lake.

I asked the drummer if they had a guitar player. He said that their guitar player was not going to make it to rehearsal, but would be there tonight. I asked if I could play a few tunes on it while they set up things. He said, "Sure! Hop on up to the stage, man." So I picked up the guitar and grabbed my pick that I always carried in my wallet. I started playing "La Bamba," by Ritchie Valens and they loved it! The drummer and the bass player were jamming to the tune. That was cool and I had so much fun. I told them I should be getting back to my grandma's house. They wouldn't let me go, they wanted me to keep playing, so I did. I snuck out of the house a couple of days during their stay across the street. It was educational and fun to listen to the music and to play during their rehearsal.

The following day, my brother and I walked over to watch the Gervais varsity team practice. We weren't in school yet because my parents were in the process of finding a house that we could rent. We could then have an address to register. We took one look at the team and thought it was their freshman team. Coming from Texas and then practicing with Moses Lake, it seemed like a freshman team. I asked one of the coaches, "Is this y'all's freshman team?" The coach looked at me and said, "No, this is our varsity team." My brother and I started laughing. He didn't take too kindly to us laughing at the team. I asked him how their kicker was, could he kick very far? He advised us to stick around to watch Russell Leach and Martin Jaqua kick the football. Russell was a senior and Martin was a junior. When I saw them kick, I turned to the coach and said, "No disrespect sir, but if I went to school here, I think the job would be mine." My brother started laughing and we walked off the field.

I called one of my coaches from Dimmitt and informed him that we were in Oregon. He gave me some advice. He wanted me to attend a big school if I could. He said I would get better looks from college scouts. I didn't know what to do, it was a stressful and confusing time in my life. I felt so alone despite the fact that I was with my family and sharing the struggles. My knowledge in Jesus was limited. I still prayed and hoped that He would hear me. What I didn't realize was that every answered prayer is in God's timing.

We were close to being thrown on the streets because of the government finding out that we were staying with our grandma. Some social worker came by and warned my grandma. Maybe she was getting some kind of benefits and we couldn't live with her, I'm not certain but that could have been the reason. Luckily, my parents got hired at Stayton Canning Company in Brooks, Oregon. We were able to rent a house on Alder Street. Unfortunately, it was falling apart. The good news was the rent, it was only $250.00 a month. God was with us even when we didn't know it.

I had Louise drive me to North Salem High School in Salem, Oregon, where we were going to try and register at a bigger school than Gervais. We were told by the office workers that we could not register at North Salem because we did not live in the district. My sister tried arguing with them, but it didn't work. I said, "Louise, let's go, it's okay ... I'll just register at Gervais."

We drove back to Gervais and walked straight into the office.

"How can I help you," the secretary asked.

"We want to register for school."

"Do you live in the Gervais district?"

We both looked at each other, "Yes."

"Okay, you'll need to fill out these forms."

"Yes ma'am," I said depressed.

"Why so sad?"

"Long story, ma'am."

I was not thrilled to be enrolling in a small school. My sister went home after we were done filling out papers. I stayed in the lobby area and I watched all of the students go by as it was time for them to get home. The front doors were opening and slamming just like the gates at a feedlot back in Texas with cattle running through them.

I was feeling down. How did I end up in this world so far away from home? It was like my previous life had vanished to be non-existent. There were only a few students left inside the lobby. I remember a girl asking me if I was a new student. I just responded, "Not by choice." She laughed and walked away.

I can't believe how much of a punk I was to respond so negative to the people there at Gervais. I guess you had to have been in my shoes and gone through what I was going through to understand better. My attitude had never been so negative, it seemed like everything I wanted was going against the grain. I wanted the life I had back in Texas, I believe that my anger inside caused my negative attitude towards people. I knew that eventually I had to face reality.

God was putting something in front of me, and I had no clue what it was. I wish I could replay that part of my life, my attitude would have been a little different. Despite my struggles I had so much to be grateful for. Most of my family was back together again, I was no longer trapped in a one-bedroom rental in Moses Lake. I was about to step into a team that I could help as a running back and as a punter-kicker. God was about to help me rise from this downward spin. He was about to put something in front of me and I was unaware that it would be the best thing that ever happened to me. I'm not talking about my sports adventure, you'll find out a little later.

This was the time of year where my coaches would say, *it is policy that if you play sports, you need to get a haircut.* I didn't cut my hair and my parents never asked me too. My hair had grown so much over the summer, it was down to almost my shoulders. It was a pain to take care of, but it was cool in the 1970s to have long hair. Again, I wish I could replay that part of my life, I would have cut my hair in a second.

My eye was starting to give me problems, it was hurting a lot and it was swollen at times. It needed to be cleaned, this I would deal with for my entire life. In Dimmitt, the chlorine from the pool would do the job pretty good. I had to find an ophthalmologist in Salem somewhere. I couldn't because we had no money to pay for the medical bill. I was struggling with so many things in 1976 when we arrived at Gervais.

As soon as we were settled a little and had a physical address, I wrote my cousin Cat and my cousin Jimmy. They were the two that were my pen pals. I kept them up on how things were going in Oregon and they did the same for Moses Lake. It was fun writing to them. That lasted a few weeks and then we just phased the letter-writing out. I never heard from my cousins until years later. Today, I keep in contact with my cousin Paul and his family – it's nice with the iPhones which we did not have back in 1976.

The following day we moved into our new rental home! I didn't go to school that day, we were all trying to figure out where everyone was going to sleep. This house was literally falling apart. It was tilted, and crooked as if one of the major studs in the framework was cracked. It was still strong enough to stay up. The exterior paint was faded and still had an ugly-white color remaining in spots. The small sidewalk was cracked just in front of the house. The homely house had a small attic that had been converted into a room – the ceiling was the slanted roof on both sides. That's where my brother Richard and I shared a room. The painting inside of the house was worn out to an un-maintained look, which fit our profile at the time.

I took one look at the house and thought to myself, *how on earth did we get here?* I walked up the steps to the attic, the sound of the creaky steps were a little scary. Some of the boards were loose and about to collapse. We needed to do a lot of work to the unfit conditions. The house had one bathroom with no shower and a plywood floor that was very uneven with cracks visible.

I eventually learned about the huge rats that would visit now and then. Oh my gosh, I hated living this kind of life. There were railroad tracks just across the street from the house. I looked out of the window and saw one apple tree on the other side of Alder Street – not much of a view. At least in Texas we had the city park with trees, a playground, a tennis court, a basketball court, and a baseball field.

My mom picked up one chair at a garage sale. It definitely didn't match the ugly-torn-green carpet that had stains all over. My two older brothers remained at Moses Lake, they were both working there and making a living. Here at Gervais, it was me, my brother Richard, Louise, and Diana that were all together and about to start an adventure in Gervais.

This house might not have been the dream house I always wanted, but it was ours to live in. And, for the simple reason of seeing my dad and mom so happy with their own place instead of living with relatives, or what could have been out on the street, was enough reason for me to make the best out of this situation.

My mom and dad both landed jobs at the cannery working on the belt. They would pick out any kind of garbage from the clean vegetables – rats, snakes, rotten vegetables, and more. It was a boring job, but paid well enough for room and board on Alder Street.

There was a Catholic Church about four blocks away on Douglas Street. We started attending that church. It was then that I slowly stopped going to a priest to confess my sins. We were so disoriented with everything going on that my mom was happy if we just went to church. Not confessing my sins to a priest was such a great relief. I still confessed my sins to God and I knew that he would hear me, he's God.

The only problem with not confessing my sins to a priest is that I couldn't receive communion. So, many times I didn't receive communion. Then much later I started going to confession once a month just to receive communion. I didn't agree with this about the Catholic Church, but this was just me, I didn't know how my brothers and sisters felt about the whole Catholic experience. It was a religion and this religion had some of the toughest rules.

When our house was finally livable due to the many repairs we completed, I went back to school at Gervais, I missed almost two weeks of school, so I was a little behind. I wore this light-blue hat that was made out of denim. It was like a beach hat, not too big but circular. It looked a little funny and no teacher asked me to remove it during class, so I left it on. This was less stressful for me, since I wanted to hide my eyes from the students I didn't know. The only time I removed it was during P. E. class. I liked it when no one was noticing my eye. The best part was that no one was making fun of me – I treasured this moment.

After a trying day at school I finally walked into my last class of the day. I think it was basic math. My accent was definitely southern at the time and every student at Gervais noticed immediately. The common question was, *where are you from?* All day long I heard that and I'm sure my brother and sisters did too. Diana was still in grade school, so I had less than an educated guess of what she went through.

I was confused when I kept hearing *you guys* when it was directed at girls. Wait a minute, those aren't guys those are girls. I could understand if they said, *you ladies*, but guys? I was saying, *where y'all eat at?* And of course, the laughing and joking about my southern accent was born at Gervais, which was just fine with me because I didn't mind that kind of joking around. It was definitely better than anyone joking about my eye.

I walked into my last class of the day. During this class several of the kids just stared at me for minutes, they knew I was the new kid on the block, and I was different. The teacher asked me to go up to the board and solve an equation. I had done these before in Dimmitt and it seemed pretty easy for me. The teacher might have been testing me to see what I knew. So as I got up, with my boots on, I walked slowly to the front of the class. All you could hear was my boots as everyone stared. A kid started making fun of my Texas background. He was sounding like a cow. Okay I got it, I was wearing cowboy boots, jeans, and a country shirt.

"Moo ... Moo!" He repeated those words a few times.

I stopped and turned around and looked right at him.

"Hey, that's pretty darn good, I have a friend in Texas that owns a feedlot, he gets about $20.00 a head, he'd probably get $40.00 for you."

The entire class busted out laughing, and I think I also made a few friends that day. I'm not going to say that I didn't enjoy the fresh start at Gervais High School. It was a new environment and quite the contrast from Dimmitt, Texas. There was less pressure to be the best at everything and the geographical surroundings were mesmerizing.

The huge evergreens, the rivers, and the mountains were such a joy to observe. At Gervais I was welcomed by many and I was looked up to by many, which I didn't expect. I was still a little disappointed because I wanted to attend North Salem High School. It was one of the biggest schools in Salem.

After school that day, I went to my locker to get my old-worn basketball, it was pathetic looking, but it was mine. My plan was to shoot around in the gym where there was no one and then go watch the football team practice and introduce myself to the coaches. I didn't care, I knew that when they saw me kick and punt the football, they would add me to the varsity team instantly. Again, my attitude was never like this before, but for some reason I was depressed about how things were going here at Gervais.

I was shooting around and making just about all my shots, I loved basketball and I always had a basketball in my locker. I liked the Gervais gym with a huge cougar painted on the wall. Wow from a Dimmitt Bobcat to a Gervais Cougar. I thought to myself, *at least they have a cool mascot name just like in Dimmitt.*

As I continued making shots from way outside, the head basketball coach was walking past in the hall. He spotted me and watched me for a while. He then walked over to me and introduced himself.

"Hi, I'm Coach Gary Sparks, the basketball coach ... you shoot the ball very well, you new here?"

"Yes sir, I'm from Texas, I'm David Espinoza."

"I hope to see you come out for the team this year, you could help us out."

"Yes sir, I definitely plan to."

"Okay, nice meeting you, talk to you soon."

I just tipped my head and kept shooting as he walked away. After twenty minutes I decided to jog out to the football field to watch the freshman-looking team practice. I had to walk across this grass field with a baseball diamond off to the side before I actually arrived at the football field.

I saw the assistant coach putting on his shoes at the bleachers as he watched the team execute some plays. They were all in white practice shirts with full gear, helmets and all. My attitude was not the greatest, but my emotional state was in a downward-spiral and I was feeling depressed. It wasn't fair to these coaches, but at the time I was only thinking of myself, which was totally un-Christian like. I started the conversation with Assistant Coach John Welch, who I hadn't met.

"Is this your freshman team?"

"No, this is our varsity team."

"Y'all have some pretty small lineman."

"Y'all? Where you from, Texas?"

"Yes sir. Who's your kicker and punter?"

"We have some pretty good ones, Russell kicks pretty good."

"I've seen him, I'd like to go out for the team and take his job, would that be okay?"

"I don't know, he's pretty good ... you think you can beat him?"

"With my boots on."

"Ha-ha! You're pretty confident huh? I've heard your kind before, all talk."

"Oh, no sir, any chance I can punt the football with my boots on for you coaches?"

"Yeah, how about after practice so the other coaches can see too."

"Okay sir, I'm not going anywhere."

John Welch and I continued to talk football for a few more minutes and then I went up to the bleachers to sit down and wait for my moment. I started thinking that I could probably even play halfback here at Gervais. Back in Texas, I would never get that opportunity with some of the great athletes that were ahead of me.

The practice had finally ended, and the moment of truth was about to happen. I was introduced to Head Coach Marklund. I remember his words so clear.

"Hi, I'm Coach Marklund, so you want to try out for our team?"

"Yes sir, I'd like to try out for the kicking and punting position, maybe the halfback too."

"You gonna kick with your boots on?"

"Yes sir, I don't have any football shoes with me."

"Okay, well, first of all you can't suit up for another week, and you can't play in a game until you've practiced at least a week with us."

"I understand, sir."

"Okay, get this young man a football."

I had been in so many pressure situations in Texas on a varsity team that was five times better than this team. It was easy for me to perform very well even with boots on. My first punt went about fifty yards in the air. My second punt went about fifty-five yards. The coaches were shocked that a kid would walk in from nowhere and punt a football with boots on that well.

They all looked at each other and said, "Let's get him some equipment today." I was glad that they were good sports even with my bad attitude. I did feel bad after that day and was about to change my attitude. God was with me even when I had a bad attitude. God loves us unconditionally, it's up to us to make choices and to learn from our mistakes or bad attitudes.

My Gervais days were amazing. I felt like some kind of celebrity. Word was getting out about me, and my sister was making friends left and right, she was the more social one. I wasn't too social, I usually kept to myself depending on situations. I talked to very few selected athletes at school. And as far as girls, well, I didn't think any girl at Gervais would want to ever be with me. I saw myself as not very attractive with my eye situation. I saw myself as an outstanding athlete among the student body, which is what kept me going at Gervais. I was also going to make sure that my academic progress continued.

I was proud that I finally got to take a typing class. I improved to be one of the fastest typists in our class, but I could never beat this one girl, Loretta Henry. I came close a couple of times. Loretta would just smile at me because she beat me every time. This drove me crazy because I was a real competitor at anything.

If it weren't for me talking to Johnny Hampton back in Dimmitt, I don't think I would have taken a typing class. Johnny was the one who would sit on a stool or stand outside of his typing classroom. Early in the morning he watched all of the students walk around the hallway. I asked him about typing, he encouraged me to take the class.

After a few weeks of football practices and adjusting to everything, God put the most beautiful human being in front of me. This would brighten up my world at Gervais, and this would make me thank my dad for moving us to Oregon. It was a blessing in disguise.

I was sitting on the wooden bleachers in the gym listening to my P. E. teacher give instructions. I turned my head to the left, and up one level there was the prettiest girl I had ever seen sitting quietly. She had blonde hair with a reddish tint, light-brown eyes, and about 5' 5" tall. She was sitting there very quiet. Through the week I would never see her talk to anyone. She was shy but very smart. I found out she was a sophomore ... I was a junior that year.

I had my eye on her every day, and I myself was shy about approaching girls, especially with my insecurities. One day, my nerve finally resonated, I didn't want this opportunity to pass by, no way. I went over to sit by her while we were waiting a turn at some game we were playing in class.

"Hi, what's your name?" I asked.

"Candi."

"You know, I have all these Starbursts and I can't eat them all, would you like one?"

"Sure, thank you," Candi took it from my hand.

Our conversation was short, and each day our conversations stretched longer. I can remember falling for this girl like no other girl I had been with in Texas – Kylene, Karen, or Joy. To tell you the truth, Isabel had vanished from my mind after I met Candi R. Cover. I could not stop thinking about this Gervais-Caucasion girl. Previous to asking Candi out on a date, I struggled on how I was going to ask her. After I met Candi I never thought about asking anyone else on a date again – Candi was it for me.

I would look forward to P.E. just to see Candi and talk to her. I was starting to make her smile and she was starting to talk to me more. The way I asked Candi on a date was funny – it all worked out though.

We were playing volleyball in P.E. and she was on the oppo-site team. I've been told that I have a soft-spoken voice, and sometimes people don't understand me clearly. I leaned forward under the volleyball net and asked, "Would you like to go on a date with me on Friday?" Candi thought I asked, *would you like to go skate with me on Friday?* So she responded, "Yes, I'd love to."

Later that day in the hallway, she was getting ready to catch the bus, she lived out in the country towards Salem on Waconda Road. I asked her what time I should pick her up and I also asked her if it was okay with her parents. She said she would talk to her mom and let me know the next day.

At school I was informed that it was okay with Candi's mom. I was in for a shock, because I had never skated, but I didn't care, I was going out with one of the nicest looking girls at Gervais High School. I didn't want Candi to know how poor my family was or where I lived. I knew that my parents were doing the best they could, but there was something about my pride and how I wanted better for myself and my family.

That Friday, I borrowed my sister's Impala, which was the nicest car we had at the time, and I drove to Candi's house to pick her up. Both her parents, Joe and Elaine, were teachers and her family was middle-income. Compared to my family, they were very wealthy. They lived on an acre with some huge evergreen trees surrounding their house – a beautiful setting.

I have to tell you my humiliating experience while stopping to pick her up. I had developed this fear of dogs going back to the Texas days. Often we would get chased by dogs that were trained to attack anyone that walked by their territory, especially in my old neighborhood. I have so many dog-chasing-me stories, if you ever meet me, you're welcomed to ask me about them.

When I pulled up to her house I was so impressed with everything about it. They had a huge carport that covered a concrete driveway. And they had a guest room with a breezeway connected to their house. About 100 feet away they had a huge shop. I stepped out of the car and as I began to walk I heard two dogs, a small-black mutt and a large St. Bernard. They were coming after me barking loudly! I was quite alarmed and did not know what to do. As her dogs got closer to me, I jumped on top of the car hood and stayed there.

Out came Candi yelling at her dogs to get back. She tied them up and apologized to me while she laughed. I felt stupid and embarrassed. She explained to me that her dogs didn't know me and were just being protective and territorial.

That night we laughed about her thinking it was just skating and not a date. The result for me was a fun date with an amazing person that was beautiful inside and out. We went to a place called Skate Palace. I fell down a few times and she laughed again and again, helping me up and showing me a few things about skating. The best part for me was when she held me while I put one arm around her to keep from falling over. I did get a little better at it that night, thanks to Candi. She never knew that I purposely fell down a few times just to get close to her.

We were having so much fun together that it was like we didn't want the night to end. I didn't wear my hat and my glasses would help hide my eyes. She never suspected anything, or at least she never said anything about my eye. That was good news for me at the time. In the long run I knew I had to tell her, but not just yet.

Candi played volleyball and was also on the drill team, which was a dancing team that normally performed at halftime during our football games. It was rare that I saw Candi perform, because I was always in the dressing room with the team during halftime.

When I started playing football with the team, not only did I get the punter-kicker positions, I was also selected to play the halfback position. We ran out of the "I" formation, I was familiar with it, but I liked the wishbone formation more with two halfbacks and one fullback.

I still remember who the fullback was, Jim Hupp. Jim's sister, Lynn, was one of the first girls I met at Gervais. My brother and I were invited to a birthday party and I remember talking to Lynn that night, which was before I met Candi. We would also go to Jim's house to play ping pong in a backyard shack that his family had. Slowly I started making friends at Gervais. The Gervais Market was always a place we could walk to for a snack. They normally had fried chicken, burritos, or Jo Jos. Tasty food but not the healthiest.

After the third game I was becoming a well known person. It seemed like the whole town knew who the Texas transfer was. In one game, I came out for the last three minutes. Our team was ahead and we pretty much had the victory.

There were three people on the sideline that started asking me questions, Rick Klampe, Scott Ramp, and the librarian, Mrs. James. The librarian was also the statistician for sporting events. They were asking me what other sports I played, and in particular about track and field. They liked that I ran the hurdles in 15.9 seconds and had cleared 6' 0" in the high jump. It was crazy how everyone knew who I was and how many people came to watch my brother and I punt and kick the football. During warm-ups was so much fun. My punts would go up past the lights, just like in Dimmitt. I had a little bit better hang time than my brother did, but he was great too. It was magical to have him next to me during warm-ups. It started way back in a small Texas town on a dirt road called, Dulin Street. My brother Richard and I were best friends and we did a lot of things together around Gervais. We were also great teammates.

At Gervais, we met people like, Russell and Greg, they had a sister named, Mary. We met Curtis, Roger, and Kent. These guys were some of the kids we met playing basketball with at Parkersville. Oregon has many small farm schools way out in the country. It was nice to know that Gervais had some nice kids that were supportive of my brother and I despite our poverty situation and despite us being Texas transfers.

It was on a weekend and during football season. It wasn't Dimmitt and the basketball coaches never said we couldn't play basketball during football season, so we played basketball on weekends. Armando was a kid that would always hang around us. He would even come over to our house and sit on the porch steps. All nice kids and sports oriented, those were usually the school friends I had.

I kept expecting to see a fight at Gervais, it was something that I had been accustomed to in Dimmitt, especially the junior high days. I was surprised that the school was very calm and laid back. Kids were friendly, with the exception of a few Caucasian kids. I could tell they were a little discriminatory, but not as much as people from the South. This made it less stressful for me to go to school.

I started learning a lot. I loved classes like John Welch's class. I was not a history-type person. In Dimmitt I would almost fall asleep in history class. With Mr. Welch's class it was fun, because I could tell he had a passion for what he taught. He would always open his class with, "Anything to discuss?" He liked current events and so did I. He liked sports and so did I.

He also had us get into groups to do class assignments, we'd work as teams to accomplish something constructive. It was a great change of pace for me. I also liked social studies with Mr. Rice's class. He was a teacher that I could steer off the subject with NFL talk or NBA talk. He loved sports and it always amazed me when we made it through a chapter we were studying. One of my favorite classes had to be, English class, I enjoyed writing and reading some of the material that I had never seen before.

Sadly to say I don't remember my English teacher's name for my junior year, but for my senior year, my Honors English teacher was, Gary Everett. He gave me opportunities that no other

English teacher did. He asked me what I thought about something he read. I was shy and afraid that I might not be as smart as other kids.

One of my favorite teachers at Gervais was Susan Arndt, she was teaching personal finance at the time. Susan was pretty young for a high school teacher and could relate well with the young kids. I was always more of a visual person and when I didn't understand something, it frustrated me. Mrs. Arndt always explained something that was complicated in a logical way that I could understand. That, to a teacher, is not always an easy thing to do.

I was stoked when I found out Gervais was offering a guitar class. I didn't take band, but I definitely took guitar class. What a fun class that was, taught by Mr. Havens. We learned simple things like basic chords and notes on the guitar. We also played and sang songs, which was my favorite part of the class. I had a little more experience than most in the class since I played a lot of guitar back in Texas. My final for that class was a song called, "Beth I Hear You Calling," by Kiss. I received an A on my final for that class.

These were a few of the classes that I enjoyed at Gervais. I am so thankful that I met these teachers. Thank you for the huge impact you made on my life. I remember asking some of my teachers about college and how bad I wanted to get a degree in a career that would provide for my family some day. They all told me the same thing, *you can do it, David, don't let anything stop you.* Especially Mrs. Arndt, she was so supportive of me. We talked about the future and many important things about life and education.

I was beginning to spend a lot of time with Candi. We would go watch movies and sometimes just hang out at her house. One of the first movies we watched together was *Rocky*. Great movie, we both enjoyed it. When I hear the theme song to that movie I think about one of the first dates I ever had with Candi. Our relationship was escalating to a higher level, and I loved where it was headed.

One morning at school, Candi invited me to dinner at her house. I was freaking out a little because I had never met the parents of any girl I ever dated. She was excited about me coming over to meet her folks. I said, "Sure, I'd love to." Keep in mind that I was a long-haired Hispanic and she was Caucasian. The way Hispanics like me ate, was quite the contrast to how Caucasian people ate, or at least the Caucasian people I knew.

On the evening of the dinner I was a little nervous and did not know what to expect. I had no clue that her parents had been coming to my football games. Their daughters, Kelly and Candi, were always involved in school activities.

Kelly was in my art class and I remember drawing weird creatures. For some reason I liked experimenting with creatures, I guess from watching some scary movies or something. Now that I'm older, I don't think I've drawn a creature. I also liked drawing basketball pictures and then writing some kind of a short story to them.

Kelly would walk by my drawings and say something like, *I don't know about you dating my sister*, and then she'd walk away. I never got the impression that she liked me, but that was just my assumption. She kept to her own project, some important painting she was working on. When I caught up with Kelly in later years, she said, *I really didn't mind you dating my sister, I could tell she was happy, and that's all that mattered to me*.

In my mind I was expecting Candi, her parents, and myself at the dinner table. When I knocked on the door, she opened it and the only other person there was her mom, she was cooking the dinner. I was introduced to Elaine, she was very nice to me. I shook her hand and then we sat on their nice living-room furniture – definitely ten times nicer than what we had at our falling-apart rental.

Candi and I sat and talked while her mom went back to the kitchen to finish up cooking dinner. I was unaware of what we were having, and if you knew me, I was a picky eater, well, I guess I still am. It smelled good and I was hoping it was food that I liked. All of a sudden, Candi's sister, Cathy, walks in and I met her. Her dad, Joe, opens the front door and walks in. He gave me this mean look and said, "Who is this dude in my house!" I have to admit it startled me a little until he smiled.

"Nice to meet you David, you're doing a heck of a job for the Gervais football team."

"Thank you sir, nice to meetcha."

"Hope you like steak."

"Sounds good, thank you."

Joe walks off to the kitchen as he looked at Candi.

"For a minute there, I thought he was mad at me," I whispered.

"Naw, that's just how Dad is," Candi said.

I also met her little brother when he came in from playing with his friends. The table was all set and I looked around to see what everyone was doing and listened to what everyone was saying. Cathy started with a prayer and I noticed none of them did the sign of the cross. I started to and then stopped. I had never used a knife or a fork to eat steak. My dad liked chuck steak. We ate with a flour tortilla and with our hands, forget the silverware. Well, Candi's family used forks and knives and they even had green vegetables which I stayed away from.

Candi was watching me and seemed surprised that I didn't know how to cut the steak. I was a little embarrassed and felt out of place. I tried to emulate what Candi was doing. I leaned over to her and whispered while others were conversing.

"Candi, I've always eaten meat using my hands, I guess y'all eat with a fork and knife."

"Ha-ha, David, most people eat steak with a fork and knife."

"I see, okay."

I started seeing the difference in our cultures, at least the culture I lived in. I'm sure many Hispanics use forks and knives. I also started seeing how their house was arranged, and how the kitchen was laid out. It was like some of my wealthy friends back in Texas. It was definitely not like my poor life. Heaven forbid she ever asked me if she could come over to my house. My thoughts were, *I don't know if she would want to continue dating a poor-Hispanic kid.*

I learned a lot about the Cover family that evening. They were all very nice to me and welcomed me. They were down-to-earth people that didn't discriminate against Hispanics. Thank you Cover family for accepting me without judgment and assumption.

Thank you for giving me a chance to be your daughter's boyfriend. I'll never forget their response when they found out I didn't like cheese, "You don't like cheese!"

After that night, Candi started liking me a little more. I would walk her to class many times, or she'd walk me to my class. She inspired me to study hard and to step up my game in studies. I don't know what it was, but I was so caught up in coolness and sports that I only put in enough effort to pass my classes. I might have snuck by with a B average, barely. Sometimes I would carry a C average. The point is, that Candi knew I could do better. In my mind I knew I could be an A student, but for some reason I just didn't put all of my energy into studying. When I wasn't with Candi, I was mostly playing football, basketball, or hanging out with my brother playing foosball at arcades.

I knew that school was important and I did have a few semesters with straight As, but not enough of them. My grades never went below a C average, I always made sure they stayed above that, I'd say more B averages and few A averages.

My junior year was flying by and I had never been more thankful to God for putting such wonderful things and people in front of me, especially bringing a girl like Candi into my life. That in itself changed my entire attitude about attending Gervais High School.

When football season came to an end, our record did not shine in the Capital Conference. I was a little disappointed because in Texas winning was very important and we had winning teams. At Gervais I didn't get that message. I think because we were competing against bigger schools that had bigger guys, it made it tough to have a winning record. We also didn't have Thompson or Leon as running backs, like back in Dimmitt.

The coaches were not as pressure-oriented like some that I knew back in Texas. My brother and I introduced some drills to our coaches, and they implemented them. We felt honored that we could contribute to a small school that we had become a part of.

At the end of the football season, I received several awards at the sports banquet. The one that stood out was the All-League Kicking Specialist Award. I still have that one along with others. I remember the Statesman Journal doing a story on me for leading the league as a kicker and punter.

Craig Fertig, who was the head coach at Oregon State University at the time, started calling me, his assistant coaches called me as well. They wanted me to come watch an OSU game on the sidelines on a Saturday. It seemed like I always had a date with Candi and that was my priority. I also didn't have a way to get to Corvillas and I wasn't comfortable enough to go on my own.

It was a strange feeling living a private home life because I didn't want anyone at school to know where I lived. I would have died of shame if Candi ever saw where I lived. It was such a sad case, especially when I came home after practice and there wasn't any food. I would often walk over to the Gervais Market to buy a burrito, they were super cheap and they tasted good after a hard practice. I drank a lot of water when there wasn't any milk, but preferred milk. Picking apples from a tree across the street along the train tracks, became a regular thing for me until they all ran out.

I always thought to myself, *I don't want this kind of life when I'm out of high school, I want something better. I don't want to take cold baths in a bathroom worrying if there would be a large rat running across the floor. I don't want to walk into my home and see an old carpet that has torn pieces with stains that are visible. I don't want to walk into my house wondering if there is food to eat.*

I don't blame my parents. They did so much for us and they always managed to find a minimum-wage job to feed us and to pay the bills. I loved my parents and saw how hard they tried to make ends meet. There was a time when they were laid off from the seasonal job at the cannery. We ran out of money and the landlord came knocking at the door. He wanted his $250.00 for rent. I don't know what happened and my parents never told me.

The next thing I knew there was talk about us moving to Woodburn to live in the housing projects. These apartment-like homes were like a village, all connected together. My cousin, Tony Villarreal, lived there. He was one of the few cousins we spent time with. We tried to get him involved in sports. He was a kid going through a rough time himself in a different way.

While that was going on in my private-home life, basketball season was underway and I was making my mark on the Gervais Varsity Basketball Team. Coach Sparks was good to me. He immediately put me as one of the starting five. He saw me shooting in the gym during football season, and he saw the talent I could bring to the team.

I was nominated to something called, Snowball Court, and I made it! I never heard of such a dance. The dance would be coming up and I would be escorting, Tracy Wells. Tracy was a nice looking girl and I was worried about what Candi would think. Candi understood but was still showing signs of getting jealous. I think for me it would have been the same, I understood how she felt. We talked about it and Candi would be my date for the snowball dance, yet I would escort Tracy.

This was a little confusing and I did feel bad for Tracy because I'm sure she assumed I would be her date that night. It all worked out in the end. I spent time with Tracy during the snowball festivities and announcements and I even danced with her after the photos and all. After that, I went out to the hall, because for some reason Candi was waiting for me out there. I just told Candi that there was no other girl more important to me than her. I kissed her and we walked back to the dance floor. The rest of the evening was spent with my high-school sweetheart. I have a song planted in my memory from that night, it's "Dancing Queen," by Abba.

Despite my downfalls and my struggles with my half-vision and insecurities, God was always there for me when I didn't even know it. Who would have thought that I, a Texas transfer, would be having the normality of a boy at Gervais High School, in such a short amount of time.

I was having the time of my life with the most beautiful girl I had ever seen. I was learning so much about people and life in general, and I was absorbing it all in and letting it dissolve into my brain. I mean, nominated for the Snowball Court? Wow! I never imagined it. I'd hear about the wealthy and popular kids always having the advantage on this kind of thing, but a poor-Hispanic kid that had just come into this school? I truly felt proud, honored, and blessed.

18.

Half-Year at Woodburn High School

God always had a sense of humor and found a way to keep my head from getting too big. My parents delivered the news that we were moving to Woodburn. My heart took a downfall. Okay, I made an incredible adjustment, like my brother and sisters did. I also made a few friends and my sports career had returned to where it once was back in Texas. My most important part of attending Gervais, was my favorite girl, Candi. This could not be happening, I was shattered and disappointed.

The housing projects were new and they had more civil living conditions than where we lived in Gervais. So I completely got it. The first night I slept in that cold attic at that old house on Alder Street, I was in my rapid-eye-movement stage. All of a sudden this roaring noise comes from nowhere. I thought it was a tornado hitting, it brought horrible memories back from the Texas days. My bed was bouncing and moving because of the off-balanced house. I hit the wall with my bed and then the noise stopped. I realized it was that train going by our rented house. At least with this new place in Woodburn there would be no train.

I talked to Candi about it and we were trying to figure out how to continue our relationship. I did not want it to end, I loved her so much. My parents were saying we could still attend Gervais High School. That lasted a week until someone talked to the school about us not living in Gervais anymore. We got pulled into the office and we were told that we needed to transfer to Woodburn High School. They gave us a week and they allowed my sister Louise to stay at Gervais. They made an acceptation for her because she was a senior.

We had a chance to say goodbye to the friends we made at Gervais. They were all disappointed as we were. The coaches were trying to do whatever they could to keep the best kicker-punter they've had in a long while at Gervais.

I immediately showed up to basketball practice after school at Woodburn High School. It was so bizarre, the level of separation anxiety was so strong and I was starting to get depressed. I missed seeing Candi and her mom was getting tired of me calling her – it was the only time I could connect with Candi. I couldn't use my sister's car because she was still attending Gervais and had gained a lot of friends.

I showed up early for basketball practice, I was angry and depressed. I started shooting baskets and realized I had this energy in my legs. Maybe the rest between changing teams? I don't know. I started dunking the basketball on the side hoops. Coach Sam Spicher walks in and says, "You're the new kid on the block, welcome. I didn't know you could dunk a basketball, no one told me."

I didn't say too much to him but he knew who I was and he was looking forward to me being on the basketball team. Later that day, the football coach from Woodburn came and talked to me. Dale Yuranic definitely knew who I was. It wasn't too long until he had me catching passes with his son, who was the quarterback. Woodburn was always pretty successful in football. This kind of attention distracted me from my Gervais friends, but it did not phase me on how I felt about Candi. I thought about her a lot, even during classes at Woodburn.

The last time I talked to her, she said that her mom was strongly suggesting that she date other boys. That didn't go too well with me and I got into a further depression because I knew deep inside that we loved each other very much.

It took me a few weeks to semi-adjust. I started hanging around with my best friend and brother, Richard. We did all kinds of things, but mainly we spent a lot of time walking around downtown Woodburn and playing a lot of foosball. We mastered this game learning all kinds of techniques to maneuver the ball and score shots. We would clobber everyone in doubles anywhere we went. It was so much fun, but at the end of the day when that was all over, my thoughts went back to Candi and how much I missed her. I was only three miles away from her school, but it seemed like a thousand miles. My heart would ache, I didn't think it was fair. Candi had my phone number for the housing projects. I did what her mom asked of me, I stopped calling her and I assumed she was going to date other boys.

I didn't want to date any girls despite the fact that Woodburn had some pretty amazing looking girls. I kept hoping Candi would call me, she was the only girl I wanted to date again. Her mom made it clear that she didn't want me dating Candi anymore and that she hoped we wouldn't get married in the future.

God had something else in mind though, and it was in His timing not mine. It was when I put all my selfish ways aside that He started putting more things in front of me, but it was my decision to take advantage of those things – Jesus gave me that free will.

That was the time I would listen to a song called, "How Deep is Your Love" by The Bee Gees. The lyrics and the music to that song say a lot about love, the kind of love that I had for Candi. I just had a feeling that her love for me was deep, but there were people that made it difficult for us.

My family started going to St. Lukes Catholic Church in Woodburn. My mom made us go to church every Sunday. I often prayed at church as I looked up at Jesus on that cross. I wanted things to work out with Candi and myself.

Candi had introduced me to a show called, *Little House on the Prairie*. I liked watching that show with her. I remember in some of the episodes, Charles Ingalls would pray by saying, *show me the way*. I started saying the same thing at that church as I prayed about my situation.

As the weeks went by I was adapting well with the Woodburn basketball team, but I was coming off the bench and I wasn't used to doing that. It was hard for me and I knew we had a game coming up against Gervais. I would be playing against my former teammates, Curtis; Roger; Bill; Clay; Ray, and Kent. It was a game that I was looking forward to and at the same time brought a different kind of stress to me. I had no money, I had no girl anymore, and I was living in the low-income housing projects. I could only see half of what everyone else could. I was forced to cut my hair and didn't know if anyone would recognize me. Despite all of that, I had a competitive spirit and I knew that Candi would be there. I was going to do my best to play the best game possible.

On a Friday night I was in Gervais watching the JV play while waiting with my Woodburn teammates. I was sitting by myself about five rows up. I noticed Candi walking across the gym and I remember hoping she was coming to say hi to me. The sight was so real and delightful. I hadn't seen her in weeks. She stepped up to the bleachers where I was sitting by myself with my game bag.

"Hi, I thought I'd come over and say hi," Candi said.

"Hi, so glad you did ... I've missed you."

"I've missed you too ... how's Woodburn?"

"Different, I think sports is the only thing keeping me going."

"David ... I'm sorry."

"It's okay. I'm looking forward to track season, my coach says I have a chance to make it to state."

"That doesn't surprise me, at least you'll have a better high jump pit."

"Yeah, that's true."

"I wanted to call you the other day, but my mom said no."

"Yeah, I got the message loud and clear. I haven't asked any girl out at Woodburn, although there is this one girl, her name is Tonia. She's a hurdler like me."

"Hmm ... I'm starting to get jealous."

"Don't worry Candi, she has a boyfriend and besides all I can think about is you. I know if you went out with another guy, I'd be super jealous."

"Ha, no need to worry about that, every guy thinks that if they ask me out you'll beat them up."

"Ha-ha! Naw, I wouldn't do that, but I would definitely be jealous."

"You got your hair cut ... you look even more handsome now."

"Thank you, that's encouraging."

"Well, I should get back to the Gervais side, hopefully we can win tonight," she smiles.

"Yeah, thank you for coming over, it was nice seeing you again."

"I'll try to call you sometime, I just don't know when."

"Sounds good, I'll see you later ... and don't give up on us."

"I won't," she smiled.

During warm-ups I dunked a couple of times just to get into my ex-teammates' heads and the Gervais crowd. On a good day, I could dunk off of one leg. My high jump practicing gave me that leaping ability. I was 6' 0" tall and had Woodburn teammates taller than me.

That game was one of the most memorable ones at Gervais. I was playing against my old teammates and the gym was packed. I remember making some great defensive plays. I once blocked Curtis' shot – all ball, very clean. The referee called a foul. I took one look at the referee and from that point on I knew it was going to be a long night. Curtis even told me as we were running down the court, "That was a clean block, you got nothing but ball."

The Gervais crowd was definitely harassing me in a fun way. They would yell out at the same time, "You! You! You!" and Candi was in that crowd. I looked up at her and she smiled and pointed at me. I just shook my head and smiled back. I could tell she was having fun watching me play against her school. That game I was on fire, unconscious to another level, in a zone. Every shot that I took was going in. I had to shoot from way outside because the Cougars were keying on me, they knew I could shoot the ball. The referees fouled me out, only two of the fouls were mine, and we lost by a few points. If I hadn't fouled out I think the outcome would have been a little different.

After the game I took time to talk to all my friends from Gervais, and they all congratulated me on a great game played. I ended up with a perfect 100% 8-for-8 from the field, and 4-for-4 from the stripe. I think I made Candi proud that night and I think that night flared up her love for me even more. God was with me even when I didn't know it. All glory to Jesus for that incredible performance that night.

As I left the gym floor I raised my hand and waved to the crowd that had embraced me when I was at Gervais. The loud cheers from them I will never forget. Most of my team was already dressed and out on the bus when I ran into the dressing room. My coach tolerated why I was so late.

Coach Spicher was waiting for me, and complimented me on how well I played. I asked him if my playing that night was good enough to make the starting lineup for his team. He explained to me that his seniors had been there all four years and that he couldn't do that to them. He assured me that I was going to be playing a lot of minutes though. I just looked at him and for the first time I didn't think about my selfish ways. I was grateful that I could be a part of this Woodburn team. I shook my head up and down while sweat was soaking my royal-blue uniform and running down my face. I understood his position and his loyalty to the seniors. I said, "Coach, I'm sorry, you're right I shouldn't have even asked." I think Coach Spicher understood my competitiveness.

At Woodburn, we definitely had a winning record in basketball, but we still fell short of the playoffs. The basketball season ended and the new school was about to be completed. Half of the track season would be spent at the old school on French Prairie Road. We were sharing this school with the middle-school kids. It was crazy for a while and I remembered attending school half-days for part of my Woodburn days.

I was so excited for track season, the high jump pit was great. I started practicing as soon as the basketball season was over. I felt great out on the track, it was counseling for me. I practiced an hour a day on the 110-meter high hurdles, which had converted from yards to meters. I also worked on the high jump for another hour. This was fun for me, I sometimes spent more than two hours on the track. As I recall my history, I feel that God put sports in front of me to help me deal with my poverty situation, eye issues, and emotional issues. God loves us and will always be there to lift us up.

Coach Pat Carey was a good coach. He taught me about how important steps were in high jump – a vital part of this field event. He had great confidence in me and encouraged me to do all sorts of jumping drills.

I made a decision to start waking up at 5:00 a.m. every morning to run two miles. It was challenging because I was never a morning person. My goal was to make it to the state meet, which would take place at Mt. Hood Community College in Gresham, Oregon.

I started out clearing 6' 0" in the first duel meet. Before I came to Oregon, I never heard of a track-and-field duel meet. In the hurdles I started out running a 16.1 and three stepping all ten hurdles. Coach Carey was big on running a lot during practices to build endurance and strength. He didn't want me practicing on jumping over the bar every day of the week. He did, however, work with me on my arch going over the bar. He perfected it a little more. I never realized that when a jumper gets over the bar, if the head is flipped up, the heels automatically flip up and will not clip the bar. A natural body reaction causes that movement.

We had just returned from the Rogue River Invitational, where I had placed first in the hurdles and first in the high jump. This was a cool meet because they gave out little trophies to the winners of each event. That was the first time I experienced a large stage watching me in the high jump. I was competing against a local kid that was a great jumper. I had my Woodburn teammates cheering for me, and he had the entire town cheering for him. I cleared 6' 2" and he cleared 6' 1". What a fun invitational that was.

I hadn't talked to Candi since that basketball game at Gervais. She was definitely honoring her mom. It was mid-season during track and field and we were set to compete against Gervais in a duel meet at Woodburn. We were still at the old school, but the high jump pit was great – all-weather turf and large-blue mats.

My friend, Ray Eder, ran the hurldes very well, and also high jumped well. I had no hint what to expect, everyone from Gervais told me that Ray was very good at both of those events. He was a senior and I was a junior. The Gervais crowd was pumped anticipating the battle between Ray and I. Ironically I knew more Gervais students than Woodburn students.

I remember being at the starting line and shaking his hand, "Good luck Ray." We both heard the starting official's signal and we got down on our blocks to start the race. I didn't have any spit in my mouth I was so nervous, but that was always a normal thing for me before a big race. There were a lot of people that showed up to watch us race – we were both top hurdlers in the Capital Conference.

When the gun sounded I took off and so did Ray. We were both neck to neck for the first five hurdles, and then through the eighth hurdle. We were leading everyone else by at least ten yards. When we came to the tenth hurdle, Ray's height at 6' 1" outdid me by a tiny margin. I ran a 15.8 and I think he ran a 15.79 – it was a fun, competitive, and close race. Breathing hard after the race, I walked over to him and shook his hand.

I knew the high jump was still going on. I had passed to 5' 8" which was a good height for me to start jumping. I knew I had a chance to take Ray in the high jump, but I wasn't totally sure. Ray was also a good high jumper.

It didn't take too long for us to start high jumping. Ray started jumping at 5' 6" and I started at 5' 8". After I cleared my starting height effortlessly, I went and sat close to the grass area far from the high-jump pit. The bar was set at 5' 10" and I was waiting for the remaining jumpers to take their attempts. The Woodburn school record was 6' 2 1/2". At the beginning of the season, Pat Carey told me that I had a chance to set a new record. To tell you the truth, I didn't believe him.

I was talking to one of my Gervais friends, a 300-meter hurdler. He whispered at me, "Hey, I think someone's watching you back there." I turned around and I saw Candi in her track sweats sitting on the grass area twenty feet behind me. I immediately got up and walked over to sit next to her.

It was so uplifting to see her again. We talked in-between my jumps. I was encouraged that maybe we would start seeing each other again. It certainly sounded positive. She said she missed me a lot and was looking forward to this track meet. I told her that I admired her for honoring her mom and not calling me. I felt in my heart that it was going to be okay in the long run.

The bar went up to 6' 1" and I think that's where Ray exited the competition. My teammate, Stromme, also exited the competition. After I cleared 6' 2" on my first attempt, I asked if we could move it up to 6' 4". I wanted to try and break the school record by an inch. The bar was set to meet my request since I was the only jumper left. I clipped the bar with my heels the first try, I could hear everyone cheering for me. I knew that I could do it. I heard Candi, "Come on Espinoza, you can do it!"

Those words gave me the energy and strength to go all out. My steps were right on so no worries there. I walked back to my starting spot, which was normally fifteen steps from the bar. I looked at the bar and visually counted my steps to where I would plant my left leg and throw my right knee up swinging my arms as I would reach up and arch at my most highest point of the jump. I took a breath and went for it. After the jump I landed on the mat and the bar was still on the two stands on each side! The crowd went crazy as I had just set a new record! It was totally official. The judges came out with the measuring tape. Since the middle part of the fiberglass bar was dipping a little in the middle part, that's where they measured – it had to be a valid measurement. The word was, that I had set a new record at 6' 3". I attempted 6' 5" but clipped the bar with my heels all three times.

I was so happy that I not only proved Coach Reese in Texas wrong about what he said, but also I had set a record with Candi watching. Witnessing the smile on her face and then her walking up to me and giving me a big hug, was priceless and something I'll always treasure. Again, all glory to God for my amazing record-setting performance.

Track and field was an individual sport, and because I was one of the highest-ranked athletes in the state, I felt like all eyes were on me every time I competed. My physical imperfections were overlooked. I had so many friends that looked up to me and respected me. If you've ever experienced what I did, you know what I'm talking about – it's a great feeling to be able to entertain people when they are totally engaged in a talent. To me it was something that I had worked so hard for since my seventh-grade year.

When people told me, *wow, you're lucky you can jump so high,* they had no evidence of what I had gone through as far as intense training and sacrifices to be that good. It wasn't luck, it was hard work doing something I enjoyed and it was Jesus putting this in front of me and giving me a lift in life when I needed it. I always thanked God for anything I accomplished, but I never understood the whole picture. I still don't understand the whole picture, but I'm learning every day.

While we traveled on away games, I would look out of the window and just think to myself, *this is all great and something I've worked so hard for, and if I could somehow have Candi back in my life, my accomplishments would be ten-thousand times more fun.* Yes, I would look out of the bus window and I would get sad. My teammates would ask me, *Hey Dave, why so sad, man ... you're like the king of high jump.* I would just smile and say, "Thanks, man."

I didn't know any of the Woodburn kids, they had real-established friendships that they developed for years, where I didn't. Here I was the new kid on the block once again. It was a lonely world for me. During practices I socialized with a few field events' athletes. One time during practice, Susie said, "There's the new kid in town." She would then start singing that song, "New Kid in Town," by the Eagles.

Woodburn was a little bigger than Gervais with a larger enrollment. I focused on my studies and got by with a B average. I took a class on government and learned a lot of new things. I also took choir and sang a lot. I did the best I could, but I walked around with a down-hearted feeling when I wasn't around sports.

On Sundays I went to church with my mom and brothers and sisters. Somehow we all ended up together again living in the housing projects. My memory is a blur on how that all happened, but it was fun having them around again. My older brothers and my dad were all looking for jobs. My brothers and sisters were my best friends at Woodburn, especially Richard who was also at Woodburn High School. He was dealing with an ankle injury during track season – he struggled that year a bit.

My track and field season that year under Coach Pat Carey was the best I ever had. I put myself on the Oregon map as one of the best high jumpers in the state. At the district championships, with a huge crowd all around us, once again I faced Ray Eder of Gervais.

In the high jump I beat him clearing 6' 2 1/2", I was able to advance to state. In a close down-to-the-wire hurdle race, I was taken by La Salle's Mike Swanson, Central's Mark Genishi, and Gervais' Ray Eder. Ray took third and I took fourth. I felt bad for Ray, because I wanted him to advance to state with me. He was a good friend of mine from Gervais. The times were close and it was fun running with such talented athletes.

The race was a little frustrating to me, Mike was 6' 7" and he was next to me on lane three. His arm kept hitting my shoulder every time we'd run over a hurdle. I think I ran like, 15.7 or so. Ray was so close to getting that second place, but he fell 100th of a second short.

I remember that all-expense-paid trip to Mt. Hood to compete in the state championships. I couldn't believe my eyes. I had always dreamed of one day making it to the state championships in something. It finally happened, all of my hard training paid off.

There were a few athletes from Woodburn that made it to state. We all traveled together. We stopped to eat and I don't know what came over me, but I ate a lot of good food at a nice restaurant. I wasn't thinking of my high-jump event. Hungry kids don't think, they eat.

It was a cold and rainy day that May of 1977. We were warming up on a wet runway to the high jump pit. I was raised in Texas where the weather was warm this time of the year. I learned quickly that in Oregon the weather can change in thirty minutes.

Despite a full stomach and the cold-wet environment, I still managed to come away with the 5th-place medal. I cleared 6' 1" in challenging conditions and I couldn't feel too bad about that. The winning height was 6' 5". I was not accustomed to less than first place that year. For some reason I didn't feel too bad, I was satisfied, because I saw my competition, and how much shorter I was than some of my competitors. Most of the jumpers were 6' 4" and taller.

I made the all-league team and was selected to the all-state team. I'll never forget my track and field experience at Woodburn High School under Pat Carey, a coach that had a passion for track and field. This coach set such an amazing example for his team.

During our practices he would join us in four-mile runs. He was fit and knew the technique to many field events and even how to start from the blocks. His time spent with the high school athletes was priceless. He pushed me to a level I never thought I could reach. This coach cared so much about his team and he displayed it so well. I learned so many things from Coach Carey, and it was mostly during our long-distance runs we executed as a team. He would lecture us on how to be good people and good athletes. He encouraged us and introduced many workout drills for our specific events. Thank you, Coach Carey, for the time you invested in me and the sacrifices you made for our team that year.

19.

Summer Before Senior Year

My brother and I would talk to the Gervais football coaches now and then, they kept asking us where we had gone and if we were going to come back to Gervais. My dad was struggling with the rent costs rising at the projects and feeding his large family.

We had friends at Gervais that we stayed in touch with. One of the football coaches started looking for rental houses that might be affordable for our family, because to tell you the truth, we were flat broke and my parents had just received a call from Stayton Canning. The harvest season was beginning again and we were on the verge of possibly getting evicted from the housing projects, that's my assumption.

My brother and I were told by this coach that there was a house that wasn't in any living condition, it needed a lot of work. The good news, he said, was the rent, it was only $75.00 a month.

What I didn't know at the time was that this house was along 99E, and that one of the Gervais cheerleader's dad owned it. That didn't matter at this point. When we told my dad, he said, "What! ... $75.00 a month?" He was already wanting to go check out the house. So, we did just that the following day.

When I saw the house, I was like, *this is the ugliest, smallest, oldest, and worst place I have ever seen* – definitely a step below that old rental next to the tracks on Alder Street. I even thought of maybe pitching a tent behind the house and sleeping out there. The good news was the amazing privacy with no other houses around. It was out on acres of farmland behind us. My dad loved it and started cleaning it up. It hadn't been lived in for quite some time.

That summer before we started to move, I received a surprising call. I walked over and picked up the phone that was hooked to a long cord. The housing projects were pretty decent and they had a small kitchen and a living room. We only had one chair in the living room, that's no joke. We all had a tiny room and there was a long hall to get to the rooms. At Woodburn, it was rare that we all ate together. We all just took our food to our rooms and ate there or we ate at the kitchen bar standing up.

"Hello," I said.

"Hi, this is Candi."

"Oh wow! I didn't think I'd ever hear from you again, but I was hoping."

"I missed you too much, I had to talk to you."

"What about your mom?"

"I think she could tell that I wasn't going to go out with anyone else."

"Well, please tell your mom I said that I'm sorry for calling you so many times."

"Okay, I think she's okay with me coming to see you, I have the Cadillac."

"Really ... today?"

"If it's okay, I'd really like to see you and talk."

"Yeah, that sounds great. Do you know where I live in Woodburn?"

"No, I'll need directions, and also, how about I come up at five?"

"Five sounds great."

My mood took a huge upswing and I had the most amazing smile the rest of the day. My prayers to God had been answered. In His timing everything was going to work out, but at the time I had no vivid imagination of what Jesus Christ was bringing to me. Now that I think back, I feel so blessed and thankful for how Jesus guided me. He put patience in my heart. I decided to distance myself from Candi while I was in Woodburn, and I allowed her to make her own decision about us.

That evening she came over to see where I lived. I introduced her to my brothers and my sisters. She knew some of them already. She met my mom for the first time, my dad wasn't at home at the time. She drove me to Salem and we walked around Bush's Pasture Park. We talked about so many things while we held hands. Candi wanted to know everything that I went through in Woodburn. So I told her everything. I asked her about Gervais and what she went through. We must have spent three hours there just talking, but it seemed like ten minutes, time just flew – we were catching up on so many things. When we got into her car, which was a nice comfortable car, I told her that I needed to tell her something about me that I never revealed to anyone. I wanted to be honest with the girl of my dreams.

"Oh ... should I be concerned?" Candi asked.

"No, not at all, at least not on my account. I need to tell you something that might affect how you think about me."

"I'm listening."

"Well, I hope you will still like me, and this is so hard for me to say."

"What ... are you moving back to Texas?"

"No ... no ... nothing like that. I'm just going to tell you because I love you a lot."

"David, it's okay, I love you a lot too, please just tell me."

"Okay, when I was five years old, I had a major accident that affected my left eye. I can't see out of it. I don't want anyone to know."

"I kind of knew something about it, I overheard one of the coaches. They were talking about you playing the left side as a halfback because you couldn't see out of your left eye."

"Did it bother you, is that why your mom didn't want you to see me?"

"No, not at all. David, you are such a good-looking guy ... I like so many things about you. I'm glad you told me, now you won't have to worry about that."

Candi wanted to know the entire set of details on how it happened and what I went through. That sequence of events are planted pretty clear in my brain. I feel that because those events were so traumatizing and vital, my long term memory stayed sharp over time.

Candi did inform me that several kids at school had asked her, *what's wrong with his eye?* She just responded, *I don't know.* I learned yet another thing about people. Some will never change. I now have in my mind, that people notice the difference in my eyes, I love glasses for that reason. At Woodburn and Gervais, I never had any kid ask me directly about my eye, even when I rubbed it. It bothered me a lot during school.

Sometimes the flesh around the eye would itch so bad that it was hard not to rub it to stop the itching. Several times I accidentally caught my eye and it rotated upward. In the middle of class I would rush out to the bathroom with a pencil. I would use the eraser to move it gently to its original position.

One of my teachers asked me, "What happened, why did you run out of the classroom?" I just responded, "I had something in my eye and it hurt, I got it out."

Anyway, back to the summer with Candi. We started going out every weekend and sometimes we would go swimming in a river or a pond. In Oregon there are so many beautiful areas to swim in – it's unbelievable.

I told Candi about the cannery and how my dad got us all jobs there. We applied and then we received a call in a week or so. I encouraged her to come work there with me. The previous summer she had worked for a dog grooming place that didn't pay well. She agreed and applied at the Stayton Canning Company, at the time, in Brooks, Oregon.

We both started working there the swing shift which paid a little better. My family was moving into the little house on the prairie, as I called it, and we were also working every day. My mom, my dad, Richard, and Louise worked the day shift. I loved picking up Candi at her house for work every day and dropping her off at her house after work.

Sometimes we would go swimming or to a movie before work. I'd give her rides on my brother's motorcycle, or she would introduce me to some Christian youth group adventure. It was nothing like the Catholic Church. I was a little nervous not knowing some of the young kids that attended these trips, but Candi filled me in on what was going on. She definitely shared a lot about Jesus with me. She was not Catholic, she attended an Evangelical church. They studied the Bible at this church according to Candi.

We didn't discuss the difference in religion, and we knew that we both worshipped the same God by comparing Bibles. We let that issue rest and never argued religion, we just knew that we loved each other. I could tell that she was happy and that made me feel great about us.

That summer was one of the best times I had with Candi. Our love for each other just got stronger and I think her parents knew that nothing was going to keep us apart. My parents liked Candi, they thought the world of her.

At Gervais there were a few Hispanics that brought back some bad Texas memories. They would question me, *why are you always with White people and never with Chicanos?* Some even wanted me to play on a Chicano basketball league. I never got caught up in that conversation, I just said, "Have a good day," and I walked away.

Toward the end of summer, we had completed the job duration at the cannery. We both gave our resignation notices two weeks before school started to enjoy the rest of the summer. I also had to start football practice soon.

My savings account grew to about $900.00 – I was going to buy some clothes and I was going to have money for away trips in sports. We had moved into our small house and we had painted the walls and cleaned up the floors. Once again, we had no shower! The housing projects did have a shower, that was heaven to me.

We had no heat in that house, my dad bought a woodstove. I hated that smoke in the mornings when he was getting it started with a match and newspaper. I slept in a small area next to the woodstove on a piece of plywood with a small mattress on it. Diana and Louise shared a small room, and my parents had the other room. Richard slept in a bigger area in the same room as me. Loop was also in the same area with Richard. Gilberto found a place to sleep, he wasn't home much.

My brother Loop started working at Stanton Industries, a furniture builder. My parents both eventually got jobs there and the income was a little bit better than they had experienced in the past.

My brother and I started playing in foosball tournaments for prize money. This was a skill that we both perfected through practicing a lot. Foosball was mega-popular in 1977. We won several tournaments taking home the prize money, and we never placed below third. After high school I went on to play in singles tournaments and eventually was ranked *pro* because of my winnings. There were three levels that I knew of, beginners, novice, and professional. Some tournaments would not allow professionals to enter because of the disadvantage to the beginners and novice. It was a game that I excelled at and was driven to be the best. I could have played foosball all day before getting tired. Foosball became a regular part of my life, I enjoyed it that much. I guess the competition part of it and the money that I won in tournaments was appealing.

Later, this table sport died fast when the video games started evolving. People started losing interest in this manual game, and turned to the sophisticated computer-graphics games. What a summer my brother and I had playing in foosball tournaments – those memories will be in my head forever.

I'll never forget the summer of 1977. Two days before school started my dad bought me a car, it was a 1970 Ford Galaxie 500. It had a white-vinyl top and the body was painted maroon. The front bench seat was an off-white color. The car was fairly large and comfortable. My Grandpa Pedro had it parked in his front lawn for a long time. My dad asked him if he could buy it from him. He sold it to my dad for $150.00 thinking it was broke for good. My dad figured out what the problem was and he fixed it. He gave me the car. Thank you Dad for giving me the first car I ever owned.

During the summer of 1977 I thought about something for a long time, and I wanted to talk to Candi about it before school started. After I drove the car for a bit, I headed toward Waconda Road to pick up Candi. She looked so pretty, a tan and her blonde hair with a reddish tint, looked flawless. I liked the few freckles she had on her cheeks during the summer – so beautiful. I drove her to a place that overlooked the Willamette River. We parked and ate some burgers. Afterwards I worked up the courage to ask her something that I was afraid to ask.

"Candi, you know how much I love you, right?"

"Yes I do."

"Well, I know that this will be my senior year at Gervais."

"You're moving back to Gervais?"

"Yes, we found a house for less rent, but it's a lot older and smaller."

"Who cares, you're moving back to Gervais!"

"Yep, and I will be in school with you and graduate from Gervais."

"That is so exciting!"

"You have no idea how that makes me feel ... which helps my next question."

"What is it?"

"With me getting ready to go to college and all, I mean, Oregon State is looking at offering me a scholarship to play football there and all."

"David, that's great, I know that's important to you."

"Yes, but not more important than you."

"So what are you trying to say?"

"Candi, I bought this bracelet for you to wear if you wish. After we both graduate high school would you marry me?"

"Oh wow, beautiful bracelet ... thank you, David. We're so young ... when we're both out of high school?"

"Yes, definitely ... we would be engaged and no one would know it, just us."

"I think that's a good plan, I wouldn't have to worry about those girls at OSU when you go there – ha-ha!"

"You wouldn't have to worry about that no matter where I go."

"Okay, then my answer is yes, I'll marry you."

Candi and I were engaged shortly before my senior year and no one knew about it, just her and I. I was so excited and relieved at the same time – she said, yes!

Like we agreed, we did wait until we were both out of high school to marry. We had our plan and that made it easier for us to focus on studies and other adventures in our lives. I'm not sure a situation like this would work for other high-school kids, but for us, we were pretty committed and invested as a couple. It just seemed right.

After that we drove back to Woodburn, where I knew about a small carnival at this mini-mall. We had fun with some rides and eating some carnival food. Then we hopped on this ride called, the hammer. What are the odds of us being upside down at the top and the chain breaking on the ride? Wow, I hated that feeling and Candi's head started hurting pretty bad. I kept yelling at the attendants, "Hey, how much longer, my girlfriend's head is really hurting!" They apologized and said they were working as fast as they could. After twenty minutes they finally got us down. When we got off, the attendant looked at us in an apologetic way.

"We'd like to offer you guys two rounds of free riding on the hammer."

"No thank you," we both responded.

That was the first time Candi told me about the headaches she would often get. The doctors always told her it was just a migraine and to take Tylenol. I didn't think anything of it then, but I sure felt bad for even suggesting we ride the hammer. That was the last time we ever rode that ride.

20.

Senior Year at Gervais

It was so hard to believe that I made it to my senior year after that life-changing accident I had when I was five-years old. I knew that some of the Gervais kids were aware of me being a half-blind kid. I never expected to be treated any different. I tried my best to avoid any kind of conversation having to do with my eye. As far as the girl thing, well, Candi knew me and the type of person I was. I knew her and that's all that mattered. If anyone asked her what was wrong with my eye, she would just say, *I don't know.*

I was full of energy and so was Candi. I encouraged her to go out for the volleyball team, the basketball team, and the track and field team. She was shooting the basketball releasing it with two hands the previous year, but this year I worked with her and helped her improve her shooting form. She improved tremendously in just a short time.

I enrolled in an Algebra II class, which consisted of juniors and seniors, just to be in one of Candi's classes. She helped me so much. Algebra was tough for me, but the way she explained the equations to me made it easier. I started enjoying algebra class – thanks to Candi.

I enrolled in an Honors English class, which was like an AP (Advanced Placement) class. I loved writing stories and reading short stories. In this class I learned that my teacher, Gary Everett, saw something in me that no other English teacher had seen before. I was shy and intimidated by smart kids. This class was full of intelligent kids, and with my interest in reading and writing stories, maybe that's why I liked it so much.

Some of my athlete friends that weren't into school studies would have probably laughed at me for having this interest. It was okay because I didn't share that with anyone in high school, except with Candi. I tried to explain mythology to her, but it was the furthest thing she would take interest in. She was impressed by the pictures I drew though. It was just a fun thing for me though, nothing I dwelt on.

In this English class I normally sat back and listened to all of the smart kids that knew each other well. I thought to myself, if I was back in Texas, that would be me with some of my smart friends. I didn't know any of these kids well. I knew Curtis from basketball and I knew Martin from football. I knew Joe, who became one of my good friends in high school. We often played guitar together and sometimes we would run together since he was a long distance runner. I couldn't take Joe in anything more than 800 meters, but I had him in anything shorter than 800 meters – he was fun to workout with, driven just like me.

I would normally sit by Robin, she was an attractive redhead and one of my class friends. Mr. Everett would ask certain individuals questions about complex stories we were assigned to read. He never asked me anything and I was too shy to raise my hand up. One day he asked me, "David, what was the author trying to say?" He caught me by surprise and I saw everyone looking at me quietly. My mind went straight to, *how can I respond to this intelligently?* I was glad that Mr. Everett called on me for the first time. I don't remember what I said, I wish I could, but what I do remember is the teacher gaining confidence in me. I got the impression that I wasn't a stereotypical Hispanic that wasn't into books.

Mr. Everett continued to keep me involved in discussions in any topic during class. I'll never forget the Q&A contest we had on Latin words. There were three kids to a team. My teammates answered a few questions, but because I knew Spanish it was a stronger subject for me. I was a huge help in our victory. We had the most correct answers, and this was in a class of smart kids. Thank you so much, Mr. Everett, for giving me the confidence and taking the time to reach out to a Hispanic kid in a tough English class.

Another teacher that inspired me to strive in the education world and in life, was Mrs. Sue Arndt. She was my personal-finance teacher that had us work on real life situations. It was perfect, because I was secretly engaged to Candi my senior year. We did this mock-marriage project where we pretended to be married to a person in the class. I'm sure I tried to pick the nicest looking girl in class, I just can't remember who she was. Some things I can remember better than others.

Mrs. Arndt was the type of teacher that could relate to me, and to high school kids in general. I think I actually inspired her to start working out again. I'd help her with sports questions she had for me and she'd help me with my financial questions, like saving money, interest, investments, etc. Thank you Mrs. Arndt for teaching me many things about living a good life, I did capitalize on many of your suggestions.

During algebra class, it was always fun when Leslie dropped by and asked if the band could borrow me to play guitar. Sometimes they needed another guitar player. That was so much fun, I'm sure Leslie remembers those times. She was a good guitar player and taught me how to play a few songs. I still remember one of the songs she taught me, "Day Tripper," by the Beatles.

School at Gervais was so much fun for me. It was a diverse school with mostly Hispanics and Caucasians. I don't remember having any African-Americans at Gervais when I attended. We did have a couple of Hawaiians, Bill and Clay. They were my football, basketball, and track and field teammates. The Caucasian population was far larger than the Hispanic population that year.

One of the things I learned from my wealthy friends back in Texas was the importance of a college education if I wanted to live a better life. When I was in Texas I visited some of my friends. Donny was a great friend of mine. I once hung out with him at his house. A beautiful house with nice furniture and a clean and comfortable carpet. He got a mini-bike for Christmas when he was in junior high. I always thought to myself how nice that would be to someday be able to afford things like that.

Johnny M. was another friend that played on one of my basketball teams back in Texas. I went over to his house, a sophisticated brick house. He wanted to hear me play guitar because he was just learning. As I was showing him how to play certain songs, I kept admiring the nice kitchen table and the large hallway leading to the bedrooms. Their entryway was immaculate. I just told myself, *some day I would love to have a nice house*.

My mom taught me about God. I knew there was a God because of her. She also taught me to keep a house clean, no matter how old or how falling-apart it was. She taught me how to display love to a family member. I was around my mom for so many years, I can still hear her caring voice or her firm discipline voice.

Although I was different than my parents in hobbies, personality, goals in life, and other things, the fact is that I learned a lot of great things from them and I could never be thankful enough. It meant so much to me when they showed up to a homecoming game or a senior night, despite the fact that it just wasn't their bag. They did that for me, and it always made my day. I remember my dad wearing overalls during one of my picture days in sports. Every other parent was wearing some nice clothes, some even wore a tie. When I saw my dad in overalls, I just thought to myself, *that's my dad and that's who he is. I'm so proud to be the son of this hard-working man that provided for his family*.

The first part of my senior year I was flying high with confidence. As a junior I had made a huge mark as one of the top athletes in the state. I had everything going and one of the prettiest girls in school would some day be my wife.

Football season was in the air and we were practicing hard. This was the year that my brother and I would be playing halfback together. Since we would be running out of the wishbone formation we would both be on the football field together. My friend Jim was the fullback. Bill was the quarterback and his brother Clay was the backup quarterback. We had a new coach that year, Coach Russ Lynde.

After a few weeks of practice we were ready to go. I was still the kicker and punter, but this year my brother would kick extra points. I was pumped because there would be college scouts coming to watch me kick the football. The college I heard from the most was Oregon State University. Craig Fertig and his assistant coaches were definitely after me.

It was the day before our first game, and we were having a light practice. We were executing a drill where the coach would toss the football, emulating a fumble, and two players would run hard to seize the football and cover it.

I was in a ready stance, and the football was tossed to the grass. I took off quickly and beat my opponent to the football. I was about to land on the ball to cover it with my arm when my cleats caught the grass and forced my ankle to go one way and my entire body a different way. I started screaming in pain. If you've ever torn ligaments around the ankle area, you would know about the excruciating pain it caused.

I lay there for a few minutes, and then I tried my best to walk it off. I couldn't walk, and I kept trying, but my limp got worse. My ankle was loose and it started to swell pretty bad. That moment in time, I was trying to decide what hurt most, my injury or the emotional pain when I would think about the games I would miss with scouts coming to see me?

Depression and frustration was an understatement. I set up an appointment to see the doctor – some clinic in Woodburn. After the doctor examined me, he ordered some X-rays. When the results came back, the good news was that my ankle was not broken. The bad news was that I tore several ligaments around my ankle. The doctor said I was going to be out for several weeks before he could clear me to play again. He also said that ligaments sometimes take longer to heal than broken bones. I didn't need to hear that.

What I didn't know was that when we fall, God is always there to help us rise from that fall, and believe me I prayed for a speedy recovery, but healing was not of the speed I wanted. All I could think about is myself and what I would be missing. I didn't think about my brother getting an opportunity to punt the football in games. I didn't think about Martin, who was the kicker before I came to Gervais. Despite the injury and my falling down emotionally, God was always there for me, He heard my prayers, but at the time I didn't know it.

Psalm 145:14-15 The Lord upholds all who are falling and raises up all who are bowed down. The eyes of all look to you, and you give them their food in due season.

My popularity continued and I received a lot of attention even after my injury. Everyone kept asking me when I was going to be able to play again. My high school sweetheart would hear it all day long too. She was amazing, helping with my books as I hobbled along to each class. That was much appreciated and I thanked her every day.

When we played Jefferson, the coaches from Oregon State University were disappointed when they saw me with crutches on the sideline. It turned out great for my brother, Richard, because he punted the ball well, and it was no surprise to me. I knew how much we practiced together since we were grade-school kids back in Texas. I was happy for him.

The weeks went by and my ankle started healing slowly. It was close to halfway through the season when I finally got to play again. I had lost a lot of practice time – I needed to get back into it. I once again had the opportunity to kick the football.

Before the homecoming game I was stoked that I was nominated for homecoming king. It was me, Mark Sinn, and Martin Jaqua. I was so flattered, I mean, never had I ever been part of a popularity figure of this magnitude at any high school. I thought to myself, *Martin and Mark are pretty well-known at Gervais and they have been here forever.*

How could a poor kid like me, living in an old shack that we rented and being at Gervais less than a year, possibly have a chance to win? I just thought it was amazing that I got nominated.

The homecoming game was amazing! I don't remember who we played or if we even won. What I do remember is Kathy Henry being crowned Homecoming Queen and me voted as her escort, Homecoming King. Wow! This was such an honor. There were so many people happy for us, and there were a few that were mad because I hadn't been at Gervais all four years.

I know that Candi had a friend that complained because her brother wasn't chosen. Well, I didn't do the voting and I didn't feel bad because I was selected. I always tried to be nice to classmates and I always tried hard out on the football field. School activities were fun for me and I tried to help in however I could. I knew that I won based on popularity, I must have done something right that all those students voted for me.

During the homecoming dance, the king and queen were highlighted with their first dance. Candi was jealous. I could relate to her because I would have been the same way if she was in my position. Kathy Henry had a boyfriend as well. While we danced and people took pictures, Kathy looked at me and said, *my boyfriend got jealous when he found out I had to dance with you.* I told her I was dealing with same thing, she just laughed and we kept dancing to the song. I was excited to be done with it and get back to Candi, she was getting jealous and waited for me. Relationships in high school are so tough, but if you make it through like Candi and I did, it's all worth it. The homecoming dance turned out to be a lot of fun.

My ankle started healing better after football season was over. Basketball season was getting started and we would have a new coach. I was hoping to see Coach Sparks back – I liked his coaching style. We acquired Coach Patzer. He was a competitive coach and winning was important to him.

We were looking like a pretty good team and this coach had us doing things that were physical during early practices. One of the drills he had us do was a lot like the fumble drill we did in football. He would toss the basketball on the floor and two players had to dive after it. He made us sacrifice our bodies to scramble for the loose ball. In a game, that's probably what a lot of scrapper players do.

It was my turn to go after the loose ball. Glenn was the other player. We both took off when he tossed the ball. I beat Glenn to the ball, however, he came down on my clavicle (collarbone), and I heard a snap. I couldn't pick up my arm and it was hurting. The coach had me step out while he continued practice. The athletic director, who was Roger Moore, looked at me in the dressing room. I told him it was broke, I heard it crack.

After waiting in the locker room the rest of practice, I was expecting the coach to take me in to get an x-ray. Instead he asked some of the team players if anyone could take me to the doctor. My friend, Bill, volunteered to take me in.

I was trying to hold my arm still on the way to the Woodburn clinic, but every bump made it hurt. When we finally arrived, the doctor ordered some x-rays. I called my parents and told Bill that he could leave now and I thanked him for bringing me. I waited for my parents. I can't recall how or where I had the x-rays done, but the results were not good. I had a clean break on my left clavicle. The doctor gave me a brace that I had to wear for a month. This brace would hold my shoulders back so the bone would come together evenly when healing correctly. I still today have aching problems that come and go in that same area.

I truly don't feel that God gives us more than we can handle, and my faith was tested at an early age. I ran out of the summer money that I saved. Food, gas, clothes, and dates with Candi took up most of it. This freak injury ended my basketball season. This was my favorite sport that I was looking forward to so much during my senior year. My left eye was bothering me a lot, it was hurting and I needed to see an ophthalmologist. And to add one more level of emptiness, my family had just been literally robbed.

A few days prior to my injury, we had just arrived from the grocery store. The back door was wide open. Someone broke in and stole a rifle, some clothes, my dad's briefcase, and a few other items. They didn't take all of the clothes, some were laid out on our kitchen table. This was scary and the first time I had ever been in a situation where we got robbed. Who would want to steal from us? We were one of the poorest families in town. My dad and brothers chased after the robbers but could not catch them. They took off running on the backside and it was too dark to see anything. My dad called the police and reported it. We never recaptured any of our items. I'm pretty sure these robbers were pretty disappointed, because we didn't have much. Whatever we had was bought pretty cheap.

My mom and dad were stressed that night, but there was nothing they could do. The one thing I remember my dad saying was, *the important thing is that we are all safe, those are just things we can buy again.* I think he was right. He fixed the back door with a stronger lock and left the outside light on all night. Even to this day I leave my outside house lights on at night.

Back to my injury. I took some painkillers that the doctor prescribed for a day or two, but after that I stopped taking them. I did not like taking pills. The doctor did advise me to only take them if I was dealing with unbearable pain.

Sleeping was difficult and I was tired. I was used to rolling over on my stomach, but with the brace I was unable to do that. I did manage to fall asleep when I found a comfortable position. That night, I felt something within my entire body driven to my heart area. A bright light and a warm sensation that made me feel like it was Jesus telling me that everything would be okay. Candi explained to me many things about Jesus and how people would experience different things. I had a tough time convincing myself that what I'm about to tell you was a dream.

After that night I woke up in the morning and my attitude was more positive. I was still a little down, but I kept thinking about what Jesus went through and the sacrifices he made for us. At church every Sunday I would see the cross, and that morning a few things about Jesus came together for me.

I stayed home two weeks, I was getting behind on my schoolwork, and I was getting bored at home doing nothing. We didn't have a TV, however, my older brother and sister would be home sometimes, since they were both attending Chemeketa Community College.

After my second week of bondage, I got so bored that I decided to play a game with my brother and sister. We placed an empty can against the wall. The torn parts of our floor were visible and looked dirty since the floor had not been mopped in awhile. We ate oranges that day and decided to use the peelings to toss into the can. We were keeping score and laughing. It was nice that I could do something fun with my right arm.

I heard a knock on the front door, I didn't have a shirt on, it was much easier with my brace to not wear one. My brother and sister ran to the other room and shut the door! Oh great, I walked over to answer the door and to my surprise, it was Ella and the entire squad of the Gervais cheerleaders. I thought to myself, *what the heck?* I did not expect that at all.

That was my first ever cheerleader visit in anything. I didn't know whether to feel embarrassed or to be flattered by the visit. They brought me a box of oranges. Ella was my neighbor and her dad was our landlord. They lived about a quarter mile away.

I told them, *wow what a nice visit, I'd offer you guys a seat but we don't have one.* We only had a small bed in the living room. They came to cheer me up, I guess they were cheerleaders, right? We talked for a while, I gave them the whole scoop on my collarbone and when I was expected to return to school.

They encouraged me to hang in there and they also said that I was missed at the games. When they left, I thanked them for coming and then I went back to my bed and felt like crawling in a hole and never coming out. To have five Caucasian girls, some that were wealthy, come into our low-income rental, was so embarrassing to me. I guess on the bright side, we had more orange peelings to continue playing our game.

I now more than ever, wanted to someday get my college degree and chase after a job that paid well for my future. If Candi and I ever had kids, I would not want them to go through what I did.

My senior year, athletic-wise, was a total nightmare that I did not expect. I did not continue practicing with the team, but I did watch the practices on the sideline all season long. I was able to spend time watching Candi play basketball during the boys' away games. I cleared it with the coach and I did not travel with the team my senior year. I did manage to play in the last game of the season. It was nice to get a standing cheer from the crowd when I started that game. I managed to play half of the game as I was not in shape from sitting out so long.

The Oregon State coaches stopped calling me when they heard about my injuries. That was disappointing, because I was looking forward to kicking for Oregon State. My principal, Mr. Ingles, was calling some Universities for me. He kept telling me that I needed to play college football, there were still colleges like, OCE (Oregon College of Education), that were interested in me. He was right because during the spring I drove to OCE for a recruiting trip. That same college is now called Western Oregon University, located in Monmouth, Oregon.

It was cool, they had a student there show me the college and then feed me lunch at their cafeteria. After lunch, I was taken to the head coach's office. We talked and he said a lot of nice things about me. He watched me my junior year at Gervais and was impressed. Before I left, they offered me a full scholarship, including room and board, to play football and to be a bilingual teacher. I know that anyone in their right mind would have jumped at this chance. What a generous offer and opportunity to play football.

I told the coach I wanted to think about this for a few days. I was still exploring other options. The Gervais coach had called OSU and they wanted me to come down to kick for them so they could watch me before offering anything. We scheduled a visit with them for the spring.

In the meantime the track and field season was beginning. I was weak and had lost some muscle strength, I had half the season to train and make it to state in the high jump or hurdles. I knew Mark from Central would be back this year, he was a great hurdler. There was also Mike Swanson, the other hurdler that was better than I was. I had my work cut out, but with my lack of training all year, it was going to be a tough challenge. We also didn't have the nice facilities that I had at Woodburn the previous year. I was just going to do the best I could.

At the Happy Rock Relays, which were held in Gladstone, Oregon, I was part of a record-setting discus relay. The discus was not one of my best events, but I was the third best thrower for Gervais. There was Martin, my brother Richard, and then me. We broke the meet record for the discus relay. Our combined total, I believe, still exists as the record today. There was no high jump or hurdles since it was a relay meet.

I took the first-place trophy in the high jump at the Willamette Invitational and at the Meet of Champions. My jumps were not as good as the previous year due to my injuries that set me back. I still managed to get over 6' 0" and sometimes 6' 1".

At the district meet, I failed to qualify for state, I couldn't get over 6' 2". One person cleared 6' 2" and one other person had less misses than I did at 6' 1". So I took third just missing state by one place. In the hurdles I placed third by a tenth of a second. I was down after those two heartbreaking results.

I went over and sat on a bench away from everyone and tears started running down my face. I didn't want to talk to anyone, it didn't seem fair to me, I was supposed to be the top high jumper in my district my senior year. Susie Breshears, a high jumper and hurdler from Woodburn, came over and sat next to me. She was a talented athlete and was favored as well.

"Well Espinoza, we can both sit on this fish bench."

"You didn't make it either?"

"Nope, I hit the bar with my heels all three times."

"I tore ligaments in my ankle and I broke my collarbone this year."

"I had no idea, it didn't look like you when I saw you high jumping."

"That's the way it goes sometimes."

"I'm really sorry, Espinoza."

"Yeah, thank you. I'm really sorry for you too."

Susie was one of the girls that I worked out with in Woodburn. We had to share the high jump pit at times. We often just hung around and talked too. She was a fun practice partner along with Needham, a high-jump friend who I helped at Woodburn. Needham had that drive to get better at the high jump. I helped him with the technique. The Woodburn days flashed through my mind as I sat there with Susie. The funny thing is that despite my failures due to injuries, I was still glad to be at the high school where I would see my high-school sweetheart every day. The few friends that I made at Gervais for just that short amount of time was a self-esteem builder and a priceless memory.

It was tough moving so much. As a kid I never felt like I established friendships that would last a lifetime. I envy, and am happy for people that have those friends that know them like a brother or a sister. They went to school together the entire twelve years.

With me it was always a challenge to have that kind of friendship with anyone. Not only because of my inconsistencies in residence, but also because of my appearance, especially my younger days. I think many kids were nice to me because that's how they were raised, to be nice to kids that are different. In reality, it has to be the individual kid's choice to want to be someone's real friend. I was okay with it, I understood. I had gone through much worse growing up and facing many bullies that were a lot bigger than I was.

I was proud of the mark that I left in Dimmitt, Texas, as one of the best punter-kickers that played varsity football. At Moses Lake, Washington, though I never played in a game with the team, I impressed the coaches there while practicing for one week before moving to Oregon. At Gervais I was the Capital Conference All-League Kicking Specialist, and record holder of a discus relay. At Woodburn I set a new high-jump school record at 6' 3" and a personal best in the hurdles at 15.7.

I didn't want to feel too depressed about my performance at the district meet when I was sitting there on the bench with Susie. My coaches, Hal Mugass and Gary Everett, told me that I had nothing to feel bad about. One of them said that placing third place in two events was amazing and he was proud of the comeback I made after my injuries that year.

I also ran the third leg of the 4 X 100 relay. We didn't advance to state, but we competed well. It was Richard, my brother, that ran the first leg, Julio Najera ran the second leg, I ran the third leg, and Jeff Bell ran the anchor. Jeff and Richard were pretty close in speed.

I knew nothing about the kind of love God had for me. We all fall and we all rise at different times in our lives. We all have challenges, they are different for everyone. I overcame so many obstacles during my grade school, junior high, and high-school days. I didn't do it alone, Jesus was right there next to me guiding me, even when I didn't know it. Jesus always put something in front of me to help me rise from the failure.

My senior year should have been the best year. I was even nominated to be class president of the student body at the beginning of the year. It came down to three finalist and we all had to make a speech in front of the juniors and seniors. The three finalists elected were Rick Klampe, Myself, and Pat Lederer. Pat probably gave the most entertaining speech out of the three. Rick gave the most experienced speech, he had served the previous term. I hate to even mention how unprepared I was. I think that day I learned the importance of preparing for a speech. I'll never forget the opportunity I had to possibly become class president. It was my own fault for not preparing. In simple terms, it was just a living-nervous nightmare and a valuable lesson for me. After that day I always made sure to prepare for any kind of speaking I would do.

Candi and I did not go to the junior-senior prom. I just didn't have the money for an expensive meal and I guess it just wasn't that big of a deal for me or Candi. We just went for a drive to Wheatland Ferry and then to eat at a small restaurant. It was great quality time for both of us and we had a chance to talk about our future together. She would have one more year of high school.

I enjoyed listening to her that night. She told me some facts about the Wheatland Ferry that I did not know. Pretty fascinating stuff. Its primary service was to get a few cars across the river. The cars were on top of this wooden deck. It had a generator on board for power. The ferry also had cables that pulled it across the river and then pulled it back returning to its original location – cars loaded up on both sides of the Willamette River.

The next day I was asked if I was willing to perform at graduation with my friends, Joe Dasso, Greg Leach, and Mark Sinn. I jumped at that opportunity. We practiced regularly to prepare for Graduation. I asked Robin Clark if she would walk at graduation with me. She was the redhead in my Honors English Class. She said yes and I was so glad because I didn't want to be one of those students that walked alone down that aisle.

There were several senior activities that occurred working up to graduation day. There was a senior skip day, but I chose to not participate in that. I wasn't into the social scene that much. I was more of a small-group type person. I did however go to a chaperoned senior party after the graduation ceremony.

Graduation night was one to conclude my high school education. It was a beautiful setting with flowers and decorations everywhere. The theme was, "May Our Yesterdays Light the Way to Tomorrow". I had a royal blue cap and gown and it was hot in there. During our performance of, "Friends," by John Denver, my glasses started sliding off and I kept reaching up to keep them on while playing the guitar. Luckily I wasn't doing the singing. Joe and I were playing the guitar while Greg and Mark were doing the singing. It was fun and I was honored that they asked me to be part of the show.

My parents were there, up in the bleachers. I was so happy for my mom, and I can't imagine what she must have been feeling when she saw her son receiving a high school diploma. She had spent so much time with me, from way back in the Texas days, to now sitting there watching me become a high-school graduate. Thank you Mom and Dad for taking such good care of me. And thank you God for loving me and guiding me even when I didn't know it.

The chaperoned senior party was held at Lydia Ruiz's house. I hung out with Candi and my family and then I went over to Candi's house and hung out with her family for awhile. By 11:00 p.m. I asked Candi if I should go to the senior party. She said, "Yes, go hang out with your senior class, you may not see them again for a long time." I got her blessing to go, so I did.

There were all kinds of desserts laid down on the table. When I asked the parents if they had some milk, they looked at me funny and said, "You want milk?" I said, "Yes, I always drink milk with cookies and pie." I think it must be a southern thing or something. There was music playing and graduates dancing. I was talking sports with some of the guys while eating cookies and drinking milk. I remember dancing with Ella Harper, she was our landlord's daughter and one of our cheerleaders.

That was a time in my life that I did like a few girls in my senior class, but my heart told me that Candi was the one for me. Ella asked me if I wanted to dance. So I did and we talked while we danced. She knew that I was Candi's boyfriend. What she didn't know is that I liked her as a friend, just like Robin Clark from my English class. Because I was secretly engaged to Candi, I didn't feel right dancing with Ella Harper, although it was nice.

So after that dance, I said my goodbyes and I left. It just seemed fitting and right to not stay there too long.

As I got into my car, I had a sad feeling. I would miss high school and the friends that I made. I would miss the game nights with the football-field lights shining as I watched my punts or kicks go past them. I would miss my teachers that were such an impact on my education. I would miss the camaraderie with my teammates. I would miss the pep assemblies and fun school activities. Never had I ever dreamed of being selected to be one of the hottest guys to be auctioned for a fundraiser. Never had I dreamed of being selected to participate in a donkey basketball game until I came to Gervais. I found a way to overcome and to somehow be recognized as someone that stood out, someone that people looked up to and respected. I overcame huge obstacles, despite my physical imperfection – my blind eye. God was with me even when I didn't know it.

I was so proud of holding the honor of Homecoming King while escorting Homecoming Queen Kathy Henry 1977-1978. I was so proud of playing one of the halfbacks in football with my brother – we both worked so hard for that. I was so proud of making it to the final two on a disco-dance contest with my high-school sweetheart.

I was so thankful and felt so honored that the senior class voted me, a kid that used to be a nobody, the *Most Considerate* of the senior class of 1978. I held my head up with pride and felt thankful for those students. I thought to myself, *my parents did something right in the values they instilled in me and the love they displayed towards me*. Most importantly, God was with me and I was starting to believe it one year at a time.

I considered myself to be a lucky guy, because when I met Candi I never thought a beautiful girl like her would ever be interested in a poor-half-blind Hispanic like me. Gervais High School was the high school that I believe God put right in front of me and allowed me to make choices – I think I did okay.

The best thing that ever happened to me at this high school was meeting the love of my life. I had never loved anyone as much as I grew to love Candi. My passion for her was so strong at times that my stomach would hurt when I couldn't be with her –

that's how strong it was. My proudest moment with Candi was when she didn't give up on me despite her mom wanting to split us up. I was at peace and I was engaged.

21.

Tough Decisions

After graduation day all of the seniors were gone from the school. The underclassmen had to continue for another week or so before they could exit school. I was about to travel to Oregon State University for a recruiting trip. I was excited about kicking and punting for the coaches there. I had never driven farther than Salem on my own so I was a little nervous about this trip. OSU resides in Corvallis, Oregon, between Salem and Eugene – about a forty-five minute drive.

I arrived there and parked where I was instructed to, close to Parker Stadium, which was the name back in 1978, now it's called Reser Stadium. I walked to the locker room and encountered this lineman that was about 6' 9" and 280 lbs. I looked up at him.

"Howdy," I said.

"What's up man?"

"Could you tell me where I could find Coach Fertig?"

"You must be the kicker huh?"

"Yes, I'm here on a recruiting trip."

"Great man, Coach will be here in a few minutes."

"Okay, thank you."

I was waiting for the coach while I watched some linebackers and linemen lift weights. It was scary how much bigger these guys were than the high school kids I played with. I could bench press around 250 lbs. at the time, but these guys were doing repetitions with 300 lbs. It was nerve-racking to think that I would be playing with guys this size. Thankfully I would just be the kicking specialist if they still wanted me.

One of the assistant coaches came in and introduced himself. He also brought a linebacker with him, who happened to be his son and a key player for the next year's team. Head Coach Craig Fertig did not show up. The assistant was to handle my tryout and recruiting trip.

We went out to a practice field and I started out with a few punts. The coach did insist on me punting easy the first few times to warm up. He knew about my injuries during the high-school season. I'd say that my punting and kicking went pretty well, but I wasn't 100% quite yet. I still managed to get some great kicks in.

The coach was impressed with what he saw. He explained that they had a senior that was the kicker, and this year would be his last year. He said he liked what he saw and encouraged me to enroll at OSU. So I told him I would do that. We talked about many things, some that I didn't understand. This was all new to me, and to be honest I was a little lost on the Division I college scene.

"David, you are an amazing kid that has talent."

"Thank you, sir."

"I talked to Coach Fertig, and here's what we decided, we want to offer you a walk-on spot for your freshman year as a Beaver. We want to work with you the first year, and then we will offer you a full ride the last three years."

"Coach, I don't know if I can afford a school like this."

"Have you tried applying for financial aid?"

"No, I don't even know what that is."

"Go talk to one of our college counselors, they can help you."

"Okay, thank you for your time, Coach."

"Oh, thank you, David. I wish you the best of luck and maybe we'll see you this fall."

His son took me to eat and we talked about many college things. He showed me where the counselor offices were. Visiting OSU was such a fun and eye-opening experience. I never knew how much there was to college athletics.

When I returned home, I called Candi immediately and asked her for some advice on this situation. I wouldn't get a scholarship until the following year. I didn't like the financial bind my family was in and I wanted a better future for myself career-wise, even after sports. I didn't want to live a life like my parents did struggling from week to week.

Candi talked to her parents about my situation. They were educated people, both teachers and intelligent. I knew that from spending a lot of time around them. They took us to the coast often and we'd walk on the beach. Those were some fun times, I'm so thankful they invited me along. They had a small cabin about five blocks from Gleneden Beach at the Oregon coast. I asked them questions about different topics at the dinner table or at barbecues outside. I basically picked their brain for my own knowledge.

Candi told me that whatever I decided was okay with her, but it had to be enrolling in college somewhere, even if it had to be at Chemeketa Community College – a two-year school.

The following week, I drove to Oregon State University with my brother, Gilberto, who was interested in the ROTC (Reserve Officers' Training Corp) program there. He attended Chemeketa the previous year, but just exploring subjects. It was soon after our OSU trip that he decided to enlist in the Air Force. I would never see my brother again for a long time. He did help me get my student identification card to be a Beaver, I was thankful for that since I didn't know what I was doing.

My eye was not a problem as I had seen a doctor in Salem, the cleaning was a huge help and it kept me going on my college introduction experience. I wasn't thinking about anyone making fun of me, and most of the people that I talked to were educated and mature. I started feeling normal and my confidence was building up slowly.

I felt that I was going to be playing football at OSU. I know that I should have been jumping up with joy, but after talking to the counselor that wanted me to take 19 credits for the first term, well, that scared me. I knew how tough it was to pass challenging high-school classes. I was looking at the medical field or the engineering field.

I knew how difficult it was for me to learn things. I was stressing over the entire concept of Oregon State University. The counselor also told me that classes were not thirty or forty kids, they were as large as an auditorium. He said with football practices, meetings, and away trips, I would have to find study time.

I had just received a downward-emotional lesson. I was worried about the studies, could I possibly pass 19 credits in one term? Most athletes take 12 credits during the season, is what I would hear.

My next stop was the financial aid office. I applied by filling out a ton of papers. I thought to myself, *no wonder people don't go to college, this is a lot of work and I haven't seen summer yet.*

In a few days, I received a letter from the financial aid department. It wasn't good news. My parents landed a job working for Stanton Industries, a furniture builder. They were working on an assembly line and the money was a little better than the cannery work. My brothers and my sister, Louise, were also working there.

This affected the amount of money I would get for college. I was short a few thousand. I had already applied at OSU and was accepted, I had my student card with my picture on it.

That Sunday at church I remember praying to God. I asked my heavenly Father to show me the way, I was lost on what to do about my college decision.

The next week I went to Chemeketa and talked to the counselors there. They told me that I could attend college there and not pay a penny. I could live with my parents and financial aid could pay for my school. They even told me that I could possibly receive a living-expense check every month based on my poverty-income level.

My dad wanted me to join the family at Stanton Industries and to bypass college. He told me that it was a waste of time and that I needed to help out with the family. I had my disagreements with my dad and I guess I understood where he was coming from. He had seen Louise and Gilberto attend college and nothing positive as far as a job had come out of that. I tried to explain to him that I was going to earn a degree in a job that would pay me good money. I don't think he believed me and it was tough for me to make a decision without his blessing. I loved my dad, he sacrificed so much for me, but this time I had to go against the grain. I was old enough and ready to start making my own decisions.

I passed on the offer at Oregon State University. I enrolled at Chemeketa Community College in the fall of 1978. My plan was to take 12 or 14 credits a term, and to search for a career while taking different classes. Writing was a must, I enjoyed that too much and would eventually need it. I was frustrated because I knew I had the potential to be a professional football player.

My long-term plan was to have an open tryout with the Seattle Seahawks. The message I got from them was to play college football and rack up some stats, or try to get into a minor-league professional team. That was another way I could get stats. Then I could give them a call and set up a tryout since I didn't have an agent. For a young kid like me that was learning so much, my priority was to get a good job that would start providing for Candi and I, because I was going to marry her after she graduated high school.

Candi was in full support of my decision and at the same time she knew how bad I wanted to play college football. She also knew about my struggles with my dad about enrolling to attend college instead of going to work.

"David, look at the bright side, I'll get to see you more."

"That is true, and I can still look for opportunities in a minor league."

"Yes, that's true," Candi smiled.

When I started college it was different, but it was a good different to me. I had been to so many different schools and I spent a lot of time by myself. This was a blessing in disguise because it made college easier for me. With college it was another similar experience. The first year flew by so fast, I looked at several careers. I thought about the medical field, but realized how many years of school the high-paying positions required. That was a simple, *I don't think so.*

I went to a counselor and asked him about high-paying jobs and the required years it would take me to graduate and get a job. All he talked about was the computer field. He ensured me that computer science was the way of the future and that there was a demand for COBOL programmers.

In the final term of my first college year, I enrolled taking a couple introduction classes in the computer science field. I took data processing and I took keypunch operating. In 1979 there were no online tools to key in data. We used cards in a keypunch machine. These cards were ran through a compiler and then generated information would come out on a printed piece of paper.

I liked typing class and I had developed those skills already. A career in computer science is what I was looking for. Two more years of school and I'd earn my associates degree in computer science. The first year I had completed taking all of my electives, and I could focus on just the program classes the next two years. I would be able to get a job soon after that. That was my plan, it felt right and I went for it. As far as football, I could keep training to work on getting stronger, I still had that dream of kicking for a professional football team.

God was with me, there was no doubt. I prayed every night before falling asleep. I learned that God answers prayers in His timing not on ours. I knew a little more about God, but I didn't have a relationship with Jesus. I understand the Trinity ... God the Father, God the Son (Jesus), and God the Holy Spirit. When I refer to Jesus, I'm referring to God in flesh, He walked on earth and on water. Jesus is there right next to us in spirit. He hears us when we talk to Him. During this time of my life, I did not talk to Jesus much. It's amazing that despite that, He still loved me and had my back in many challenges throughout my life.

The next two years of college would be a mental grind of studying every night. For me, computer languages didn't come easy, I had to study hard and I had to ask a lot of questions to the instructors. When I learned something, I retained it well. During the summer after Candi graduated, we worked at the cannery to save money for food, gasoline, clothes, and entertainment. Candi and I would be working at the cannery for our final summer. We both got drained with the boredom of that job.

We announced our engagement before she enrolled at Chemeketa Community College. Our secret was no longer a secret and everyone was happy for us. All of my brothers and sisters were overjoyed. I can't speak for Candi's family, but I knew they were supportive of us.

Candi decided to give computer programming a chance as well. She was bright and could figure out the coding pretty fast. We worked on several assignments together. It was fun for me, but Candi was thinking she didn't like programming. She wanted to change her major to become a teacher some day. I supported her on this while I continued with my computer science classes.

It was not easy coming home and watching my family in Gervais. They were tired from working all day. My brother had joined the family at Stanton Industries. I was the only one going to college and expanding my education. I had trust in what the counselor told me about computer science. The instructors confirmed his words about this field and the job security in the future. I was tired of watching my parents go from job to job. I didn't want to live a life like that.

I studied hard until past midnight sometimes, while I heard the breathing of my family as they slept all night to wake up early in the morning for work. It was tough listening to some of my brothers and sisters tell me that I should go to work at Stanton Industries. And my dad, when he was in a bad mood, he would let me know his thoughts on my waste-of-time going to college.

I explained to him that I wasn't paying for my school and that I got living-expense checks from financial aid. I think he felt that I should be contributing like the rest of the family. My mom would talk to me when my dad wasn't around.

"David, don't listen to your daddy, you keep going with college. Education is important. You don't want to end up like us."

"Thanks, Mom. I'm glad you see how important this is. All of my rich friends in Texas had parents that went to college. That's why they have great jobs."

"I know mi hijo, I understand. We're doing okay now, and the rent is only $75.00 a month."

I was so glad I had my mom encouraging me. She was such a blessing to me. I thought of the days when I had that accident at five-years old. She spent hours with me at St. Anthony's Hospital.

She spent hours with me at doctor clinics. She attended to my intense medical needs that kept my eye flesh from getting infected. I didn't know how she did it with five others kids to keep up with. God was with me even when I didn't know it.

While I was attending college I took a little break to experience the beginning of a wonderful life with a special person. Candi and I were married on December 6th, 1980, one day from the anniversary of the war at Pearl Harbor. I think this kept our marriage from a war – ha-ha! We bought a pretty decent single-wide mobile home from her Grandma Alice. The home was on her grandparent's farmland. It was brown with almond-colored stripes and looked new inside. We were beginning our life together and it sounded great to us. I had never seen such a big smile on her face.

Before we got married the priest met with us a few times for some counseling sessions. Candi was an evangelical and I was a Catholic. He specifically explained to us, that as long as we didn't argue religion, we would be fine.

The evening of our wedding day, after a long tiring day, we drove to the Oregon Coast, where we would spend our honeymoon. We stayed at the Cover's cabin. Candi's sisters had snuck their way into her suitcase. I have never been the type of person that was into pulling pranks on people. They filled up her suitcase with birdseed. When she opened it, all of the seed dropped everywhere and if I can recall correctly, she said, "I'm going to kill my sisters!" I wasn't too happy about that, but now that I think about it, I guess it was their culture to do stuff like that at the expense of someone else.

When we returned from our honeymoon, again, another prank. We found newspapers all over inside the cabinets and in the rooms of our mobile home. I can't believe how much work they put into this prank. I felt a little better knowing it was going to be easier cleaning it up than what they went through. If you ever get married, don't ever leave your keys alone anywhere.

Candi and I had debates on which church we should attend. I heard her case and she heard my case. I explained to Candi that if she wanted to continue going to her church, that was something I would have to accept and live with. I told her I was going to continue going to the Catholic Church and would love for her to join me. She was doing a lot of thinking because there were many things that she didn't understand about the Catholic religion. She would try to explain to me the differences and how she didn't totally agree with some of the Catholic rules. I was so bullheaded that I didn't do any kind of research on what she was trying to tell me. I wish I could have that moment back.

Candi's sisters were not too happy with me, because they thought I had influenced her to start going to the Catholic Church. Candi did inform me that she talked to her sisters and explained to them that it was her choice to start going to the Catholic Church. She wanted to be with her husband. It was great, because I could now listen to what she was telling me about the rules she didn't agree with. One of them in particular was praying to the Virgin Mary.

Candi's answer to her sisters was solid. Since one of her sister's husband didn't attend church at all, she simply just said, *I love my husband, and on Sundays, he goes to church with me.* That was the end of that conversation.

We often had our talks and discussions about religion and the differences. We never argued and we listened to each other open-minded.

"Candi, I don't pray to Mary, I never understood why we do that. I was raised Catholic and what I don't agree with I just toss out. I pray to God."

"Well, that's what my church does, we pray to Jesus."

"We aren't allowed to go to another church, I was told it was a sin," I said.

"David, I don't understand that at all, but how about I start reading the Bible to you every night?"

"Every night?"

"Yes, I'll go to your Catholic Church and all I ask is that I can read you the Bible every night."

"Okay, sounds like a good compromise."

"I love you, the important thing is that we are together finally."

"You are so special to me," I said looking into her eyes.

"Ditto." She reached over and kissed me.

We were in agreement with our beliefs and we would go on to attend the Catholic Church on Sundays. She did start reading the Bible to me consistently, maybe not every night, but at least three to four times a week.

My college experience was phenomenal! I joined the track and field team, my coach was Ed Ford. He was a coach that had a passion for track and field and he remembered me from my high school days. In my early college years I was practicing with the team. We had to drive out to Willamette University to practice the high jump – they had a nice high-jump pit. I practiced the hurdles at the Chemeketa track.

This was not working out for me because the amount of time I spent training was taking time away from my studies. I know there are students that can do sports and studies at the same time in college. For me, I was enrolled in some pretty tough classes and I wanted to focus on them. My passion at the time was to graduate with a college degree for a high-paying job and to play professional football at some point. I eventually talked to the coach and informed him that I would discontinue my track and field career at Chemeketa. Ed tried to encourage me to stay on, I could tell he was disappointed that I was quitting the team.

During basketball season I was taking a basketball class as an elective. The teacher was Rick Adelman, who also happened to be the men's basketball head coach at the time. He approached me and gave me some compliments on how well I played. In that class we just played basketball games the entire hour – a fun class. We would drive to the Salem Armory, which is where the Chemeketa games were played in 1980. Rick asked, *why don't you come out to our tryouts this year? I would really like to have you on our team – you shoot the ball extremely well.* That was a huge compliment from Rick, who years later became the head coach of the Portland Trailblazers, an NBA team.

As much as I loved basketball, I was too short at only 6' 0" and not quick enough to ever make it to the NBA. I just wanted to have fun playing one of my favorite games. My studies were too important and I was the type of kid that needed that time to study. The sport I had potential in was football, and Chemeketa did not have a football team that I could kick for.

Attending Chemeketa was not only educational, but I was also exposed to many foreign students that I got to know from hanging out with them at the student-union building during lunchtime. There were all sorts of activities for college students. Sometimes the college would bring a band in to perform in the quad area at the center of campus or inside the student union. There was a ping-pong table, a pool table, and a foosball table. I mastered the skill set to become a great player at all three games.

Foosball was my game, and at this point I was still a novice player. In the second year of college I decided to enter the tournament on all three recreational games. The winners in each category would advance with an all-expense-paid trip to Washington State University in Pullman, Washington. I was so pumped for this. In one year's time, I was one of the best ping-pong players, the best pool player, and the best foosball player. All because of my willing to learn the techniques of each game and master them during lunchtimes.

I won first place in the billiards tournament. I won first place in the foosball tournament – singles and doubles. My partner in doubles was Nick. I placed third in ping pong behind some amazing ping pong players. The coordinator asked me which game I wanted to advance on because I would not be able to compete in two. They would all be played in different buildings at the Northwest Regional Championships of CCs. I decided to go with foosball, my favorite recreational game.

The trip was so much fun. I kept calling Candi and I would give her updates on what I was doing and explained to her how big Washington State University was. I had never seen foosball players as good as what I saw at the championships. I was so used to clobbering everyone at Chemeketa. I realized that there was always someone better somewhere else. I ended up taking 5th place in singles. I was ranked number five in the northwest, which was a pretty high honor.

Candi and I continued to struggle financially. I was on my last year of college and she decided to stop going to college and apply for a job for the State of Oregon. She landed a job for the Employment Department. She would work to keep us going with the mobile-home payment and food while I studied hard to complete my degree.

It was challenging for both of us. She would come home tired and I would come home from school tired from studying. We had our good days and bad days, but we never went to bed angry. She started explaining many things about the Old Testament and the New Testament. She told me before that the way you get into heaven is by *accepting Jesus as our Savior*. I don't know why I forgot that message for the next several years. She witnessed to me many times before we went to bed. I heard her reading scripture after scripture. Later in my life I heard some of those scriptures and recalled her words.

God placed Candi right in front of me in Oregon. I made that choice to start talking to her in a P.E. class. She was the best thing that ever happened to me. And now this wonderful young lady was my wife. I felt like I was already in heaven.

We did everything together. We traveled to the coast on weekend vacations. It was cool that her parents owned a cabin there – we used it free of charge. We often had a fire going down on the beach ... we'd cook some hotdogs or hamburgers. She introduced me to something called S'mores, which is Hershey's chocolate, marshmallows, and Graham crackers. We went looking for shells on the beach. To this day, when I'm at the beach, it always reminds me of the fun times we had during our newlywed days.

We also went to gatherings with her side of the family and my side of the family. That was another adventure. Whose house and what day and time? We somehow made it work. The holidays were challenging, but it was always fun.

During this time, as for many years, I would go fishing with my brother, Richard. We fished together many years, even back in Texas at some small ponds that were stocked with fish. In Oregon there were many places to fish. I recall going to the Canby ponds, the Willamette River, Diamond Lake, and the Oregon City Falls. At the falls we normally fished for salmon. We would walk down this mountain to get to a dock where all of the anglers would stand and cast their lines with a hook, and then reel it back slowly in hopes that a salmon would be attracted to the bait. My brother talks about how those were his best days spending time with me. I agree with him, it was nice not to argue over a foul playing one-on-one in a basketball game.

I remember the last time we went fishing at the Oregon City Falls. There was some kind of a mill company there. They were holding a strike and the angry workers didn't want anyone around. We had no knowledge of what was going on. As we were fishing on the dock, we started hearing these large boulders splashing next to us on the water. The strikers made it pretty clear that they didn't want us around there at all, so we left and never returned after that scary day.

When I graduated from Chemeketa with an associates degree in computer science, I chose not to walk at the commencement. The cap and gown were too expensive and we needed the money to survive. No one in my family seemed to care about how big of a deal it was for me to have a college degree in a professional field that was booming. I was the first in my family's generation to graduate from college with a meaningful degree. I took that with great pride.

When I told my mom, she was super happy for me. I can't recall what my dad's thoughts were. When I was living with my family at Gervais on Highway 99E in that small shack, I would work on my homework for hours. My brother walked by on the way to his room many times and said things like, *sure glad I don't have to do homework anymore.* I'm sure he remembers how many hours I spent studying, not counting my brainwork at the college, lab work, meetings, early-morning cram sessions – I could write a long list.

I started looking for a job right away. Candi was so excited because it meant that she could quit her job and start her education to someday become a teacher. She wanted to be a kindergarten teacher, she liked teaching the little kids. She couldn't quit her job until I was hired. I applied at many places and finally started getting some interviews.

I was ready, I had my resume and what I thought would land me a job. One summer I even worked as an intern for minimum wage to be able to count that as paid experience. This experience would be a great addition to my resume.

Every interview I got called for was discouraging, the answer was always, *we're looking for someone with more experience*. All of my interviewers were managers that were Caucasian, except for one, she was a Latina lady. I thought that since I was Hispanic she might hire me. I remember the state agency, it was the Public Utility Commissioner. I thought, *this is it, this could be my opportunity*.

I received a letter the following week telling me that they offered the position to someone else. I was so mad, I crimpled up the piece of paper and I threw it at the TV. Candi looked at me and said, "David, keep trying, something will come up, be patient."

I was almost in tears, she always found a way to cheer me up. She said, *let's go get some dessert somewhere*. She knew a hot apple pie with vanilla ice cream would always cheer me up. She would often make me a batch of chocolate chip cookies. Candi was one of the best at baking.

The weeks went by and we were living on a tight budget. I felt so bad because Candi helped put me through school. One day, she arrived from work. I cooked some food for us. A candle was a great idea to place on the table. I had a long talk with her.

"Thank you for this nice dinner, David. I didn't know you were a cook."

"Ha-ha! I'm not, it was difficult."

"Ha-ha!"

"Candi, I'm thinking about going to work with my family at Stanton Industries."

"Your dad's gonna say, I told you so."

"I know I'm prepared to hear it from him. I'm not giving up though. I'm still going to keep applying. I applied in Portland today."

"That's good, I agree, something will happen, Jesus is watching out for us."

"Yeah, well, I wish he'd get some binoculars to watch us a little closer."

"David, it will happen, you'll see."

"Okay, I'll keep at it."

"By the way, I have some news," Candi said.

"What news?"

"We're going to have a baby," she smiled.

"Oh wow, really!"

"Yes, really," she chuckled.

I was about to become a father. I can't describe the emotions, I experienced the happiest feeling and the scariest feeling at the same time. I wouldn't be honest with you if I said it didn't matter what we had. I definitely wanted a boy, but if we had a girl I would still be happy and she would become an amazing basketball player. She also wouldn't be allowed to date until she was thirty – ha-ha! Just kidding.

The following weekend I went over to talk to my dad and brother and I also shared the baby news to my whole family. They both agreed I should go to work at Stanton Industries. My brothers, Richard and Loop talked to their foreman. Richard was getting to be an expert at running a warehouse full of furniture. He had saved enough money to buy his own brand-new car, I remember that silver Chevy Monza.

I still remember the first day I showed up for work at Stanton Industries in Tualatin, Oregon. I filled out some paperwork and walked over to meet the boss. He was a jokester. He reached under my coat and rubbed my back saying, "Okay, he's dry, he'll do." I got the joke right away and started laughing. My intense training started that day. My brothers gave me a crash course on Loading-at-the-Warehouse 101. There is a skilled way to load furniture inside a semi-truck. The trucks would all back up to the huge doors and seal the rubber frame to keep the cold weather out.

It was another labor job that I wasn't looking forward to, but we needed the money to make our utility payments and mobile-home payment. We also needed another car as mine was starting to fall apart.

There were mostly Hispanics and Russians working at this furniture plant. I felt so out of place once again. I had gone to college and here I was working hard all day and physically wearing myself down. Every day after work my muscles would be so sore, and I was tired. At night I would mail out more resumes and applications to state agencies or private companies in Portland. I wasn't happy, and if it weren't for my beautiful wife that was waiting for me when I got home, I don't know what I would have done. I looked forward to seeing Candi after work. She was always encouraging me to keep applying and she was always giving me hope that something would happen soon. She prayed for me every night. Sometimes we would pray together.

I would carpool every morning with my family driving my car to their house and picking them up. I had plenty of room in my 1970 Ford Galaxie 500. They would help with gas. Every morning I would rise at 4:30 a.m. – this became routine. Candi and I lived on Lakeside Drive, which was located on the outskirts of Salem.

We started planning on buying a house. We talked to a real estate lady that her mom knew, Terry Judd. There was an FHA program that was giving loans to young couples in a lower-income bracket. The interest rate would be low and as pay raises occurred the interest would increase. To me it didn't matter, I just wanted to get into a home that was new and had a shower. We applied for the loan, but the underwriter rejected our application. It was disappointing. What Terry told us was that the job at Stanton Industries was not secure enough. I explained that I was applying for a computer-field position and that I had a college degree. She said that when I was hired for that job to give her a call. She would try to hold the house we were interested in for a few more months – we agreed with her.

A month later, during the month of October 1982, I was loading a huge trailer with furniture that was going to Levitz, a retailer that bought wholesale from Stanton Industries. My foreman walked over to me and said, "Hey Dave, you have a call on line 2." My first thought was, *I don't think Candi would be having the baby this early.* I walked over to the office area, which was visible to the warehouse with chairs, sofas, and loveseats standing on their arms on the concrete floor.

"Hello," I said.

"Dave, this is Darrell Climber from the Department of Transportation."

"Oh, hi Darrell!"

"How are you?"

"Oh, I could be better, just loading a truck at work."

"Well, things are about to get better for you, we have decided to offer you a job in computer operations."

"Oh wow! Thank you so much."

"When would you be available to start?"

"I can start tomorrow!"

"Ha-ha! Dave, easy. Here's what I want you to do, give your employer a two weeks notice and report here on the first of next month. Does that sound okay?"

"Yes sir, thank you so much, I'm so excited to start work there."

"Ha-ha! Congratulations, we look forward to having you."

After I received that call I went into the trailer and sat there almost in tears. I couldn't let anyone see me, that place had some pretty hard fellows. Some would spit out the F word as an adjective every sentence. I was far into the trailer behind all the merchandise I had loaded. My hands were dirty from the pads I used to cushion the furniture. My mind took me back to Coach Reese, my seventh-grade coach, who told me I would never be a high jumper. Here I was about to embark on a higher paying job and the possibilities for future advancement in my career as a software engineer focusing on applications development.

I sat there and thanked God for answered prayers. I had a few tears running down my face. My eye was a little dry and the moisture helped a lot. I would have great medical insurance finally and I would be able to fly to Texas soon to see my doctor for a cleaning and evaluation of my eye.

When I got home I saw Candi through the kitchen window as I drove up to the mobile home. I kept thinking to myself how lucky I was to have her in my life. She deserved all the happiness and all of the nice things I could buy her in the near future. More importantly, she deserved the most amazing love from me as her husband. I truly believe that Jesus brought Candi to me for a higher reason than I could ever understand, especially in this time of my life.

When I told her about the phone call, she had such a huge smile on her face. "Sometimes you have to have a little faith, David," she said with her kitchen apron on. She was right and I learned yet another valuable lesson from her.

I contacted Terry Judd immediately, our real estate agent, and we set up a meeting the following day. The paperwork was submitted to the underwriter once again. She kept our file, so it was much faster and easier to submit everything.

22.

Our New Home on Indiana Avenue

Our loan had been approved the second time around. We finally moved into a brand new house that we actually saved a little money on because we requested no landscaping. I would do that myself. It was a crazy-exciting time for us. Candi had given notice to quit her job on November 5th. We were already moved into the new house and I was varnishing a new dresser I bought for the baby's room. That night Candi went into labor early the next morning and our first-born son, Jacob, entered this world.

I attended the necessary training to be allowed inside the delivery room. I was with Candi when our son was born. We already had names picked ahead of time. If it would have been a girl, she would have been called Rachel, the name came from one of Candi's grandmothers.

Our entire world became about our little guy. I bought him a basketball and some sports shirts. We were so proud and happy. I can't describe the wonderful feeling of another family member coming into this world to share many years with us.

The following year, while I continued working at the Department of Transportation, my wife had a miscarriage. It was a sad day and we worked through the sadness. No doubt our child is in heaven now. We went to the coast and spent some quiet time together. We knew that we wanted another baby, we didn't want Jacob to be raised as an only child.

The doctor said Candi's health was good and we should try again for another child. On December 22, 1984 we had our second child, Matthew. Both of our sons' names were picked from the Bible. Jacob was already two-years old and he was full of smiles when he heard about his little brother. We were flying on cloud nine. Our parents were happy for us and celebrated with us.

Candi decided she was not going back to school until they were older, she wanted to see them walk for the first time. She wanted to teach them the Word of God. She wanted to play with them, feed them, laugh with them and love them as much as she could. When I came home from work, it was my turn to play with them and to love them as much as possible. Candi was in need of a break after a challenging day with two little ones. I think if you are a caring mother you understand what I'm talking about.

While I was working and learning more about my job, she was grinding at home with the boys. I need to say that she was an amazing mom to our boys. I saw how much time she put into being productive in a loving way.

We knew some of our neighbors, but we weren't that close to any of them. Candi made a friend that lived two houses down on Indiana Avenue, in Salem, where we lived. Her name was Sheri Ober. Sheri was over at our house many times when I arrived from work. She knew it would then be time for her to head back to her house. Sheri also had kids so it was nice that Matt and Jake could play with Robby and Michael, and I think even Sarah. It was great because while Sheri's husband and I were at work, they had time to visit a lot.

I was still working out and trying to stay in shape. After work, three days a week, I would take my footballs over to the Chemeketa field or the McKay High School football field and I would kick and punt for an hour or so. When the boys were a little older I would bring them with me and they would retrieve the football for me. These were priceless memories to me. My kids were getting exposed to sports at a young age. I knew how much fun I had with sports and how much I learned from sports. I wanted the same thing for my boys.

In 1985 God put another opportunity in front of me. I read about the Portland Steelheaders, a minor-league professional football team. They played in the Northwest Football Alliance League and they had moved to Salem, Oregon. They were holding a meeting and tryouts in a week. They were changing the name to the Salem Stars. Their corporate headquarters would be in an upstairs building on Lancaster Drive, which was close to where we lived.

This was almost perfect and I was not about to miss the tryouts on Saturday. I was ready and my ankle was 100%. I had been punting the football 55 yards in the air and I had been kicking the football into the end zone consistently.

I talked to Candi about it because I knew we had two kids and I had a full-time job. She told me to first find out as much as I could at the meeting and then we could talk again. I attended the meeting on a Thursday, because tryouts were Saturday.

If I made the team, this would mean away trips on weekends and I would not get to see my kids much. After the meeting with the Salem Stars' owners, BJ Winchester and Ron Stutzman, I found out that practices would be three times a week and mandatory.

When I returned home, I talked to Candi about this opportunity. I was so excited, this is what my dream as a kid was, and I knew that I could build stats up for the NFL tryouts or CFL tryouts.

"Candi, I totally understand if you don't want me to tryout. I don't want to play on a team if I don't have your blessing on this."

"David, I know it's something you've wanted to do since the OSU recruiting trip. I think you should go for it if it's something you really want."

"Yeah?"

"Yeah, I'm behind you and so are our boys, isn't that right Matt and Jake?" She turns and smiles at both boys.

"Thank you sweetheart, I love you!"

So it was set and I attended the tryouts on Saturday. When BJ Winchester saw me take my first punt, his eyes enlarged and his mouth stayed open for a few seconds.

"Do that again!"

"That's just my warm-up I haven't really punted hard yet," I said.

"What? Man, you're hired."

So I did it again, except this time the football went about 62 yards in the air with a clean spiral. He looked at me.

"You're hired, practice starts on Monday, show up."

"Really?"

"Yes, really! Good work man, we're glad to have you on our team."

I asked if he wanted to see me kick some field goals, but the answer was, *no need, you're in man.* I was thrilled that I was going to play minor-league professional football. I would be the starting punter-kicker.

As the season got going I was working at my day job and was waiting with anticipation to being promoted to a higher-paying position in information technology. I was also being a dad to my active little boys and a husband to my wife. I felt that I was a good husband to Candi, and I don't mean to boast, she was happy.

Our first game of the season took place in Spokane, Washington, against the Spokane Fury. This team had three or four players that were released from their NFL teams. They were trying to get back into the league. The Spokane Fury were stacked and we were a new team that was coming together. BJ was still working on acquiring our quarterback, Steve Smith, who had played for Oregon State and had been attending NFL training camps. We didn't have Steve for our first few games but when we got him, it turned our season around big time.

Our first game's attendance was probably around 1,000 people I'm guessing, which was great for a minor-league game. The lights, the all-weather turf, the fans, and the environment brought back so many good memories of playing football. This time I would focus on just punting and kicking the football.

We were getting killed, our defense was adjusting and learning how to play together. The established Spokane Fury had more experience than our team. Without our quarterback it was going to be a long night. Our backup quarterback, Eric, did a good job but it just wasn't enough. We found ourselves trailing in the fourth quarter, 0 - 45.

Ironically, I had no idea that this moment was about to become one of my all-time highlights of my sports career. There was less than two minutes in the game and we had the ball on fourth down and fifteen. I heard one of the players yell out, "Let

Espinoza kick it – what do we have to lose!" The ball was sitting on their 40-yard line, plus 10 yards from the goal line to the goal post, plus another 6 yards where my holder would place the ball on the turf. This would mean that if I made this, it would be a whopping 56-yard field goal. That would be better than most NFL kickers could do.

The head coach thought about it for a few seconds and looked at the players pleading for him to put me out there to try and kick the field goal. He looked at me and said, "What the heck! Espinoza, get your butt out there and kick it!" I was freaking out a little as I had never tried anything farther than a forty-yard field goal.

I snapped my chin strap on and I ran out onto the field. I felt pretty good, but I thought to myself, *there's no way I'm gonna make this, but I'll give it my best shot.* I kept thinking that I would never get an opportunity like this. It was the perfect night, the Saturday-night lights were gleaming and there was no wind. As I was listening to the holder's count, I had a quick flashback of my brother and I practicing on Dulin Street and also when we watched the Dimmitt Bobcats warm up kicking the football past the lights.

I also remembered what Coach King told me at practice back in Texas, *keep your head down and don't lift it up until your right foot hits the ground.* The Bobcat's head coach would strap a belt to my face mask and tie it to my belt so I would never lift my head while practicing field goals.

My head was numb and I was zoned on the spot where the football would be placed by holder, Bradley Joel, one of our wide receivers that could catch the ball well. I heard the count and saw Bradley catch the ball as he placed it on the ground. I started my motion with a tad bit of a delay, I wanted to be sure Bradley had enough time to turn the laces on the football and place his finger on the tip of it. I made my forward motion and kicked the football as hard as I could, keeping my head down – *boom!*

When my right foot came down I saw a defender just barely miss me. I looked up and the football was spinning and floating through the air. It was so far away and it took several seconds to reach the end zone. The crowd went silent for a moment while watching the football in the air. To be honest, I could not tell if it went through the uprights or not, it was too far away. And then, both officials raised both hands straight up high. I was speechless and my heart was pounding with joy, shock, and surprise! The entire crowd at Joe Albi Stadium erupted and most of the people were from Spokane. My teammates were jumping up with joy and they all mobbed me when I came to the sidelines. We lost the game 3 - 45, I led all scorers. I had never been happier despite a loss.

After the game I probably signed about fifty autographs, some during the last minute of the game. Kids kept coming down from the stands and reaching out with a piece of paper or a program and a marker. What a good feeling that was, I'll never forget that moment. The entire team went to eat at John Stockton's restaurant, well, his dad's place.

Our season improved when we acquired Steve Smith. I also talked to BJ and Ron about my brother, Richard, who was a better punter than I was. They couldn't believe it because they thought I was pretty darn good. It didn't take much to convince them when they saw Richard punt the football. This made it easier on me and I could focus on just kickoff and field goals. My brother and I were playing professional football together, what a dream come true.

We went on to make it to the Northwest Football Alliance championship game against Auburn in the Seattle area. It was raining a little but not too bad. That night I kicked a couple of field goals, one was from 45 yards out. Auburn had a wide receiver that was headed to play for the San Francisco 49ers. He was tough to handle. Our quarterback showed up late, there was a communication problem with his ride.

At this game I also witnessed my brother punt the football 75 yards in the air. He nailed a clean spiral with a perfect connection on the football. To this day I have not seen a punter hit one that far, even from NFL punters – wow!

It was a long season and a tiring one. I missed my kids and wife during away games, luckily there weren't too many. It was nice when I could drive to the games with my family and meet the team there. I got the full experience of playing professional football. Only a few players got paid in this league. For me, my salary was based on ticket sales, some days were better than others. I was able to buy my wife a brand new Chevy Cavalier, a four-door economy car. With my day-job pay, this was just extra money for my wife and kids.

The second year I didn't finish the season. I had a try out with the Portland Breakers, a USFL (United States Football League) team. That was a great experience because of the NFL kickers that wanted to play for the USFL in Portland. Some were on the rebound from injuries or recently getting released from their team.

The tryouts started out with fifteen kickers including me. We all kicked once starting at the 20-yard line. Everyone made it straight through the uprights. They moved us back 10 yards and we all kicked again. I had no idea that there were going to be that many talented kickers. Three kickers would get signed to a two-year contract is what I was told.

When the football was moved to the 45-yard line, everyone missed but three of us. I made it and I jumped up for joy with the other two kickers. One of the other kickers had played for the Dallas Cowboys, my favorite team. We talked for awhile – it was a fun day. They gave us all a document to fill out and return right away. We were to report to camp in a few weeks.

I was excited, especially if I could sign on for two years and then end my football career. I had a good taste of traveling and being around a team of all kinds of personalities. It was awkward staying at the hotel while most of my teammates went out to enjoy the nightlife. I didn't drink alcohol and I wasn't the least bit interested in going to the places that some of my teammates went. Sometimes I would just hang out with the big linemen. They would hit an all-you-can-eat place and we would eat a lot of food. One time, at a Skippers restaurant, they told us that they were out of fish. The linemen were not too happy.

Sometimes my heart would get crushed, and I didn't understand why things happened like this. The USFL folded. In negotiating with the NFL, the owners made a deal and the NFL signed off on it. I don't know all of the technical details, but there would be no more USFL. I was so down about this entire dream I was chasing. I finally made it to the big times and this happened.

My minor-league coach contacted me, he told me that there were a few CFL (Canadian Football League) teams after me and I should jump on this opportunity. I had to talk to Candi again, I was torn in decision making and I was pretty stressed about the possibility of leaving the country and being away from my wife and kids.

"Candi, my coach said that there were a few Canadian teams after me."

"Well, what did you tell him?"

"I told him I needed to talk to you first."

"What about Seattle, can you still get a tryout with them? It's a lot closer."

"The problem is, that I don't like being away from you and the boys."

"We don't like it either, but if it's something you really want, we can make it work."

"I think I'm done with my football career. I got hit pretty hard in Auburn, it scared me. I want to be around for our boys."

"We do love it when you're around."

I decided to end my football career. I had a good taste of the professional football experience, and nothing was more important to me than my wife and kids. I missed my family on away trips. I had no doubt that eventually I would have made it to the NFL, but it wasn't worth the headaches and the missed time with my precious little boys.

If I would have gone on and made millions playing in the NFL, what good would that have been if I missed out on helping my kids with their skills and watching them grow every day? It wasn't worth it to me. I prayed about it and I felt at peace with my decision to end my professional football career.

23.

It Started With a Datsun Pickup Accident

In 1986 I bought a little Datsun pickup to haul all kinds of stuff and for me to drive to work. I felt more comfortable leaving an old vehicle parked outside all day than Candi's new car. I wanted her to have a dependable car. We were done with her driving used cars, especially when she was driving the kids around.

Everything was going great, we were having the time of our lives as a family and bonding with our kids in every way possible. I was beginning to show them how to shoot the basketball inside our house plus many other things. We were taking them to all-comer track meets, and whatever else was happening in town. I was gaining quality experience in my computer-field job. We were having barbecues with my family on Sundays, and we were spending time at the coast with Candi's family. I was feeling like a normal person with full vision.

One day we were driving back home on Checkerboard Road toward 99E from Gervais, where my brother lived at the time. We were hauling a piece of furniture that we bought from Stanton Industries. Candi had Matt on her lap and Jake was sitting in the middle resting his head on the back part of the seat and we all had our seatbelts on. I came to the stop sign and looked both ways ... 99E was a busy road and still is today. All of a sudden, an unexpected rear-end collision – *bam!* A white car slammed into the bumper of our pickup. We slid close to the middle of 99E.

It was such a hard jolt that I was stunned and a little out of it. Candi was in tears and the boys were crying. I got out of the car and yelled at a person that came out of a tavern that was close by,

"Call 911!" The person that hit us was not intoxicated or any-thing, he just wasn't paying attention.

I don't believe that God wants these accidents to happen to us, I don't totally understand why these things happen, including my terrible accident when I was five-years old back in Texas. I do understand that to be human is too error, we are not perfect, and we have been given free will. Jesus died on that cross for us. He gave us the freedom to do as we choose, to make our own deci-sions.

Maybe that's what happened, this fellow that smashed into our pickup on Checkerboard Road was not perfect. I don't feel that his decision was to plow into an innocent family. I strongly feel that God has the power to prevent things from happening. He must have His reasons for not preventing my accident back in Texas or this accident with my family. I just don't know the reason and never will. What I do know is that He was with us even when I didn't know it.

The funny thing is that I would always look up and ask God, "Why?" Those hard and difficult times in life have given me more reason to think of others and to have compassion toward people that are less fortunate or people that are struggling with body imperfections – there are too many kinds to list. This world is so temporary compared to infinity in paradise with Jesus. I didn't feel like that when this accident happened to my family, trust me.

We all went to the hospital and got checked out. Candi had a concussion and my two boys, Jake and Matt, were fine. Matt had Candi's body for cushion and Jake had padding from the bench seat. I received a pretty bad whiplash, but Candi was injured the worst.

We did talk to an attorney and went through the necessary procedures to eventually get some kind of compensation for repairs to our vehicle, doctor bills, and the pain we went through. That was the first attorney experience I had ever gone through. I learned a lot about how lawyers can help you deal with mishaps like these.

As days went by and I recovered from my injury, I applied for a higher-paying job as a software engineer (computer programmer) at Children Services Division. I was called to be interviewed. I expected two people to interview me, at least that's how the last few interviews went. Boy was I surprised. There were five managers and one systems analyst as I walked in and sat down. They all looked at me, some disappointed, and some with smiles on their faces. Carol Jackson was the systems development manager who was doing the hiring. He introduced me to the rest of the interview panel.

I was a little nervous but that faded away fast as I was prepared to answer any kind of computer-language questions, or questions about jobs that I had worked, basically my experience. The funny thing is all of the questions I was anticipating were never asked. I remember one question that I didn't expect, *why should we hire you?*

Carol was the first man that I ever met with a female name, I was expecting a female. He mentioned that he had followed me when I was kicking for the Salem Stars. That was a good connection, I talked a little bit about that experience. They were impressed on how I was able to juggle so many things in my life, kids, sports, family, and still have hunger for knowledge and advancement in the computer field.

Another thing they asked me about was my college transcript that I had to submit with my application to get this interview. I had one term at Chemeketa where I did not do well. Gary Hanson was the I.T. manager and was hoping Carol would hire one of his friends that had a bachelor's degree in computer science from the University of Oregon.

"David, to honest with you, we have other candidates that are more qualified than you, would you be able to produce right away for us?" Gary asked.

"Yes sir, when I learn something I don't forget it. If I don't have the answer to a complex solution, I know where to get it. I'm a hard worker and I want this job."

"I noticed something on your transcript, one of your terms kind of bit the dust, what happened there?"

"I apologize for that term. I married my high-school sweetheart during college. I don't know how it was with you guys on your honeymoon, but for me, well, school was the last thing on my mind." They all started laughing except the I.T. manager.

"I guess that would explain that," Carol said while he continued laughing.

I could tell that with Carol I maybe had a chance, but I was worried when Gary Hanson asked me about the one low-performance term in college. I remember that term, not only was I taking 17 credit hours, but I was also taking several classes that were computer languages, one being assembler (machine instructions), that class was tough. I was also taking trigonometry. I never took that many challenging classes in one term again. And also, I got married and went on a honeymoon which put me a little behind. Despite the fact that in one of my terms I had a 4.0 GPA, the one bad term brought my GPA down fast.

In a few days I received a call from Carol, he offered me the job and I accepted it. He said I would be getting a letter in the mail and I could officially start on the first of next month. I don't know about you, but I had no idea that God was with me, how could I have possibly been selected over candidates that were more qualified than me? I'm so glad that this agency gave me a chance.

Children Services Division, System's Development Unit, under Carol became one of my all-time best places I ever worked at. I learned so much at that place. My programming skills climbed to a higher notch while working there. This wasn't coding for school projects, this was coding in COBOL, my favorite computer language ever and it was in the real world.

At school I was taught flow-charting, at CSD, I learned how to design computer programs with Warnier Diagramming (brackets). The information was stored on a large mainframe computer. I had experienced everything with mainframes and mid-range computers in my previous jobs for ODOT and at Dept. of Revenue.

Children Services was like a family. Our building was located in downtown Salem, a fun place to take breaks and eat lunch. I made some great friends at CSD. Probably the most I ever had in my life outside of family. I'll never forget Jill Ertsgaard (Jill Petersen now); George Shellenberg; Frank Koscher; Steve McGoldrick; Don Crossley; Pam Ryan; Beverly Shuford; Charles Peterson, and Linda Lennox.

When Jill Ertsgaard became our manager, she started giving me opportunities that no other manager did. She trained me to become a more efficient developer. She saw something in me that no one had before. She realized I was a visual person, I was struggling on certain technical coding abilities. Jill helped me understand, and that was my turning point of being able to contribute to the agency. I was assigned to be in charge of the Provider System – a major foster care system. One of my all-time favorite applications that I developed was a Foster Care Match Screen. The application was to help match foster kids with foster parents. Don Crossley was my lead analyst and we both trained the users in Portland, which was Multnomah County. I started gaining experience on public speaking, I didn't realize how much work it took to plan a training session.

I found out fast that my job wasn't just about writing code and testing. It was definitely about the end user. We provided a service for them. There were requirement meetings; staff meetings; systems' standard meetings; agency training; security training; software update trainings; HR training; sexual harassment training, and much more.

Thank you to Jill, George S., Don, and Charles, for sharing your knowledge with me. You all showed me many things about working in a high-pressure world while making it fun and productive. I will always treasure those moments at CSD, especially the March Madness brackets we used to post up on the walls. I still remember Penny, she picked the underdog, Ball State, to win over a higher seeded team. When Ball State won, we asked her why she picked Ball State. Her answer was, "I don't know, I just figured with a name like Ball State, they must know how to play ball."

I was making huge progress in the computer field. Most of my time was spent with my wife and kids or at work. We made it a point to visit my mom and dad and my in-laws on weekends.

It was tough for me to converse with family about work, unlike their conversations, mostly a drama situation at Stanton Industries. They worked there for a long time before the plant shut down and moved to a different location. They all had to scramble to find work at other places.

My family was still living in Gervais, Oregon – a small town about eight miles north of Salem. My parents, brothers, and sisters all lived there as well. Candi's side of the family, her parents Joe and Elaine, one brother, Joe, and sister, Kelly, lived in Salem. The other sister, Cathy, was teaching in Oakridge, Oregon.

In the month of January 1987 while we were visiting Richard and Julie in Gervais, my dad wanted help remodeling a house he purchased inside Gervais. Candi and the kids stayed at Julie's house and my brother and I went to help Dad. Late in the day about 6:00 p.m., Candi called me and complained about seeing double vision. Right away I drove over as fast as I could to pick her up. We headed to the Salem Hospital Emergency Room.

Candi was afraid and worried. Most of her lifetime she experienced headaches, but every time her mom, Elaine, would take her to the doctor, he would say the same thing over and over, "It's just a migraine, take some Tylenol." This time there was a symptom that gave the doctor a reason to give Candi a brain scan. I was worried sick and scared. On the way to the hospital I kept checking on Candi.

"Are you okay?"

"Well, I'm still seeing double and my head is hurting."

It was like falling off of a cliff and not landing yet. My stress level was rising and I didn't know what to think. I just needed to get her to the hospital quickly.

We arrived at the hospital in about thirty minutes. We had to fill out information – just normal emergency procedures, good grief. Candi and I both went in when the ER doctor examined her. He immediately said, "I think there's something going on in your head, I'll have to order a brain scan." I went back out to the waiting room while they took Candi back to the scan room. I waited nervously and many things went through my head, I didn't have any spit in my mouth and my breathing was shallow ... I knew I had to remain strong.

I waited for about an hour until finally the doctor came out and handed me the bad news. Candi had a growth that was pushing on her left eye's optic nerve. Candi was admitted to the hospital right away. The doctor explained to us that this growth had to come out as soon as possible. Our family doctor arrived at the hospital that night to examine Candi and to talk to us. He was quite honest and informed us that Candi could die.

The following day the neurosurgeon came and talked to us. He explained that he would remove as much of this brain tumor as he could without harming any delicate brain organs. We heard that Dr. Buza was one of the best surgeons around. This made me feel a little better but not much better.

It was difficult and confusing for Candi to accept what was happening to her. She was emotional and continued to be for the rest of the night. She kept saying, "God is with us ... I don't want to die." We had always been Christians, we went to church on Sundays, prayed regularly, and in general we were always nice to people. Candi took it to a further level in being extra nice to people. She would go out of the way to do things for the school, relatives, and friends.

As I lied there on the hospital bed holding Candi while she was crying, I kept saying to myself, *why?* You see these kinds of things happening in movies and to other people, but never to us. We had everything going in life with our kids, our house, and activities – life was so much fun. It was one of the longest waits of our lives, waiting for the surgery to take place in a few days.

I had my hands full with Matt and Jake. They were good kids, but still young and didn't know what was going on. Actually, I felt they were the biggest boost of support for Candi and myself. Jake was sad, he understood that mommy had something in her head that had to come out in order for her to get well and come home again. At four years old, I remember him telling Candi, "God will help you Mom, you'll see." Matt was too young to know what was going on. In any event, they both kept me busy enough that it created unbelievable support in making it through all of the stress and emotional turmoil.

Surgery day finally arrived, it was during the month of February 1987 that Candi leaned back on the hospital bed while they prepared her for surgery. The kids and myself were next to her along with her parents and other family members. I thought to myself, *this could be the last time I would talk to her*, but my heart kept saying she would make it and she would recover, *please God give her the strength to survive this operation.*

As I looked into her beautiful light-brown eyes, I told her how much I loved her and that I would be waiting for her after the surgery. Candi was in tears and she said, "I love you too, David, and all of you too." She turned her head and looked at everyone in the room, "I keep thinking of that song that says, *there are angels all around me.*" Candi looked nervous and scared. As they wheeled the hospital bed away, I waved at her and smiled, she waved back as more tears ran down her face. My two little guys waved at their mommy as well. Candi and I both questioned ourselves that night, *is this really happening to us?*

I had never felt so helpless and so downhearted in my life. I took my two boys back to my brother's house in Gervais. My sister-in-law, Julie, was so supportive – watching my kids when I needed it – so thankful for her. I then drove back to the hospital and waited in the lobby area. The surgeon would call me as soon as he was done with the operation.

Candi's parents, Joe and Elaine, were in the lobby waiting just as I was. They were concerned. Never had I seen my mother-in-law crochet as fast as she was that day. She must have completed an entire blanket during Candi's operation. We kept looking at our watches in silence. I closed my eyes and prayed to God.

Meanwhile, in the operation room, Candi's surgery was finally happening. The doctor described the procedure to me. Candi was given anesthesia and then she was hooked up to all the necessary medical equipment. Once the procedure began, there was an incision made on her hairline above the forehead. Next, the flesh covering the skull was flapped back. Now the surgeon was ready to drill four holes through the skull – kind of like setting up a square. Once the holes were drilled in each corner, a jigsaw with a special blade was used to cut the skull from hole to hole. Finally, the tumor, which was described as a white mass the size of a golf ball, was carefully removed. The surgeon didn't remove all of the tumor tissue due to delicate brain organs that could have been harmed.

The operation took three and a half hours and there was no blood transfusion needed, thank God. When the surgeon called me, I answered on the phone located in the lobby. I was relieved to hear that Candi was strong and made it through the operation. I had never prayed before as much as I did at the lobby. I wanted to see Candi but I couldn't. The surgeon said it would be a few hours before the anesthesia wore off.

When I had the green light to see her, I walked into the intensive care unit where Candi was placed. She had her eyes closed lying flat on her back with a huge turban-like wrapping around her head. I slowly walked up to her and said, "Hi." My tears slowly started running down my face. I wanted her to feel at ease so I asked her in a whisper, "Can you name your husband and your two boys?" She moved her head a little bit but not much and responded with a whisper, "David, Jacob, Matthew." My heart jumped for joy at that moment – I knew her memory was still there.

The surgeon told me that she had a good chance to recover and that they needed to take a piece of the tumor to pathology to find out if it was malignant (cancerous). He said not to worry because even if it was cancer, there would be a plan for treatment. I didn't know what to say – I was in a bit of a shock. The days went by fast as Candi continued to recover from brain surgery.

The days were long for me and busy. I tried to spend as much time as I could at the hospital, but with two kids it was difficult. Elaine, her mom, took turns with me. I started realizing how tough it was to do Candi's job as a stay-at-home mom – I struggled in that department. I had so much to learn while my wife was in the hospital. My manager, Jill Ertsgaard, was supportive and I was blessed to have *sick leave* saved up. I'm so thankful to my family members and co-workers that helped me out in many ways.

After several days, Candi was up taking walks in the hospital hallway. In eight days she was back home. Now all we had to do is wait for the results from pathology. Was it cancer or was it just a benign cyst? The surgeon called and wanted to talk to me alone.

We all went to the hospital since it was the same day the staples from Candi's forehead were being removed. As they were doing that in a room, Dr. Buza showed up and pulled me out of the room away from everyone else. He looked at me with a serious look in his eyes and whispered, "It's malignant." I felt like crying followed by an awful feeling all over my body, like a big truck had just hit me. My heart sunk low.

Dr. Buza followed those words with some encouragement. I remember him saying, "She's young, healthy, and strong. She has a chance to beat this. With treatment and today's technology, there's hope." That made me feel a little better.

I went back to tell Candi the bad news and immediately followed with the good news of treatment and what the doctor explained. Candi was silent and didn't know what to say. She felt tired and weak. We immediately scheduled appointments with the radiation physician, the chemotherapy physician, and the neuro-surgeon.

After a few weeks we were done with talking and we began Candi's road to recovery. The first thing we did was wait for Candi's head to heal from her brain surgery. Believe me that was a challenge in itself. Candi complained about painful headaches. Once she took the Tylenol with Codeine that the doctor pre-scribed to her, the pain eased up a bit. She was also taking Phenobarbital to help prevent seizures. Candi felt nauseated many times. All I could do is be there for her with as much support as possible. We couldn't have too much noise around the house for a long time.

She was taking so much medication that I had to buy a container to separate the pills for each day. This kept us consistent on the required pills she needed to take.

After Candi was well enough to move around it was time to start radiation therapy. I can't recall how many days a week I drove her to the hospital for radiation treatment. As soon as I made it home from work, we'd head to the hospital for treatment. The plan was for the radiation to kill the remaining tumor tissue.

After a couple of weeks of radiation treatment, we continued to the next step, chemotherapy. These two treatments work to-gether to combat the cancer cells. I took Candi to many treatment sessions. It was painful watching her go through the chemo-therapy treatments. The chemo was administered intravenously. It was too intense and painful to her, so the doctor had to mix the solution with Novocain. A normal chemo session would last anywhere from forty-five minutes to an hour. Afterward, Candi appeared as if she was intoxicated and sick. When we arrived home she would throw up and feel nauseated.

She would sleep for three hours and when she woke up she felt worn out and exhausted. This went on for weeks. Once a month the doctors would take magnetic-imagery scans to monitor whether there was still tumor tissue or not.

God was holding my hand. No way I could have dealt with all of this, including taking care of my two little boys, without His guidance. God has all the power to strengthen us when we feel the weakest. I prayed every night, I don't remember a night that I didn't pray while we were going through the hardship.

When the treatment process was over, Candi was beginning to come around and was delighted that she didn't need to go in and get her wrist or her arm poked by a needle, or simply the inconvenience of being there in general – at least for another month when the next brain scan was scheduled.

When it came time for the next scan we were nervous because this was going to decide whether to continue the treatments or not. Candi had been praying every night and even making a promise to God that from now on she would read the Bible every night and become a better Christian. I didn't know how much of a better Christian she could have been. I guess reading the Bible every night was a great addition, not just for her, but for me, Jake, and Matt as well.

We were finally given the results. Doctor Granitar said, "I have some good news, no tumor tissue is showing up." I smiled and gave thanks to the Lord, the doctors, and the nurses for taking part in a successful treatment process. The chemotherapy physi-cian looked at me and said, "Now I'm not making any promises, this thing could come back or it could be gone for good, but for now it's not showing." He concluded to tell me that Candi would need brain scans every three months for one year. After one year, only if she was having problems would they give her a scan. I was so relieved and happy. Candi was thankful for prayers being answered and for the talented physicians.

"David, I'm going to start walking around the Chemeketa track just to see how I feel."

"That's a great idea, I'll support you one hundred percent. Let's help you get back in shape. We can take the kids out there with us and I'll jog with them while you walk."

"David, this cancer is scary, there's no cure for it. I want to do as much as I can with the boys and I want them to always remember me. I don't know how many years I'll have left."

"Candi, miracles happen, they could find a cure, or you could beat this thing."

"I sure hope so, I hate all of this medication I have to take, it makes me sick."

"I know, I'm so sorry ... I'll be here for you."

In May of 1988 Candi began to exercise again. The first month, Candi walked two miles a day and the second month the same. The third month she jogged one mile at a slow pace. After a few months she was jogging two miles. I couldn't believe it, this was more running than Candi had ever done most of her life. She was still experiencing headaches and weakness, but the workouts made her feel healthier. The surgeon had informed us that these kinds of surgeries take two or three years to heal provided the medication was taken regularly and the person took care. There were times when Candi wanted to push herself a little more, but she realized she needed to ease back, slow down, and take care of herself.

24.

Candi's Remission Was a Blessing

Our kids were growing fast and learning many things at home with Candi. When I arrived home they would learn about sports, mainly basketball. I wanted basketball to someday pay for their college education. Despite the fact that I played football, I was not going to encourage it, unless they showed a passionate interest. I played football and had three concussions during my playing days. The pounding that I received on the football field has left me with several aching conditions. I guess I didn't want them playing a sport that would risk a serious injury.

They both started playing soccer in a peewee league. We started experiencing the joy of having little athletes. When soccer was over, we started with basketball. I built an indoor hoop with two-by-four boards and just the rim bolted to one of the boards. They used a beach ball to shoot since it was light. Later I bought them a miniature basketball and a real indoor hoop with a backboard and all. They wore out that hoop shooting baskets every day. I would do my best to teach them the shooting form. There were times where I was a little too hard on them, I was way too competitive and I wanted them to be better than good. I wanted the best for them, I wanted them to experience what I did growing up in sports.

"David! They are little kids, not high school kids."

"I know Candi, but I just want them to learn now, so they'll be ready later."

"They have plenty of time to learn, let them be little boys."

"You're right Candi. Guys, I'm sorry, it's okay if you want to play something else. I love you guys. Daddy is sorry."

Candi was full of compassion for our boys and always looking for things they enjoyed doing. She was definitely supportive of what I was doing and what my plans and dreams were for them. We both wanted the priority to be an overall perspective of raising them to be decent young men.

During the spring we would all go out to the track at Chemeketa C. C. and we would jog with Candi. The more we went to the college the stronger Candi was getting. She was healing from the tough surgery she endured. Eventually her pretty-reddish-tint hair grew back and it was how I remembered her once again. She was smiling more than ever and she would also kid around with me like the good-old days. When I was at work Candi would call me and suggest something for us to do with the kids after work. She would suggest a trip to the coast or a trip to Enchanted Forest, an amusement park just outside of Salem.

We started taking the kids to all-comers track meets at different schools in Salem, Canby, and Woodburn. I remember hearing Candi cheer for them like never before. We made a great team, because I was setting up workouts for them at home and she would do the cheering from the bleachers at games or track meets.

I have to admit that I hated myself for putting my kids through workout nightmares at times. When I felt that they weren't putting in a good effort, I would make them run a 400 meters, which is one full lap around the track. I did that several times before Candi came down on me again.

"David! They're tired, it's hot today, take it easy."

"Candi, I'm just trying to motivate them."

"You over-motivate them sometimes, there has to be a balance."

"Okay .... okay. I'll easy up, you're right. Sorry guys, I'm just trying to help you is all."

We were a family that was tight, we went everywhere together. Sometimes Candi would call me at work to inform me that her mom was taking them to the coast for the day, it was beautiful and they wanted to take the kids to play on the beach.

That happened from time to time. Sometimes I would drive there after work and meet them for the weekend.

We were the type of parents that always looked for opportunities for our boys. It didn't matter whether it was for a Math 24J contest, or a spelling bee contest. We signed them up and they participated. Matt wasn't always happy about spelling bee contests or math contests, but he did it for us. Jake on the other hand, boy was he excited about hopping in the car and getting to any place we were going. Jake was such a leader among his peers, he was always one of the tallest kids. Matt was always average in height and followed Jake in just about everything. He was always trying to keep up with Jake.

I never knew how special it was to have a family like mine. I had a Christian wife that was teaching me about the Word of God on a daily basis, and two boys that were a joy to see when I came home from work.

It was rare that I would go do something without my family. There were a few years where I was playing competitive basketball at Oregon Latino Tournaments. We would get a group of guys together and we would practice and prepare for an upcoming tournament. My brother, Richard, was always on the team, we were both pretty good shooters.

We would get into these massive arguments over a stupid foul that we both disagreed on. I think about those days and wish I could have them back. I wish that I had started a relationship with Jesus Christ back in those days. During this time, I was a Christian, but basically on my terms. Church on Sundays, prayers in the evenings, and sports with my kids and wife.

But again, despite my ignorance of what it meant to be a Christian, or in better terms, a follower of Jesus Christ my Savior, He was there for me even when I didn't know it. He loved me that much.

Candi would ask me why Catholics did certain things and why the religion believed what they did. I would always answer, *I don't know Candi, that's what I learned in catechism classes.* I told her that I wasn't comfortable going to a priest and confessing my sins, all through my childhood life I wasn't comfortable with that. I remember her pointing out certain scriptures in the Bible.

My focus at the time wasn't into the Bible. I was raised to go to confession on Fridays and church on Sundays. I was so glad that she was reading the Bible to me every night, and whether I fell asleep before she finished or not, I still heard the Word of God like I never had before.

I continued working every day, eight hours a day with weekends off. I loved my job and I started thinking about old memories I had when I was poor in Texas. I saw some of my wealthy friends' houses. I wanted a two-story house with a basketball court in the backyard. I wanted that now for my boys, to give them the things that I could never have while displaying my hard work to earn those things.

I felt it was the perfect time to build a basketball court in our backyard. When I first asked Candi if I could do that for our boys, she thought I was crazy. But when I explained to her the benefits of a concrete slab and a hoop, she agreed with me and I went to work. Every day after work I moved dirt, leveled the ground, and set the forms for cement to be poured. I hired a professional finisher to put the final touches on the court. This was one of the best things I ever did for my kids. They had a safe place to play and they would invite their friends over to play basketball.

The following year I attended a one-day training session to become a basketball coach for the Boys and Girls Club. I remember seeing my friend, Curtis Schott, who graduated from Gervais High School with me. He was also going to be a coach. He also had kids that were playing in the league.

I coached both my boys in different years and I had the time of my life. Candi would cheer for our team and support me in the practices or games. We were a team and we loved sports with our kids. I found out how tough it was to be the head coach of grade-school kids.

When Matt or Jake had a birthday party, we would invite their friends from school. Candi and I would set up different games. I normally led the *Simon Says* game. We were enjoying life with our kids. We would also take them for a visit to the grandparents. My family often had barbecues and Candi's family often invited us for breakfast on Sundays after church. Elaine made the best waffles in town. My mom made the best tacos with some Mexican-style dishes.

I was having fun at work with my friends and I was progressing with more knowledge under my belt in computer-information technology. I had several promotions while working there which began to hurt us on our mortgage loan. We were paying more interest but still not as high as the current market rate.

When I got my next annual raise, my plan was to go show my check to my dad. I wanted to clear some things with him from the past. At the time he and my mom were still working for Stanton Industries and doing well. He bought a brand new Ford Truck with a canopy. They also bought a car for my little sister, Diana.

When the checks were distributed to all of the employees at my job, I opened the envelope and put the check in my wallet. That evening, we went to my parents' house and I showed my dad what my waste-of-time in college had done for me. I was making more money than both my parents put together, and they were making good money at Stanton Industries, along with my brothers and sister. Dad and Mom were living inside Gervais in an old house on two lots. It was theirs, they owned it and they were getting closer to being done with the remodeling.

My dad's mind was wowed. He couldn't believe what I was getting paid. He didn't understand the type of work I did, but he learned that if a person goes to college and sticks with a certain field, only good things can happen in time. It wasn't long that he started encouraging my brothers to go to college. The only brother that graduated from college like me, was Gilberto. All of us siblings graduated high school, two graduated from college, which is to be commended.

One evening in 1990, Candi, myself, and the kids were driving to Albertsons to get groceries. I had just bought Candi a 1990 Honda Accord LX. It was a champagne color – beautiful car. On our way back I remember turning into Brown Road, which led us to Indiana Ave. Candi was stuttering trying to tell me something. At first I thought she was playing around, but then I realized it was serious. When we got home I unloaded the groceries and Candi could finally talk to me again. She said she was not able to talk for a few minutes.

I was so scared, and I explained to the boys that I needed to take Mommy to the hospital. I called Elaine and she came over to watch the kids for us. Elaine was always there for us when we needed her. We were blessed that she lived in Salem. I think with us, it was either Richard and Julie or Elaine that helped us through hard times, we trusted them the most. I'm so thankful for them to this day.

At the hospital, the news was unclear. The MRI showed some unidentified images, but the doctor wasn't too concerned. He ruled it as maybe too much stress. So we had to slow down on her workouts and also give her more rest. It was looking like she was back to her normal self.

We prayed that night, my two boys also prayed with us. We kneeled down in front of the bed. We asked God for healing, to help Candi overcome this cancer she was dealing with. As always it was up to God to heal, I didn't understand, I just had to trust in the Lord.

Meanwhile, my mom had been working at a hospital as a maid. She loved working there. I started seeing my parents every morning. My dad would bring my mom to our house and I would take her to work and then drive to my work. After work I would pick her up and bring her home. My mom and Candi got along super well, they laughed together about many things. We did this for a few months until one day my mom got sick.

She had walked into a contaminated room at the hospital that did not have a sign on the door warning of the danger. The procedure was clearly to hang up a sign on the door to inform the cleaning maids of a contaminated room. My mom stopped working and stayed home. She started drinking a lot of water and going to doctor's appointments. She eventually was admitted into the hospital that she worked at.

I'll never know the entire story. She told my dad that she had accidentally scraped herself on something in that contaminated room. Shortly after she started feeling sick.

My dad did everything he could to get an attorney to represent my mom. It seemed that there was a conflict of interest between the lawyers and the hospital. The hospital bill was rising and my mom continued to be taken care of for over a month. With no insurance, my dad was struggling, because he didn't have the money to pay for the hospital bill.

My mom passed away in 1990. Before she passed I went to visit her at the hospital several times. I couldn't see her regularly because I was taking care of Candi and the boys. I told my mom that I loved her and I thanked her for being there with me back during the Amarillo days. Some of her sisters and nieces and nephews were also there. It was a sad time for me. I have great memories of my mom and what she went through to take care of us kids in some of the most trying times.

Mom was the link to the chain in our family. We had family gatherings because of her. She was a top-notch cook, especially with authentic Mexican food. My mom was always there for my dad, she was a good wife to him. She was also a grandmother that played baseball with her grandkids. She would use this plastic baseball and pitch to our kids. They loved playing baseball with grandma.

She was a cheerleader to all of her six kids. I remember her supporting me in just about everything I did. The encouragement she brought to me in furthering my education was priceless. Her love for us was unconditional. Despite our struggles she was always full of compassion. She always had a way to lift us up when we were down.

I'll never forget what she did for me when I was at St. Anthony's Hospital in Amarillo, Texas, and then several years after that through my recovery. My mom meant so much to my family, it was difficult to see her go the way she did. She was only fifty-five years old. I know I'll see her some day in heaven.

25.

The Year 1992 Was Tough

In 1991, Candi began having seizures once every two months. This was scaring me. She was taking some strong medications that would help her headaches and control her seizures. She wanted to run in the 3000-meter run the following year at Bush's Pasture Park.

A year went by and she was hanging in there adjusting to the medications and staying in shape. Her goal was to someday run in the race, so she kept training while monitoring her rest and stress level. We were all rooting for her.

In the summer of 1992, Candi, Jake, Matt, and myself were training for cross-country runs that took place at Bush's Pasture Park, which was close to Willamette University. The races were held every Thursday evening and the final race would be the championship run for the first, second, and third place trophies of several divisions. Candi was training for the 3000-meter run. She never ran it before, this was a good goal for her to reach. Her hard training would hopefully pay off. She was nervous about competing in an event where other runners were around her and people watching in a big crowd. She was used to watching her kids run and compete.

In the first race of the summer she was one of the top five finishers in the women's 30-39 age group. Her time was 15:29 – not too bad for the first time competing after all she had been through. The following week Candi continued to train hard and after the second 3K run she had improved her time dropping it to 15:20 and again finishing in the top five. Candi was motivated and inspired by all of the other runners that could sprint the 3K. The third run was coming up the next Thursday. Candi was striving to break 15:00. After the run was over she fell short running 15:14. That didn't discourage her at all, it just made her train harder the next week. I would run with her to set a faster pace – this helped her tremendously.

The final 3K race for the summer had arrived in the 1992 Cross Country Championships. First, second, and third would receive trophies in each age group. Needless to say, I ran 11:59 and did not place in my age group, but wow, what an amazing race Candi had.

I hadn't thought about her fighting brain cancer. We even started having small arguments like old times. Candi's life was beginning to get back to normal and I was proud to be her husband and to see all of her accomplishments.

The championship race for her age group was finally about to get started. I was at the starting line yelling at Candi with our two boys. I yelled, "You can do it!" Jake yelled, "Good luck, Mom!" Matt just watched and smiled. As the gun went off Candi made a fast dash at the beginning of the race running at a good pace. She slowed down a little in-between to have enough energy to finish strong. At the end of the race she was cruising down the stretch. I was looking at the clock and yelled at Candi, "14:42 ... 14:43 ... 14:44!" Candi heard me and kicked as hard as she could. She placed second, winning a trophy, and she broke 15:00 with a time of 14:49. In 1992, Candi was a true champion in more ways than one.

After the summer was over Candi started having seizures more often, like once a month. They would normally happen during the night. I would wake up and see her shaking. All I could do was make sure she didn't hit herself against the wall or fall off the bed. It was so scary for me and I was worried.

We returned to the doctor once again. She received an MRI (Magnetic Resonance Imaging). The result was not good, the cancer was back. She was scheduled for a second surgery soon after that. The entire world collapsed on us. After she recovered from surgery for the second time, Salem Hospital could not help us anymore. She was referred to OHSU (Oregon Health Science

315

University). This hospital was in Portland, Oregon. We were told it had the best Blood Brain Barrier treatment program in the nation.

Candi wanted to fight this thing doing anything it took to survive. She wanted to live so bad and to continue being a daughter, mom, and wife. She had just started taking classes at Chemeketa Community College to eventually become an elementary teacher – she loved kids.

She wanted so much to watch her two boys grow up. She dreamed of watching them play basketball in high school and in college. It tore her heart up and she was depressed. I remember her words, "David, this isn't fair, I don't want to leave my two boys." I had no words, I just held her and told her how much I loved her and that I didn't understand why this was happening to her. We continued to pray every night for her health and a possible miracle-cure in the near future.

After Candi's second brain surgery my stress level had jumped higher than when she had her first surgery. Every time I looked at my two boys I knew I had to be as strong as I possibly could. They needed me and I needed to be there for them.

I started driving Candi up to Portland, Oregon. I would talk to my boss at work and request time off. Intense chemotherapy was scheduled every month. My boys were in school and I needed childcare after school. I started asking for help from relatives or my neighbors that I knew pretty well. This was not easy for me because I was an overprotective parent. Her mom, Elaine, would come with me to OHSU, and when the boys weren't at school I would bring them with me to OHSU.

This new type of chemotherapy was a surgery, we spent an entire day in Portland for the treatments. She went through surgery preparations and then the treatment took place. The way the chemotherapy was administered was painful for me to hear when the doctor explained it to me.

The surgeons would use main arteries from the leg that led to the brain. Medicine was shot in through the artery to open up the brain barrier. Then following that procedure the chemotherapy was shot through the artery so it could get inside the brain where the tumor was growing. After the surgery, Candi was weak, and always glad it was over. Every month she seemed even weaker and not herself.

As the months went by Candi would get sick as we drove up this long hill that led to OHSU, she was anticipating pain and suffering through this harsh treatment. Sometimes we had to pull over for her to throw up. I started bringing a bucket for that reason.

I was starting to feel like I was taking care of three kids, but if it meant that she was still alive and with us, It was worth it to me. I felt so bad for her and I felt so helpless during that time of my life.

Candi allowed doctors to try a couple of experimental drugs on her, Neupogen which helped reproduce white blood cells and Epogen, which helped reproduce red blood cells. This would help other patients with treatments if successful. She was one of the first patients to try that medicine. It was successful and many people were able to reproduce red and white blood cells to survive the intravenous treatments – lives were being saved. Praise God for that.

The sacrifices she made as a mother of two boys, while battling this horrible illness, was a true inspiration for me. She taught me so much about loving our kids. How to feed them, help them keep up on homework, get involved with school activities, attend church and Bible readings, take them to doctor appointments, etc. She enjoyed watching her boys play basketball or whatever activity they were participating in. She was an amazing mom – there are many amazing moms out there, and we need more. I'm so glad we celebrate, Mother's Day, a day to honor mothers like Candi. It's a tough job but rewarding at the same time.

When Dr. Nuewelt at OHSU pulled me into his office, he sat me down. He had a serious look on his face. He said, "Mr. Espinoza, we can't continue the treatments, she's too weak and won't be able to handle one more treatment. I'm giving her three more months to live, max." The news hit me hard. I just looked down at the floor and was in a mega-shock mode. Many family members heard the news later, they were saddened and it was a difficult time in our lives. I was blessed to have had the opportunity to listen to Candi. She shared many things with me, some that are private and some that I will share with you.

Candi said, *David, please take care of our two boys – they are precious to me. Some day they will both be married and have kids of their own.* She started crying and continued, *Jacob is so talented and tall, Matthew is always trying to keep up with his older brother. He works so hard to be like his older brother. One day he will be able to compete with Jacob – he'll catch up to him. I love my boys so much it hurts me – this isn't fair. Jacob is going to be fine, but please encourage Matthew. I'm going to be with Jesus soon.*

What does a dad do when his oldest child comes up to him and says, "Dad, is Mom going to die?" That was difficult for me ... to talk to my kids about what was happening.

The caring-mom nature she had was truly remarkable. She began to plan for many things. She would write notes and leave them in different places for me to find. She even left two notes in a box that we kept for our kids' memories. One note was for Matt and one for Jake. She knew her kids well and she raised them properly while I was at work.

Her thirteen years of being my wife was a love that not many people have – we were so in love and we shared two wonderful boys together – we did everything with them. We were there with her until her last breath. We had just moved into a new house on Strawberry Court N.E. It was a two-bath-three-bedroom house, a little bigger than our last. This prevented me from paying more interest due to my salary climbing fast. I also wanted Candi to see her new house while she was with us on earth. Candi's parents helped us move our boxes to the new home. I sold our appliances and purchased new ones. I took great pride in building another basketball court in this new house while Candi watched through the window. She was too weak to come outside and she was too weak to even speak much. I can't imagine what might have been going through her head.

During the last year of her life, she wanted to do everything with the boys, take them trick-or-treating; pictures; she did a glamour photo shoot for me; we prayed; we visited both sides of the family; we drove to the cabin at the coast; we went to a Blazer game; she spent time with her sisters and mom; she talked to me about many things; she talked to me about our boys; she told me how much she loved me, and she thanked me for everything. I just supported her in whatever she wanted to do, and I still felt that it was not enough for what she had done for me. Candi gave me so much love, support, and knowledge the thirteen years she was married to me.

Candi's sister, Kelly, offered to help me out, I had exhausted all of my sick leave from work and I had to return. Candi was under hospice care and she was at her sister's house. Kelly called me when Candi was in her last few hours, I rushed to her house immediately. I thought I knew how it was going to feel when she passed, but I had no idea until it actually happened. In January of 1994, Candi went to be with our Lord Jesus Christ. I was able to tell her, *thank you for being my wife and an amazing mom to our kids ... I love you so much and you will always be in my heart.* All she could do at that point is shake her head up and down lightly. She was thirty-two years old. Matt was nine and Jake was eleven. It was painful to watch the caretakers put her into a black bag. One of them looked at me, and said, *we won't cover her face until we get outside.*

Yes, I knew that she went to heaven and I knew that she was in paradise. She had accepted Jesus as her Savior, she had submitted to her husband and loved her husband. And I submitted to her and loved her as Jesus loved his church. Our marriage was fun and loving, and with our two boys it was more fulfilling, productive, and prolific.

Why was I so angry that this happened to us? I looked at my two boys and I just started crying. They would be without a mom, that was terrible and I felt I had every right to be mad about this unfair situation. I was human, and now, not only would I not have my mom around, I would also not have my wife around.

That night, I talked to my boys and assured them that mom was in heaven and that we were going to be okay. Matt was afraid and in tears. Jake was sad, his tears came a little later. Eventually they both fell asleep. I was not able to sleep all night, it felt like one big dream. It felt like I would wake up in the morning and Candi would say, *time to get up, David.* I was so exhausted.

As I fell asleep I kept thinking of the day we first met, my tears could not stop, but that was okay. I thought about her smile and her beautiful face. I thought about how lucky I was to have been her husband and to share two boys with her. I grabbed her pillow and I could smell her scent. I kept her coat the longest, it had her scent for months before it wore out. I still have her scent in my mind. I remember her wonderful scent.

Night after night I would wake up at 2:00 a.m. and turn to her bedside, I just assumed she was right there. I even thought I heard her at times. I would break down in tears again once I realized she was gone. Honestly, it took me months before I got it in my mind that she was no longer next to me at night. That was so difficult to cope with. I could never fall back to sleep when I woke up in the middle of the night.

I do want to say thank you to a few special people that helped me with my two boys *tremendously* when I needed it, Jesus Christ (God); Elaine Cover (Candi's mom); Richard and Julie Espinoza (brother and sister-in-law); Kelly Ward Ferber (my sister-in-law), and Sheri Hall and her daughters (neighbors on Strawberry Ct.). I'll always be thankful to these people for the extra help they provided. I know it must have been a disruption from your families – you displayed love in every way possible.

I think about how temporary this world is and then I think about eternity. Everlasting life in heaven is what Candi is experiencing now. One day we, believers in Christ, will see her again. She has no more pain, no more tears, no more sadness ... praise Jesus, she has everlasting life in paradise.

Revelations 21:4 He will wipe away every tear from their eyes, and death shall be no more, neither shall there be mourning, nor crying, nor pain anymore, for the former things have passed away.

That to me is a celebration. I also think about how proud Candi would have been of our two boys and the fine young men they have become.

26.

Single Parent Life

After the funeral I took some time off. It was nice seeing so many people there – the church was full. Friends from high school, my entire family, and people I didn't know showed up. My coworkers came, it was nice of them to all show up. When that day was over, it was quiet back at home. It was just my two boys and I as we did our best to start a new life without a special person that was planted in our hearts.

When I was taking care of Candi, it was a physical strain toward her last three months, for her as well as for me. I had to lift her and hold her up when she needed to get up to walk to a different room, or to use the restroom. To be honest, I was so glad I could take care of her. The boys were now in grade school and they helped me out with so much while I was helping Candi in so many ways. I loved her so much, it was difficult letting go when I had no choice, it was in God's hands.

Candi had a talk with me two months before she passed. She encouraged me to meet someone in the future. She knew I would not be happy without a female companion. Her requirements for whoever I met was, *to consider the boys and to be sure that she treated them well. Also, she had to be a Christian.* I told Candi that I was never going to marry again. She looked at me and said, "David, you won't be happy if you don't marry again, you have my blessing." I didn't know what to say. It was an awkward moment. So we started to talk about who I could ask out in the future.

Well, at least I knew that if I ever met someone, I would have Candi's blessing and I would not feel guilty. But for now I was going to try to grieve in my own way. We had just moved into this new home on Strawberry Court and we didn't know anyone around. Our home phone was different. The phone company assigned our old number to a person that got swamped with calls. People were trying to reach me to pay their respects. To those people, I'm truly sorry you couldn't reach me and to the gentleman that received all the calls, I'm also sorry.

I did call my old number and talked to the gentleman. I told him I was going to call the phone company to see if they would reassign that number back to me. He was thankful for that and the phone company accommodated me when I explained the situation to them. We also received a lot of cards that were forwarded to my new address.

When I returned to work, I thought I was ready and that my emotional state was calm, but the minute one of my coworkers came over to my cubicle to pay respects, I broke down in tears. Then several other workers came over and asked if there was anything they could do for me to just let them know. This group of people were like family to me, I had worked with them for years.

As the months went by I thought about asking my boss, Jill, out to lunch. I had gotten along well with her during my years at Children Services Division, back then. Unfortunately she was seeing someone. She did say that she was flattered and if she would have been available, she might have gone out with me.

I was at the age where everyone I knew was married or divorced and not wanting to marry again. I wanted to meet someone for my boys and for me at the same time. I was lost and I didn't know what to do next. I gave up on the lady hunt and focused on my boys and basketball. I was coaching their teams at the Boys and Girls Club. Once again, God put sports in front of me to help me deal with the pain inside that was unbearable at times. We stopped praying together as a family. Without Candi, things were different, I wasn't thinking about the Lord as much as I did when Candi read the Bible to me every night.

My mission was to take care of my boys and keep them going in sports and academics. There was not much time for me. When I did get time for myself, I would try to get some sleep, but it would not do me any good, I couldn't sleep. I wasn't eating well and I lost a lot of weight. I had people make comments like, "You look too thin, David, you need to start eating more." The strangest thing is that I didn't see myself thin, I didn't pay any attention to myself. I paid attention to my two boys, they were my first priority in everything I did. I was overprotective with them. I drove them to school before work and I picked them up after work.

Bob and Shari Hall were neighbors that had kids attending the same grade schools as my kids did. They were the neighbors I got to know. They were Christians and probably the only people I ever asked for help in our neighborhood. They knew Candi for a short while and even watched the boys for me a few times when I had to drive Candi to OHSU for treatments. I believe that God put them in front of me. God was with me even when I didn't know it. I'm so thankful for Bob and Shari Hall and their girls.

I had given up on the dating world, and most of my dates were during lunch because I didn't have anyone to watch my kids, it just worked out better this way. Oh yes, I started the dating scene at age 37 and had no clue what I was doing.

I would sometimes invite a young lady to dinner at our house, if I thought she might be the one. I wanted my boys to meet her and get their opinion. Trust me, it didn't go well while they were still in grade school.

"Dad, no, she looks too much like the other lady," Jake said.

"Okay, it's not going to work with this one either," I said.

I'm not going to sit here and lie about my manhood, there was a time while dating that I was sinning. I was praying at night, but being hypocritical and not following Jesus Christ. In contrast, I was being the best dad that I could be – I went over and beyond. I kept my dating adventures away from my boys unless there was a lady that I thought they might like. I now know that I was going about things the wrong way, but at that time in my life I was doing the best I could.

The dating world was always less appealing to me. I just wanted to meet my next future wife that would love me and my kids. For some women, the sports thing was always an issue, *why is your kid's game so important to you?* They didn't realize the passion we had for basketball, or working out. Those relationships didn't last. Or, I interviewed them and found out things about them that were not going to work out with my kids – we didn't even go past a movie date. Or some ladies didn't like that I had kids, it was too much baggage for them. They would say, "Kids? No thanks."

Some would see that my eyes weren't looking too great. I was tired at times and you could visibly see that one of my eyes was not looking too presentable. I had not gone to a doctor in a long time and my eye needed cleaning. Some women wanted a beautiful face in a man and a great body. I had the great body at the time, but my face needed work. One lady wanted me to go see her grandfather with her, who lived close to the southern Oregon border. She wanted me to leave my kids at home and just spend time with her. My answer to her was, "See you later, my boys come first."

Two of the many ladies that I dated during several months were ones that I loved. One broke up with me because I was Catholic. It tore my heart, because I did love her a lot. A few months later there was another lady that loved to drink hard liquor – she lived four hours away from Salem. I didn't drink or smoke and I wanted to keep that garbage away from my kids. We talked about it several times, but her answer was always, "I love to drink, and neither you nor anyone else is going to tell me that I have to stop drinking!" I informed her that I wasn't willing to take a chance of her being drunk one day and throwing a chair at my kids. As much as I tried to make it work with this lady, because I loved her, I knew it just wasn't going to work. She had these amazing pretty blue eyes and a beautiful face. She eventually broke up with me and I never saw her again.

There were women that found out I was single and showed interest, but by then I had stopped dating, it was too hard juggling everything, it just wasn't working out. Sometimes I found myself comparing them to Candi and they were way below my expectations. It was a bad idea dating while my boys were still in school. I wish I could do that moment over. I would have waited until they were out of high school. I made some big mistakes in life.

I decided to just focus on my two boys who were old enough to cook for themselves and to do their own laundry. I folded their clothes and put them in their dressers when they were outside playing with friends. Sometimes I folded clothes late at night. Most of my nights I didn't get to sleep until midnight. It was important to keep up with the house chores and school letters I had to read and sign.

Keeping up with their school activities, studies, and basketball workouts were great times for me and memories that I will always cherish. Planning birthday parties for both of them and hanging out with their friends from school was my life for a few years.

When Jake entered high school, we moved into a new two-story 2,400 square-foot home in N.E. Salem close to farmland. I built my third basketball court in our backyard, which was much larger than our previous house. This is the house that I still live in now as I'm writing this book.

When I was a little kid, I dreamed of living in a house like this. It was my vision and something I worked hard to finally achieve. This house was ours, my two boys and I. Four bedrooms, including a master bedroom with a master bathroom. A double-sink area and a Jacuzzi tub. We wrestled in the downstairs living room because we had no furniture yet. We had a lot of fun at our new house. The boys would invite friends over to play basketball in the backyard, or to just watch a game on TV.

I finally had enough money to go on an actual vacation to Disneyland in California. My two boys experienced some fun times with me. When we were at Disneyland, all I could think about was Candi and how much fun she would have had with us at the happiest place on earth, or so they say.

While we were in Disneyland, it was like forgetting about everything for a few days. The rides I went on with my kids and their smiles brought joy to me. The shows we watched were exciting because we had never seen any of this.

One show that we watched was called, *Honey I Shrunk the Kids*. This was the first time I realized I couldn't see in 3D. My boys were both saying, "Didn't you see that Dad!" I kept watching everyone jump when a bee was flying around, I guess it was big and gave everyone the affect that it was right in front of them. I just saw it as a normal big screen. I was a little frustrated and was tempted to ask for my money back. It was yet another thing that I couldn't enjoy due to my half sight.

Despite all, I think Jesus guided us and lifted our spirits to help us through the roughest times. My prayers were being answered one at a time in His timing, not mine.

The toughest challenges for me were getting through huge milestones my kids had reached – like high school. The first time I dropped Jake off for his first day of high school, I drove off in tears, I didn't want to break down in front of my son, I wanted him to enjoy his first day of high school and not worry about me or anything else. I felt sad that Candi couldn't have been there with me to share that experience. And it was the same thing with Matt, when he got to high school.

I can tell you that as a parent I did the best I could to love my two boys. I not only said the words, *I love you*, but I also made every effort to display love to them. The meals; the basketball practices; the games; the coaching; the birthday parties, the talks when they were discouraged; the laundry; the house upkeep; keeping them safe; the school shopping; the support with their hobbies; keeping up with their academics; prayers and witnessing Jesus to them; allowing them to make mistakes: church on Sundays; summer activities: vacations to Disneyland; holidays and cooking turkeys on Thanksgiving Day; keeping them in touch with grandparents, and much more. I could write an entire book on just the things I did for my two boys out of love.

What my two boys did for me, I could never repay. They encouraged me and gave me a reason to not give up despite our loss. Sometimes I would look at my oldest son, Jake. I would say, "I don't know if I can do this, I feel so stressed and tired." He would look back at me and say, "Yes you can, Dad, you can do this ... you're not too tired." Jesus was working through my boys to reach me sometimes, I do believe that.

They don't remember all of what happened, but they do remember most of it. It's so heart-touching today when one of them sends me a text or an email thanking me for everything I did for them. I hope that they do the same for their kids one day.

During their first basketball games in high school, my thoughts were, *this is not fair, all of these couples that have kids and they get to share this experience together.* Matt was the Student Body Class President at McNary High School for the freshman class. Candi would have been so proud of him. Jake was dominating the basketball court and was the scoring leader of his team, how proud his mom would have been. Both boys were doing well in academics. The school they attended had over 2,000 kids, it was one of the biggest schools around.

The holidays were always difficult for us, especially Mother's Day. Every time I saw someone that knew us from the past, they would ask me, *how's Candi doing?* I would have to explain and then watch them feel bad. Some of her close friends broke down and of course I had a few tears myself. As the years past every sad memory faded a little, but those special moments, like graduations, signing a letter of intent to play college basketball would still be felt in my heart without Candi there. In my book, *Noza A True Basketball Success Story*, I wrote about Matt and Jake playing against each other in a college basketball game, which was one of my all-time favorite sports' moments with them. During that game, all I had on my mind was Candi, Matt, and Jake. We were a team and we were so happy doing many things together, this game would have been such a priceless moment for Candi and I. I hope that when I die, I can see her and I can tell her about Matt and Jake and how they grew up to be amazing kids.

I was still attending a Catholic Church at the time, and learning as much as I could about the Bible on my own. I started going to a Bible studies, but was discouraged when it was ran by parents that didn't know much. I would ask questions and they didn't know the answer half the time. I'm not saying all Catholic Churches were like this, but I was surprised and did not return to the Bible studies. I started reading the Bible more every day, but just parts here and there. I was struggling with this church that I was attending. I was bored half the time, and this is just me, I'm not judging anyone else and I'm not the one to say how a church should worship. All I knew is that I didn't feel at peace.

I knew that my mom raised us going to a Catholic Church, but now I was old enough to decide a few things on my own. I prayed that night and I asked God, *show me the way Lord, I'm at a confused point.* Again, I remember watching *Little House on the Prairie* where Charles Ingalls would pray and say those same words.

I didn't have the desire to date, and for most of my kids' high-school days I stayed away from women. I did, however, work out a deal with Kimber, one of the ladies that I dated previously. She graduated from Gervais as well. We became friends and we would go out to a movie now and then. She was a single parent like me. We did that a few weekends and sometimes we would just go for a walk to have someone to talk to. We both enjoyed that and we weren't so alone during our companionship time. I was working at staying away from sin and this was working out for me – safe with no romance.

I was stabilizing my life and I was trying to find a balance. I was buying my kids the best basketball shoes on the market, I wanted them to take care of their feet and have fun while playing basketball. I'm not going to talk about the amazing success I shared with them in basketball, but I will share the title of the first book I wrote, *Noza: A True Basketball Success Story.* I was focusing on the obstacles my younger son overcame. The book tells our story, a time when I was a single parent and I encouraged them to become the best they could at basketball.

When Jake signed to play basketball at Linn Benton Community College, it was only Matt and myself at home. A few years previous to this point I had arthroscopic surgery on my left knee. It was giving me problems and then my back was giving me problems because of my knee. My back swelled up pretty bad and I could not move. Matt was a senior and was driving to school, basketball practice, and the grocery store. He was taking care of me, I took a week off of work. I could not walk or move. I was staying downstairs in the living room. Matt installed a twin-size bed where I could get comfortable and watch TV.

Matt was a huge blessing to me. He would call me and ask if I wanted a chicken sandwich or a burger at Carl's Jr., a fast-food place in Keizer, Oregon, which was close to the high school. I was hungry and always wanted a Famous Star Meal. My son would watch games with me before heading upstairs to his bedroom to do homework and then play the guitar in the late evenings. He had mastered playing the guitar and he was becoming a good singer too. Matt was my best friend that year and I will always be grateful to the love he showed me. When I watch college basketball games on ESPN, it brings great memories that I shared with my son, Matt.

He started encouraging me to come to the Courthouse Athletic Club where we would always workout. I hadn't gone in weeks because of all the health issues I was dealing with. I finally listened to him and forced myself to start going. I slowly regained my energy and strength. I had some of the best times at our dream home with my two boys. I thank God for blessing me with two boys that taught me so many things during their high school days.

With Jake, Jesus taught me to be patient and to love him unconditionally. He was a social and popular kid among his peers, and a challenge for me to keep up with, he overcame some rough times. He was dealing with what happened to his mom. Jake remembered her, he was the oldest and I can't imagine how he was feeling during his school days. I was so proud that he got an award at McNary, The Comeback Kid Award.

Jake was intelligent, he found a passion for hip-hop music. He became a local hip-hop artist, The Kid Espi. I decided to support him on his passion, our relationship improved tremendously when I did that. I used to listen to him rehearse for hours in his bedroom. Sometimes I would walk in his room and find stacks of papers with lyrics to his songs that he would rap to. He went on to produce seven albums, two solos. His work ethic was powerful – such a strong drive to achieve his music dream.

I prayed for Jake every night. I wanted his lyrics to not include some questionable language. At that point in life he was old enough to make his own decisions. My job as a dad was to encourage him as much as I could to follow Jesus Christ. I could not be more proud of the person he turned out to be. My prayers again were answered.

The day came when Matt signed a letter of intent to play college basketball. He would play his first two years at Southwestern Oregon Community College, Jake would start his second year at LBCC. Both colleges were in the same league, NWAACC.

We rented a U-Haul truck and loaded up all their needed furniture and clothes. Matt would be staying in dorms and Jake would be renting an apartment in Albany, Oregon. I drove the truck and Matt drove his car. We made it to Coos Bay, Oregon. By early evening, we unloaded Matt's things and said our goodbyes. I was feeling sad, but I knew they were ready to move on and I encouraged education as a priority.

I was taking Jake next, Albany was on the way back off of Interstate 5. It was pretty late in the evening when we made it back to Albany. We unloaded Jake's things and I gave him a hug and said goodbye. Jake told me that he would be coming to visit me on weekends when he could. He didn't want me to get too lonely.

As I'm writing this part, I am in tears. On my way back to Salem, I thanked the Lord for the blessing He gave me with Matt and Jake. It was a sad day for me. My entire life had been watching after them since they were born and even more so after their mom passed. I had done my best as a dad trying to do a *mom and dad's job at the same time*. My prayers were for my two boys to have a successful life in college and for their safety.

When I arrived at home after returning the U-Haul truck, I walked inside our house. It was so quiet, a quiet that I had not heard before. I decided to drive over to where Candi was buried at St. Barbara Cemetery in Salem. Based on Revelation 21 in the Bible, if I spoke to Candi, she would not hear me, she was in heaven with Jesus in paradise. I did talk to myself standing next to her plot. I thanked her for the great job she did with our boys when they were younger.

27.

Jesus Closed a Door and
Opened a Window

My job as a software engineer had taken off and I was at the highest pay scale for my position, systems analyst. I had been promoted to the Department of Revenue. I eventually made some good friends at work that kept me sane social-wise. I became friends with Shamus; Cheryl; Ed; Dawn; Rita; Mike, and Rick. Those people made it fun for me at work.

Throughout my career I learned how to code in many computer languages like COBOL; CICS COBOL; Assembler; JCL (Job Control Language); Easytrieve Plus; Basic; CL (Control Language); Microfocus Cobol; IMS Database Calls; Advantage 2E; FTP Scripting (File Transfer Protocol), and a touch of Java. I mostly enjoyed coding and testing in the COBOL days at Children Services Division. It was fun having skills that not many people had.

I was the only Hispanic that worked at any I.T. shop I was employed at. In the early days I was used as an interpreter in addition to developing software. Taxpayers would call in and no one knew Spanish. I was so glad when they started hiring bilingual Revenue agents.

I experienced discrimination throughout my career at different places I worked. Despite the fact that we had policies in place, it was still real. I just did my job and tried not to worry about those issues. A manager once told me that if it got to be a problem I could report it. I never did report anything on anyone. I knew I had to adjust and I didn't want it to affect my work. My years working for the state were productive, educational, and rewarding. For the most part people treated me with respect, but like any job you'll always have a few that are negative and full of complaints.

I worked with four platforms during my career, IBM Mainframe, IBM Midrange, PC, and Web. I flew to New Orleans, Louisiana, for CA World 2000 – software updates and training. I flew to Dallas, Texas, for vendor software updates. I flew to San Francisco, California, for software updates and training. I had to prepare presentations for our staff and conduct a training session. I was also required to take trainings locally, some in Portland, when I was first learning Revenue's AS400 commands and coding.

I was busy going to work and driving to Albany or Coos Bay to watch my boys play basketball when they were in college. I tried to watch Matt's games when his team was playing away, since more of the NWAACC teams were in Portland, Eugene, and Albany. When Jake or Matt's teams played Chemeketa, it was in Salem. It worked out with minimal four-hour trips to Coos Bay.

I would often invite their Grandma Elaine Cover to watch some of the away games. She enjoyed watching her grandkids play basketball – it was nice having her as company for a long drive. I never enjoyed driving far distances alone, I always invited someone that wanted to go watch with me. Sometimes I would invite one of Matt's friends from high school. Albany was a closer distance so I usually drove there by myself.

I won't be shy about this, I felt I did a pretty good job at being a top-notch dad to my two boys. They meant the world to me and still do today. If anyone were to ask them about me, they would hear it from both boys.

We experienced a ton of things together. We laughed together; we cried together; we played sports together; we vacationed together; we hung out together; we prayed together; we all shared a piece of Candi's heart together, and we supported each other. I bought them the best things on the market, like basketball shoes and more. I made sure I displayed to them that God was important and that education was power.

I can't express how proud I am of what they have accomplished in life. I have no regrets in raising my kids the way I did. I did the best I could, and I know Jesus was right there next to me, even when I didn't know it.

When the boys were old enough to start their own adventures, I started taking acting classes. I wanted to try acting – it seemed fun and I would be around people. In two years I learned so much about acting. I didn't realize how tough it was to be believable in front of people or the TV camera. At one point I thought about flying to LA and auditioning for one month to see if I could make it to the big screen.

All of my acting dreams came to a halt when I severely injured my knee. Not only that, but I learned that my passion was being around my boys and attending their games. I think God showed me that. I did manage to make some money shooting a Les Schwab Tire's commercial and during photo shoots for magazine covers or advertisements. I also played a small part at the Pentacle Theatre in Salem, Oregon. The name of the play was, *Arsenic and Old Lace.*

I joined a company called Extras Only in Portland – my agent was Danny Stoltz. The closest I came to being on the big screen was when I received a call from my agent. I was to appear on a wedding scene with Marlee Matlin. I had injured my knee and could not walk. I decided to end my acting career because of the injury and a conflict with my day job. I did enjoy all of the auditioning and fun experiences and I have no regrets.

I had given up on meeting a woman to date, and then the Lord opened a window that I didn't expect. I met Loni, a single parent that had two daughters, Darci and Kalin. The girls both had attended McNary High School at the same time as Jake and Matt.

I remember speaking to Loni for the first time when her kids and my kids were in elementary school attending Junior Olympics track meets. My boys specialized in the field events. Darci was a runner and Kalin was a field-event's athlete.

"Excuse me!"

"Yes?" I turned around and saw this beautiful blonde-blue-eyed lady.

"Could you tell me where we register?" Loni asked.

"Oh, sure, it's right over there," I smiled at her and she smiled back.

"Thank you."

"You have someone competing?"

"Yeah, my two daughters."

"Very nice, good luck."

I walked off and never saw her again until years later at some of the girls' basketball games. I would also see Loni at the Courthouse Athletic Club. I exercised there regularly and my boys played a lot of basketball there as well. I would see Darci there working out as well. Darci played basketball at the same high school my boys did.

I saw Loni again at Matt's high-school-graduation party at 4:00 a.m. I volunteered all night long and I guess she volunteered to clean up. I said hi to her as she briefly stopped to say hi, and then she continued walking in. She was in a hurry to get to the clean-up area.

Loni's daughter, Kalin, was home for the summer. She was planning on getting married in 2003. That year I saw Loni with her daughter Darci at Albertson's grocery store in Keizer, Oregon. I said hi to Loni and wanted to say hi to her daughter, but she seemed kind of shy and kept going through the aisle.

Loni stopped to say hi to me. I was totally out of character, I wanted to know if she was a single parent. My kids could tell you better than anyone that I had embarrassed them many times speaking out to people I didn't know. I didn't want to miss this opportunity though.

"Hi it's good seeing you again," I smiled.

"Hi."

"I'm so curious, are you married?"

"Uh, yes I am."

"Oh darn, okay I was just curious, I didn't notice a ring on your finger."

I can't remember what she said but she did explain why she wasn't wearing one. I was a little disappointed, but understood and didn't look back.

During the fall of 2004 a friend informed me that she didn't think Loni was married anymore. I was so excited to somehow get a hold of her. I'd go to Albertsons across town just to see if I could run into her while grocery shopping. I never did see her. Another friend told me where she worked at. It took me several avenues, but I finally connected with Loni. She was no longer married, and she accepted my invitation to dinner. Sadly to say, we went to Burger King. I was so used to eating at fast-food places. They were quick and cheap. Loni was such a good sport, she didn't complain about us eating at Burger King. Now that I think about it, I feel bad that I didn't even ask her where she would love to eat. I hope she can forgive me for my selfish and thoughtless first-date evening. But then again, I had been single for so many years that I was stuck on my own ways.

We started seeing each other and we would talk for hours about our kids, our life, my struggles, and her struggles. Everything was going great, it was just her and I for months. I started falling for her. We started spending more time together, she was an elementary P.E. teacher and worked long hours. I would get off work and wait for her to come over. At the time she was in transition living with her mom in Keizer.

A few months later, she asked me if I would like to meet her mom and brother. I said *sure, I would like that.* For the first time she introduced me to her mom, Donna, and to her brother, Scott. She also had another brother, Ed, that lived in Texas. Her dad was no longer alive.

I was happy, because to me, a female that wanted me to meet her mom meant that she was interested in me. After that night, I felt welcomed by her family and I felt us getting closer as we spent more time with each other. Loni was a blessing to me from the start. That night I thanked the Lord for putting her in front of me.

Whatever sins I had committed in the past, I repented, and I asked for forgiveness. I went to confession at the Catholic Church for the last time. After that I was done with confessions to a priest. Loni started attending church with me and people started noticing that I was dating someone. Loni would mention things to me about the differences between the Catholic Church and the church she attended with her daughter, Darci.

I listened but was stubborn about being open-minded. Candi had mentioned those same differences to me. Darci was attending a Calvary Chapel Bible College in Murrieta, California. Kalin was living in Edmonton, Alberta, Canada. I didn't get to know Kalin well, she was far away in Canada.

Calvary Chapel churches study the Word of God – the Bible, book by book, chapter by chapter, verse by verse. It was different than the red-code rules I had been raised with in the Catholic Church. I do want to mention that those red-code rules did help discipline me as a young boy, I am truly thankful to the Catholic Church for that.

The difference in our beliefs at the time were not compatible. The church that Loni attended had just gone through a major division. She was seeking a new church to attend. She would attend St. Joseph's with me during that process, but only because that's where I attended.

Catholics do worship the same God, they just worship a little differently. I'm not going to judge anyone here, because my side of the family was cradle Catholic. A majority of them still are today. That's all I was taught, Catholicism doctrine. What was funny is that Loni asked the same question that Candi asked me when we were first dating back in 1979.

"How do you feel you get to heaven?"

"Well, you go to church, you treat people kindly, and you believe in God."

"Actually, it's when you accept Jesus as your Savior."

"Oh, I see."

In my mind I remembered hearing that from Candi. I was still stubborn and didn't continue the conversation. We continued attending St. Joseph's Church. Everything was semi-stable, and I started looking at Ephesians where there are scriptures that talk about husband and wife. I wanted to understand more about Jesus in the New Testament and how a Biblical marriage worked. Because to tell you the truth I wanted Loni to someday be my wife in the near future.

She started attending Matt's games with me. Jake had graduated from Linn Benton and met a young lady that he started dating. Her name was, Jennifer Bell. Jake was supportive of me dating Loni and so was Matt. They were out of high school and knew that I would be happier with a companion for life.

I guess what seemed to be a fun and exciting time in my life started taking a downhill turn with my emotions and discomfort. When Loni's daughters first found out about us, one of them was totally against the whole idea and the other was okay with it. My thought was, *wow, her daughters are going to be so happy and excited!* It turned out to be the total opposite.

What a blessing in disguise this turned out to be for me. God put, Darci, a wonderful young lady, in front of me to open my mind and look at the Word of God. She was about to embark into a third-world country after graduating from college. She was heading to the jungles of Peru to share the love of Jesus Christ. Loni would tell me so many things about her and how she was following Jesus Christ.

I started paying attention to the things I heard about Darci and how she was spreading the Word in another country. It was foreign to me ... how could someone leave the United States to serve the Lord and live in the midst of another culture? That is not an easy thing to do. A mission is about living in the culture and then displaying Jesus' love. Teaching the Gospel to people that have never heard of Jesus Christ. Not everyone will have that calling. I started understanding a little at a time, but at this time I still struggled a little with the entire concept.

Darci was a special person that God put right in front of me. Through Loni, I got to know Darci and I had the opportunity to learn more about Jesus Christ.

I eventually proposed to Loni. My original plan was to buy a box of chocolates from See's Candies and place the engagement ring inside one of the slots. The day I was planning my proposal, I drove to the candy store, but only to see a sign, *We are Closed.* So that evening, I invited Loni to my house to shoot some baskets in my backyard. After I proposed to her, she was thinking for a few minutes. She then said, *okay, if you make a free shot and then I make one, I'll say yes.* Talk about pressure at the free-throw line. I was pretty confident about my shot, because I was a pretty good shooter. I was worried about her shot, she hadn't played in a very long time. I think Jesus must have intervened, because she made it!

We started attending different churches, but I wasn't comfortable with any of them, sometimes I would disagree with the pastors. I was so used to the Catholic doctrine that I found myself defending the Catholic Church that I was accustomed to for years.

God was finally, in his own timing, putting knowledge in front of me about Jesus and why He came down to earth, in flesh, to teach us how to love and serve.

Loni and I were planning our wedding when it took a detour. Loni felt it was too soon for her daughters to deal with their mom getting married. Loni convinced me to wait another six months, she needed time. I had been alone for a long time, it was probably difficult for anyone to understand. I loved Loni so much, and waiting another six months was nothing compared to the years I had been alone. So I agreed, and Loni had a huge smile on her face. I remember her saying, *I love you, Dave.*

I loved meeting someone like Loni, she had two daughters and I had two sons. What better combination? We could both relate to each other as far as our kids. We agreed that our kids were special to us both.

I hadn't seen Darci since that time at Albertsons. I was going to meet her in person when Loni was loaning her the car to go to church at Athey Creek off of I-205. Darci was dropping her mom off outside my house before driving to Athey Creek Fellowship close to Lake Oswego, Oregon.

After waiting the additional six months, Loni and I attended a few meetings with a pastor from a non-denominational church that was close to Silver Falls State Park outside of Silverton, Oregon. His name was Wayne Muller and we felt comfortable with him and his openness about marrying us on December 31st, 2005. I was so worried that her daughters might not attend, because the word I got was that they were not too excited about their mom getting married to me – at least that's how I felt, I could be all wrong.

Matt was playing on a full scholarship at Southern Oregon University that year. His team was playing Warner Pacific University. After the game, Jake and I brought him back with us the day before the New Year's Eve wedding. Matt was going to play the guitar and sing a couple of songs at our small wedding.

I remember Loni having feelings of whether to go through with this or not. Matt and Jake both called her and said some nice words to her. They wanted her to know that she was being welcomed into our home and they knew that this was going to make me happy.

The next day at the church I showed up early and didn't know if Loni would show up. Luckily she showed up with her daughters. I didn't see her until she was walking up the steps from the basement in her beautiful wedding dress. It was breathtaking how pretty she looked. She had this huge smile on her face. We had a small group of family and friends there.

We both memorized our vows and recited them to each other. Pastor Wayne did a great job teaching a small message to everyone. Matt did an amazing job with the songs. Kalin had a hard time lighting the candles, one of the lighters wasn't turning on. Jake finally handed his to her. That was a funny part at our wedding. Kalin and her husband, Everett, also did a small reading. The reception was fun, we joked around as we were cutting the cake.

Both of our work places were generous with the gifts they gave us. We drove out to Newport, Oregon, immediately after the reception. Our family and friends stayed to clean up and bring the gifts and items to our house. We were so thankful for the people that helped out at our wedding.

We did continue going to the Catholic Church for a few years, but it just wasn't working out for both of us. There were just too many differences and we didn't feel at peace. I never went back to the Catholic Church. What I started learning from that point on was complimenting what Candi had read to me in the past and what she tried telling me during our early days. I know that Jesus has forgiven me for not listening to Candi, I was wrong and I can admit that.

Loni and I were getting to know each other better living together and going places. I never expected that I would change so quickly. I started being selfish, I wanted things done a certain way, I wanted the house to be spotlessly clean. I didn't want to go to the places Loni wanted to go. I wanted to make all of the decisions, I was not being the same husband that I was to Candi. I found myself comparing Candi to Loni and wanting Loni to be like Candi. They were similar in many areas, but different in other areas. I had turned into a terrible husband and Loni was not happy. And then when her daughters found out, well, that just made things even worse.

I was not the same person. Anyone that knew me would not believe this was the same person. I would get so jealous, and I would want things done the way I did them around the house. I hope that some day all of Loni's family can find it in their hearts to forgive me, because to tell you the truth it took me months to forgive myself.

It's true that Satan is always trying to pull us away from Jesus. This time it was me that Satan was trying to pull away from Jesus. This evil thing sometimes comes in a camouflage. Sometimes this evil thing wants us to think we are power over God, but this evil thing is no match for Jesus.

Matthew 4:10 Then Jesus said to him, "Be gone Satan!
For it is written, 'you shall worship the Lord your God
and Him only shall you serve,'" then the devil left him,
and behold, angels came and were ministering to him.

When my two boys would come home from college I would talk to them about certain things. They counseled me on issues that I didn't understand. They were both smart kids and had learned a lot about people and how you treat people. Matt was studying the Bible and reading Christian books. He helped me through several things while I was in my early stages of marriage with Loni. I made a terrible mess of things in my marriage.

What I didn't realize is that Loni wasn't Candi. I asked Jesus to show me the way once again. I wanted that way now, but it wasn't up to me, it was up to Jesus and in His timing.

A few years went by and we would attend different churches in the Salem area. Sometimes we would attend Athey Creek, which was located in the outskirts of Portland. The more I listened to the teachings the more I started understanding the Word of God.

Darci met Gino, a young Peruvian man, while doing mission work in Lima, Peru, and surrounding villages. Their story is amazing, I'd love to write it some day. I'll explain briefly, she was eventually engaged and then planned her wedding. She would be married in Lima, Peru. Loni flew there to spend time with her and Gino two weeks prior to the wedding and I was to meet them there a week prior to the wedding. I had work and couldn't get time off until then. Jake dropped me off at Portland International Airport, since I would fly back with Loni.

I was dealing with all sorts of anxiety and stress, but I wasn't about to miss my stepdaughter's wedding, that was way too important. This would be my first time ever to leave the USA and to visit a third-world country. I was excited, anxious, and nervous all at the same time. It was a long flight and I lost my appetite during the flight. I first arrived in Houston and then hopped on another plane to Lima, Peru.

Everything was as described to me when I arrived at the Lima airport. There were custom checks and tons of people holding up signs so their arrivals would see them. I wandered around looking for Loni and Darci.

After five minutes I heard Darci, "Dave!" She ran to me and gave me the biggest hug ever. That made me feel good and welcomed. She had this huge smile on her face. And then I saw my wife and she also had a smile on her face. It was so nice to see them again. I met Gino, he was a handsome and tough-looking Peruvian. He was polite while showing me a few things in the Lima airport.

I have to admit that I was in a little bit of a culture shock, I wasn't the kind of person to take change well. The important thing was that I made it there and experienced a great time while I was there. I wish I could do that week over again, but I can't. I know that I caused a lot of heartache to Loni. I was selfish in many things when I was there. I don't want to discuss any of those things, it's too painful for me and my family – it was so unlike me.

Satan tries to steer us away from Jesus, I believe that Satan has the power to influence people of the world. But like I mentioned before, Satan is no match for Jesus.

Basically, I was thinking of myself in many situations, when I should have been supporting my wife and my stepdaughter in a special time in their lives. I'm not saying my entire time there was selfish, but some of it was totally selfish on my part. Their wedding was beautiful and I enjoyed being there. Loni did get to spend quality time with both of them – I was glad that she did.

God put this trip in front of me, I saw a deeper level of poverty. I was raised in a poverty neighborhood, but in Lima, Peru, and surrounding villages? Wow, I had never seen it close up in real live situations.

Gino took me to the markets in Lima, we paid ten cents for a large-fresh-squeezed orange juice. He gave me a tour of the city and a lesson on the people there. He explained why there were soldiers with rifles at each corner in downtown Lima. They help protect the tourists. It was cool because I could talk to him in Spanish.

One day while Loni was out with her daughters getting their hair and nails done, I stayed back at the hotel. I decided to go for a walk around the neighborhood. I noticed that many houses had eight-foot fences in front. The crime there at night was pretty bad. I was walking by a few houses and a huge pit bull started barking at me, this startled me, my heart was racing. I was relieved when the dog was on the roof and stayed there.

We spent some quality time with Gino and Darci and experienced South America. When we got back home, I shared pictures with my family and my two boys. I also brought some to my work and shared with my coworkers, none had ever been to Peru. I felt blessed that I made it back safely and that I brought back yet another memory of my life. There were a lot of positive experiences in my trip to Lima, which had over nine million people living in the city – wow!

As I was saying earlier I had always been a down-to-earth person, or at least I felt I had been. I loved Loni so much, but was portraying it so poorly, that I think I was suffocating her. I was not being a good husband. I wasn't physically abusing her, but I think emotionally she was feeling that I was being a little too controlling.

I would often tell her to not wear certain clothes, I wanted her to dress more modestly, like the Bible speaks in certain scriptures. Loni felt that it was too Amish-like and that modesty was a judgment call. I learned that a husband should be the head of household, but not in the way that I was handling things.

Husbands are to love their wives as Christ loved the church. I wasn't doing that. My boys were out of the house by then, Matt was getting ready to graduate college and Jake had just gotten married to Jennifer. Their wedding was beautiful and big, a lot of people. Jake and Jen both knew many people.

Loni started attending a small church that was planted in Salem. An elder from Athey Creek came to Salem to plant a new church and to teach the Word of God, book by book, verse by verse. I didn't attend the first couple of times, but I did get invited by Loni and Darci. I prayed again that night and asked the Lord to show me the way, my wife was not happy and I wanted to be the best husband I could be to her.

I felt in my heart that I needed to give Mission Fellowship a try. I thought I would go there and see what they knew and then decide if I wanted to continue or not. After the first time I went, I learned so much. It was amazing. I kept going back for more.

At this point I caused a lot of problems with Loni's family, they did not like me anymore and didn't want to be around me – I have to say, I didn't blame them. I was trying to learn more because I knew that God existed just because of what I went through. I loved Loni, she saw that we were struggling. I can't remember how this all happened. I agreed to go to a counseling session with our pastor and his wife.

I learned a lot about what it meant to be a husband to my wife. I'm not saying that either of us were perfect in our marriage, or right about things we discussed. What I did learn, was that loving your wife is not about controlling her. Loving your wife is to act how Christ loves His bride, the church, which translates to his people. He gave us free will. I learned that I could suggest things to my wife in a respectful and civilized manner, and if she submitted on her own free will, great! But if she chose not to, I would still love her no matter what. That concept for me was difficult, you have no idea how difficult it was, I never interpreted Ephesians that way.

Ephesians 5:22 Wives submit to your own husbands as to the Lord. For the husband is the head of the wife even as Christ is the head of the church, his body, is himself its Savior.

I was being a buffet Christian (one who picks verses that suits him or her). I was totally excluding this next verse. This is how God wants us husbands to treat our wives. I strongly recommend this next verse to husbands that might be going through what I did.

Ephesians 5:25 Husbands, love your wives, as Christ loved the church and gave himself up for her.

All it took was that one session for me to see things from a different angle. My boys both would tell me similar things, but I was too stubborn, I wanted to be right about my selfish ways. I apologized to Loni for being such a terrible husband when I should have been a lot better, when I should have been like I was back in high school and back when I was married to Candi. I created a conflict with her family. Now it was time for me to restore with Jesus in my heart and prayer. Forgiveness would not come right away as fruits had to be seen. I'm speaking for me and what I started realizing.

At first I expected Loni to forgive me instantly. I expected her daughters and their husbands to forgive me instantly. I expected her mom to forgive me instantly, and her brother. But now that I know more about Jesus and His righteousness and justice, I know that forgiveness takes time, sometimes years. My job was to produce fruits that could be displayed, and allow the restoration through Jesus, my Savior, to happen in His timing.

In no way am I perfect, I would still slip now and then, but I assured Loni that I would get right back on track. Things started slowly improving. Eventually, because of Jesus' guidance, things started coming together.

I was growing as a Christian and adapting to not making it about me. I was starting to think of others, how Loni, Matt, and Jake always displayed and talked to me about. My kids were proud of me for making an effort at changing my ways and returning to the person I used to be. I felt that God brought Loni into my life, not just to give both of us joy, but to also transform me into a better Christian. Also, to love her as much as I loved Candi. Before, I was a buffet Christian, I only picked the Bible verses that suited me. That started changing one day at a time, but it wasn't easy – it was a narrow path. I needed Jesus in my heart and I needed prayer – I couldn't do it alone.

Loni showed me a scripture that I often read. I encourage you to look at it wholeheartedly.

Corinthians 13:4-7 Love is patient and kind. Love does not envy or boast; it is not arrogant or rude; it does not insist on its own way; it is not irritable or resentful; it does not rejoice at wrong doing, but rejoices with the truth.

I was so adapted to just my two boys and I. I had a routine down and I was focusing on them and their future. I started realizing what a blessing Loni and her daughter were to me in addition. I didn't see Kalin as much, Canada is thousands of miles from Salem. I've learned so much about the Bible and I continue to learn more.

I was now attending a church that taught the Word of God – the Bible. Our pastor did a great job with analogies that supported what he taught straight from the Bible. The majority of people had their own Bible, we took notes, and we worshipped before and after the teachings with songs. Our church made it about Jesus, as many do in our community.

Slowly my family was coming together. All of our kids, Jake, Matt, Kalin, and Darci have college degrees. Loni and I support them in any adventure they are on. I feel honored that my two boys are followers of Jesus Christ, they display it every day and they are my counsel when I have a question. I feel honored to have a relationship with Darci and Gino, they are followers of Jesus Christ. I enjoy talking scriptures with all of them when there is an opportunity. Most of all, I am honored to be Loni's husband. I love it when I ask her a question about a certain scripture and she has a logical answer for it. I read the scripture and I think about it to try and understand what Jesus is saying. One day I hope to be the person my wife asks a question about the Bible and I have the answer for her.

I have shared some personal things about my life including some things about my children and stepchildren, the ones I'm closest to – *I apologize if you feel uncomfortable about what I wrote, but you all have had a huge impact in my life that has been so blessed. I thank you for that from the bottom of my heart.*

They know I'm half blind, and they don't treat me differently because of that. I think sometimes they forget that I'm physically different, which makes me feel normal. God put me in a situation where I felt restored in more ways than one. I was restored to look normal again, unlike my grade-school days when kids were making fun of me in different ways. God was with me even when I didn't know it. I was also restored to be the husband I once was with Candi. It took a decision I made, to let go of myself and allow Jesus to come into my heart.

During the second year of attending Mission Fellowship, our pastor was holding a baptism at the Willamette River. My plan was to just watch, because several people from the church had signed up for this baptism. As I was standing there next to the water on a sunny day, everyone was getting ready for this event, I walked up to my pastor, Hans Rasmussen.

"Is it too late for me to sign up to get baptized?"

"Absolutely not, do you want to get baptized?" Hans asked.

"Yes, definitely."

On a warm August day I was baptized and became a new-born Christian. I was reborn in spirit with the water of Jesus Christ. It felt good to go underwater and then come up as a newly-born Christian. It was so cool because this was my decision to accept Christ as my Savior.

John 3:3-6. Jesus answered, "Truly, truly, I say to you, unless one is born again he cannot see the Kingdom of God." Nicodemus said to him, "How can a man be born when he is old? Can he enter a second time into his mother's womb and be born?" Jesus answered, "Truly, truly, I say to you, unless one is born of water and spirit, he cannot enter the Kingdom of God. That which is born of flesh is flesh, and that which is born of spirit is spirit."

That day I felt that I was forgiven by Jesus for my sins of the past. Oh how I would encourage anyone that's going through difficult times like I was, to start thinking about allowing Jesus to come into your life. Your situation may be totally different than what mine was, but I assure you, Jesus is there with you even if you don't know it. It is up to us to grab what he puts in front of us – it definitely is our choice, He gave us that free will.

By 2012 I had written three books while holding down a day job. I found a passion for writing inspiring sports stories. I was also thinking of retiring from this great job that paid me a lot of money. I did all of the research and I prayed about it. For a full-benefit package, the requirement was that I had worked 30 years and I was at least 55 years of age that calendar year, or 59 with less than 30 years of service. I wanted to start my career as an author, I was ready for a change for many reasons. I had worked over 31 years and I was 54 years old.

On June 30, 2013, I retired from my day job with full benefits. I would get a decent salary every month and I would start my adventure as a full-time author and keynote speaker. I had previously taken a year of Toastmasters which was a huge help in public speaking. I didn't realize how bad of a speaker I was until I took Toastmasters.

For my retirement celebration, I wanted to do something for others, I didn't want to just make it about me. All that I was learning about Jesus and all that I had been blessed with, I just felt a need to invite my friends, relatives, and immediate family members. Not everyone was able to attend because of other obligations, however, most of the important people in my life were there. Darci and Loni helped me with the decorations early in the morning. I was performing a clean standup-comedy show at the Grande Theatre in downtown Salem, Oregon.

I asked several musicians that I knew if they would perform after my comedy routine. My son Jake was the emcee and performed his hit song, "Oregon Homeboy". He had been a performing artist in the previous years and his stage name was "Kid Espi". My cousin, Sophie sang a song. Loni's nephew, Matt French, played the guitar and sang two songs. A couple from my church, Kris and Carolina, played the mandolin and sang. We gave away prizes at the end and we had cake, punch, and cookies in the lobby afterwards. Loni asked some friends that she knew if they would work the reception area. I hired one of her former students and her friends to serve in the lobby. Some friends from our church kept an eye on the lobby while the show was going on. Huge thanks to those people that helped me out.

My son, Matt, surprised me when he showed up with a crew to do a video production of my entire show. I still watch that now and then. They had cameras in different locations, one up front, one on the floor behind the stage, and one on the balcony. It was unbelievable and I felt so honored and blessed by my family and friends. I think we had over 150 people in attendance.

I did my best to get all of my brothers and sisters to show up, but most of them could not afford to travel the distance. I was happy for the ones that did show up. I was also thankful for my cousins from the Moses Lake days, most of them showed up, including my Aunt Olivia, my mom's sister.

It was my dad's birthday, he was turning 79, so I added a special tribute for him. He sacrificed so much for our family when we were growing up. I acknowledged him and said some nice words after the show. Jake had everyone stand up and sing happy birthday to my dad. That was a touching moment, I was so glad I could honor my dad and thank him for all he taught me when I was growing up. He was always there for me and he was always working and providing for our family.

My author adventure started. A new chapter in my life. My goal is to someday write a bestseller. But if that doesn't happen, it's okay. It's all up to the Lord, and if it's His will. In the meantime,

I love writing and I love encouraging middle school and high school students to further their education. I also take any opportunity I get to witness, but it has to be the right time. I can't just tell someone to read the Bible and follow Jesus. I have to actually set an example and display love for Jesus. That in itself can be a tough challenge.

My marriage has improved by leaps and bounds. Jesus allowed restoration with many family members that despised my actions before. I know that some may never forgive me for the jerk I used to be, but I'm responsible for my actions, not theirs.

I still have moments where I get angry because of a minor thing, but it doesn't take me long to think about my reaction. Loni is so good to me, she'll give me examples of why I should not overreact over the smallest things. I love that about her, she's right most of the time, don't tell her I said that – ha-ha!

I'm finding that the closer I get to Jesus the less I will sin. I'm reading the entire Bible for the first time in my life. I started doing this in 2015. I'm three quarters of the way through. I read it five days a week, a few chapters at a time. I can't wait to get to the New Testament. The Old Testament has so much sinning going on and so many people going against God's words. But then again, that's happening in today's world as well.

My life has always had its ups and downs, and things that happened to me were, I would say, intense and at an early age in my life. Not too many people lose half their eyesight at five-years old. Not too many people will lose their thirty-two-year-old spouse while raising two little boys. Not too many people will lose three family relatives in a four-year span. My mom, my nephew, Evan, who got killed in a car accident when he was fourteen, and my wife, Candi. God was always with me, raising me when I would fall, showing me the way, answering prayer after prayer.

The hardship that I experienced in life has encouraged me to have more compassion for kids, teenagers, or adults that might be going through a similar hardship. I've learned that God gave me gifts I didn't expect and answers that helped me overcome the obstacles I faced.

With my Catholic brothers and sisters, well, I have found a great source for any Catholic questions that I have. My niece, Jaclyn, married Brad. I have so much respect for Brad – a highly educated Catholic. He is honest about what he has learned about Catholic doctrine. If I have a question for him, he'll answer it for me. When we debate, we are friendly about our discussion. We both have different views on how we interpret certain scriptures, and that's okay. We all have a choice to believe what we want.

Some people don't believe that God is real. With Brad and I, I have learned stuff about the Catholic Church that I never knew before. He points to me, in the Bible, where their doctrine comes from. I love Brad for that reason. While we don't agree on every-thing, we do agree that Jesus is the focus and that we should love one another as Christ loved the church. I do believe that the church I attend worships the same God as the Catholic Church. Catholics use the same Bible we do, with a few extra books in their Bible. The way that the services are held are different. Me, I like to hear the scriptures the entire hour, I find peace in that, and I can't speak for anyone else, it's just me.

How lucky have I been? Well, I never thought about it before. Not many men get the opportunity to experience solid love twice. Not only did I think I would never get a date with a girl, but to be married to my beautiful Candi for thirteen years, and then to be married to my beautiful Loni going on twelve years now? I have to feel lucky and blessed. Without Jesus, I'm nothing though, I hope my story is evidence.

Phillipians 4:13 I can do all things through Christ who strengthens me.

God had blessed me with many of my dreams that came true. Three new houses that I built, I never thought I would finally get to this point coming from a poverty neighborhood full of dirt roads. Two wonderful sons that are doing some amazing things and are believers in Christ. Two stepdaughters that are talented and are also doing some amazing things as well.

It's 2017 and I'm working on this book, my autobiography. I was scared and nervous about exposing my imperfections and sins to everyone. But, I felt Jesus in my heart saying, *go forward and write this*. I hope that with my story, I can help someone out there that might be going through the roughest times in their life.

As my marriage continues to grow with Loni, I feel at peace more than ever. We now have six grandchildren. Darci and Gino have two little boys, Luca and Josiah. Jake and Jennifer have two little boys, Tyson and Kaleb. Kalin and Everett have two little boys, Silas and Seth. Matt and Bethany are newlyweds and for now have a little dog named, Sherman.

My newest adventures for Jesus and stepping out of my comfort zone have been challenging and fun at the same time. My son, Matt, founded a ministry called Salem Hoops Project. This is our way of giving back to the community and also displaying Jesus' love toward kids and parents.

Basketball is our passion and we have the necessary skills to train kids with the needed skill sets. Matt played college basketball and even two years at the minor-league professional level. I joined him and support him to this day with this non-profit program. I'm the director of operations and I provide Gatorade or Powerade for the kids that participate. Matt is the executive director and trainer, and Jordan Carter is the treasurer and trainer as well. This is something that we do for others, it's all volunteer work. Matt calls and coordinates the volunteers for all of the free basketball clinics.

I started sponsoring a child in Burkina Faso, Africa. It never crossed my mind before to do something like this for a child in need. I don't do things like this for the purpose of getting anything in return. I do these things because I want to help others. I started these two voluntary opportunities, which were out of my comfort zone, and I feel so good and blessed by them.

I feel it's okay to have passions, and now, I try to participate in those passions for Jesus. I try hard to use my gifts with Jesus in mind. When you do for others the reward is the satisfaction that you helped someone out there.

Luke 6:38 Give, and it will be given to you. Good measure, pressed down, shaken together, running over,

will be put into your lap. For with the measures you use,
it will be measured back to you.

I still ask myself, if I had one wish to be someone else like a wealthy movie star or a famous NBA Player, or even an NFL player, who would that be? My answer still remains, *I would want to be me.*

God created me, and because of that I have my two grown-up boys that I love. And now, I have Loni and two grown-up stepdaughters. Loni and I have six beautiful grandchildren that we love. There's no amount of wealth that can buy what God has given me. Yes, I might be half-blind, and I can't even see the 3D affects in a 3D movie. That's okay, because with Jesus Christ in my life, I definitely have full sight with full vision on what's important and much more beyond 3D.

As far as the sufferings, imperfections, unfairness, and evil in this world, remember that this tiny world is temporary. Everlasting life in paradise with Jesus is what will be a mesmerizing peace. That to me, with healthy bodies and no tears from the earth that will be passed, sounds a lot better.

God bless you, and thank you so much for taking the time out of your schedule to read my life story.

1959 – I was a one-year-old baby in Dimmitt, Texas.

This is St. Anthony's Hospital in Amarillo, Texas, where I was admitted for several months as a five year-old.

1969 – I had so much fun growing up with my family.
From left, Loop; Gilberto; Mom; Diana; David (Me); Dad; Richard, and Louise.

First Grade

Second Grade

Third Grade

I won my first trophy as a 12-year-old boy in the Ford Punt, Pass, and Kick Contest. My brothers also won.

I started thinking about my future at a very young age.

Our first trip to Oregon. I was eleven-years old. We stopped for lunch by a beautiful river.

Sheryn Roberts was my good friend during sixth grade. She lifted my self-esteem to a higher level.

Karen Stevick was my eighth-grade friend and pen-pal. We had one date in Friona, Texas, while watching the Dimmitt Bobcats battle the Friona Chieftans.

I loved riding horses at Six Gun City, a tourist attraction inside Palo Duro Canyon, just outside Canyon, Texas.

Eighth-grade graduation was a rewarding night for me. I walked away with the citizenship award, a math award, and an athletic award. Thank you Jesus for guiding me in this adventure.

Eighth-grade banquet.

After working hard all summer I always had money to buy some cowboy clothes. I often wore boots to school.

My brother Loop and I next to our black and white TV. This was after Loop returned from New Mexico where he completed high school early.

We are at the city park in Dimmit across from our house, Louise,
Loop, and Me.

Summer of 1974, here I'm with my brothers and sisters at the city
park in Dimmitt.

My dad and his brother Jessie would often get together to play music. I learned from them.

Escorting my mom at the homecoming school-pep-assembly – Dimmitt Bobcats homecoming-game rally.

I made the varsity football team as a sophomore. This photo has a lot of subtext when I see it. It was displayed on the front window of a car dealer in town.

I was overjoyed when I found out my parents were attending the homecoming game.

My mom and dad in front of a house that was made out of solid rock. Hole 'N The Rock is a tourist attraction in Moab, Utah.

The summer we stayed with our cousins, the Torres family, in Moses Lake, Washington. I'm at a dance that my cousins, Cat and Margo, insisted I go to. It was a fun experience.

In 1977, this was my first school dance with my high-school sweetheart, Candi. I wore this same outfit for several formal events.

I broke loose and scored a touchdown against the Woodburn Bulldogs.

After a tough game in horrific weather. The Gervais Cougars won!

VARSITY BASKETBALL: Frank Davidson, Eric Butts, Bill Lindsey, Ray Eden, Coach Cory Sparks, Walter Konicka, Glen Davis, David Espinoza, Curtis Schott, and Ron Gelhouse. KNEELING: Rodger Grape.

I was voted to the Snowball Court. I escorted Tracy Wells.

I earned a starting spot on the Cougars' Varsity Basketball Team. This was a fun season despite not knowing my teammates very well.

I was playing some tough defense this game.

Candi and I were helping out at a school dance. She was in charge of refreshments.

Candi's mom, Elaine, would often walk on the beach with us. Her dad would stay back at the cabin. This is at Gleneden Beach close to Lincoln City, Oregon.

My first car ever! A 1970 Ford Galaxie 500. My dad bought it from my grandpa for $150.00.

Head Coach Craig Fertig from the Oregon State Beavers was heavily recruiting me. I enjoyed the phone calls on the weekends.

I played varsity basketball with Gervais the first half of the season. We moved to Woodburn and I played the second half of the season with the Bulldogs. I'm number 33 in the back.

Here I am playing on Woodburn's team against my former teammates from Gervais. This was one of the best games I ever played during my high school career. Thank you Jesus for that blessing.

I'm with my Woodburn teammates during my best track and field season in high school. I set a school record in the high jump that year and I advanced to the state meet, what a blessing.

The 110-meter high hurdles was my favorite running event. I took third at the district meet.

Thankful to the Gervais High School Cheerleaders who came to visit me when I was recovering from a broken collar bone in 1978. Senior year was a time of injuries for me – I was depressed. The Lord was always there to help me rise.

I was voted Homecoming King. It was announced at halftime during the football game. Kathy Henry was crowned Homecoming Queen.

1977-78 Homecoming Court at Gervais High School. This was such an honor that I never expected. Thank you again, Jesus, for the many blessings.

I ran the third leg on the 4 X 100 relay at Gervais. I'm handing off the baton to Jeff Bell.

The high jump was my favorite field event. I was warming up at the St. Helen's Invitational.

I was selected to play in a donkey basketball game my senior year. I'm going for the dunk!

What a fun time, riding on donkeys and shooting hoops against our Gervais staff.

My high-school sweetheart, one of her many senior-year poses.

My senior photo at Gervais High School where I was voted "Most Considerate" by the senior class – what an honor.

My parents and grandparents. This was in 1980, our first visit back to Texas. We were checking on our house. My dad eventually sold it.

My brothers and sisters at my wedding, minus Gilberto, he was in the Air Force and could not be there.

I married my high-school sweetheart on December 6, 1980. That was a special day for me. I started a new life with Candi.

Our firstborn child, Jacob (Jake), we were so excited! I became an overprotective dad. I was on cloud nine with our special addition to the family.

We were having so much fun discovering so many things about being the best parents to our little boy.

We had our second child, Matthew (Matt). What a gift from God to have two healthy boys.

Candi was a blessing to our little guys, she always put them as priority and displayed love to them.

Candi's 3K run at Bush's Pasture Park in Salem, Oregon. The boys and I cheered her on every time.

1986-1987 – my brother and I played professional football for the Salem Stars of the NFA (Northwest Football Alliance). I later made the roster for the Portland Breakers of the USFL (United States Football League).

I was so proud of my older brother, Gilberto, he served in the Air Force. He came home for a visit before heading to Desert Storm.

This was the last time my entire family got together back in 1988. I'm at the far left. This was a celebration for me ending my pro-football career.

Three months after this photo was taken, we lost Candi to brain cancer. She was a true blessing to us. We will see her again in heaven. Revelation 21.

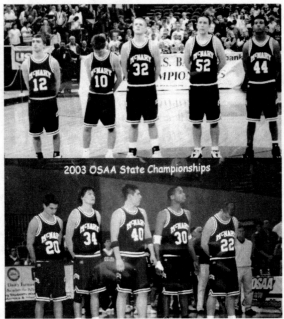

One of many great moments with my two boys in sports. Jake and Matt both helped their teams make it to the state tournament during their senior years. What an amazing experience!

Another great moment in 2004. Matt and Jake played against each other in college basketball.

I never thought I would meet another beautiful lady. God put a special lady in front of me. This was when I started dating Loni in 2004.

We were married on December 31, 2005 at a small church near Silver Falls State Park.

Jake, Dad (Me), and Matt at the wedding reception. It was a small wedding with family and friends.

Kalin, Mom (Loni), and Darci – the bride and her daughters at the reception.

My wife and I enjoying the Oregon sunshine. We are at the Volcano Stadium in Keizer, Oregon.

A favorite time in my life where Loni and I enjoyed watching Matt play college basketball at Southern Oregon University. He went on to set two 3-point shooting records and helped his team advance to Nationals in Point Lookout, Missouri.

Supporting my son, Jake (Kid Espi), was an amazing adventure. He was a hip-hop record-ing artist and a natural performer. In this picture he is perform-ing in one of his biggest hip-hop concerts in the northwest.

In 2013, our family celebrated Christmas where all three grandkids were together, Silas, Tyson, and Luca.

Winter time in front of our house in Salem, Oregon.

We flew back to Dimmitt, Texas. I wanted to show Loni where I was raised. It was amazing to see the original siding on our old house, which still stands on E 4th and NE Dulin.

After 31 years, I returned to see the football field where I once played as a Dimmitt Bobcat.

My dad and I at the Oregon Coast when he turned 80.

A special day for me. I was baptized in the Willamette River and became a new-born Christian. Jesus is my Lord and Savior.

Four generations, my son, my grandson, me, and my dad.

2017 – my awesome family on one of many holiday celebrations.

I'm so thankful for my family's support and love. In this photo we're celebrating Father's Day.

Loni and I vacationing at the Oregon Coast. We enjoy walking on the beach and eating at nice restaurants.

Oregon has some beautiful rivers. Here we are somewhere between Roseburg and Eugene along Interstate 5.

Spudnut Shop, in Richland, Washington. My wife loves trying new places to eat. This was the first time we tried Spudnut donuts.

In Portland, Oregon, having some fun in the city.

In Folsom, California, where we were visiting Loni's Uncle Allen and his family.

Loop, my dad, and me in Lincoln City, Oregon. Loop was visiting for a few weeks. We hadn't seen him in years.

My brother Rich, my dad, and me. Rich and Loop were my closest brothers, we spent a lot of time together in the past years.

My wife and I love Jesus Christ first, and then our family. We enjoy spending time with each other laughing; exercising; playing games; reading; watching movies; eating dinner; supporting our kids, and supporting our grandkids.

Sources

The material that I have written comes from my strong-long-term memory. My collection of family photos and my traumatizing experience as a five-year-old boy played a role in the true details of my life story. Dealing with intense situations as a grade-school kid enabled me to retain explicit and precise details, even fifty years later. Because of my passion for wanting to overcome, my story was, emotional, fun, and challenging to write.

Bible scriptures referred to throughout the book come from the English Standard Version (ESV).

In chapter 1, the small paragraph I used on the history of St. Anthony's Hospital was from an original plaque that still stands on the old-vacant ground in Amarillo, Texas.

Credits

Most of the photos were provided by David Espinoza. The older photos were taken by Gabriela Espinoza and Candi Espinoza.

Thanks to my son, Jake Espinoza, for the book-cover design.

The front-cover photo was taken by Gabriela Espinoza in 1976.

Dimmitt Bobcat football photo credited to Dimmitt Photography.

Thanks to Karen Stevick King for her quote in chapter 11, and for the eighth-grade photo she provided.

Sheryn Roberts photo credited to the Dimmitt grade-school yearbook.

Candi Espinoza's graduation photos credited to the Gervais High School yearbook (Willoria)

David's graduation photos credited to the Gervais High School yearbook (Willoria).

Snowball Court and Homecoming Court photos Credited to the Gervais High School year book (Willoria).

Wedding photos of Candi and I credited to her Uncle Dale Bartholomew.

Several photos of family with Loni and I credited to Matt Espinoza.

Three photos during my high school track season and basketball season credited to the 1977 Woodburn High School yearbook (Wohiscan).

About the Author

David Espinoza completed his Associates Degree of Computer Science at Chemeketa Community College in Salem, Oregon. Shortly after, he was employed by the State of Oregon. The computer field was taking off and there was a great demand for software developers. In 1982 he landed his first job. Working as a software engineer, he stayed close to his family in Salem where after 31 years he retired at age 55.

David was raised in Dimmitt, Texas, and after his sophomore year, in 1976, his parents packed up and moved the entire family of six kids to the northwest. He spent three months with his cousins in Moses Lake, Washington, working in the fields and at a potato factory. His family then moved to Gervais, Oregon, where he graduated from Gervais High School in 1978.

In football, Espinoza became an excellent kicker and punter at the high school level. Several colleges were expressing interest. Oregon State University's Head Coach Craig Fertig and his coaching staff scouted him and even called him on weekends at his house several times. An injury to his right ankle forced David to attend a recruiting trip at OSU while he was not 100%. OSU offered him a walk-on position for the first year, and after that, a full scholarship.

David decided to bypass on OSU's offer and enrolled at CCC. During college he married his high school sweetheart, Candi. He first completed his college degree and then landed a job as a computer programmer. By then, he had two wonderful little boys. He treasured his family so much that he tried out for a local professional football team to stay close. He made the team and played games on the weekends with the Salem Stars during the 1980s. He helped this team of the NFA (National Football Alliance) make it to the championship game. The highlight of his football career was kicking a 56-yard field goal against the Spokane Fury.

David later tried out with the Portland Breakers, a USFL (United States Football League) team that ran parallel to the NFL. He was overjoyed when he was picked as one of the top kickers at the tryouts. Before reporting to the first practice, the USFL folded. It was a sad day and the next option was to head to the CFL, the Canadian Football League.

There was word from the Salem Stars' coaches that some teams were interested in a field-goal kicker like Espinoza. David had a family and did not like being away from his wife and two boys. He made a decision to end his pro-football career. He valued his family more than the fame and money.

The author was a three-sport athlete all through high school and continued to play at the professional level. His experiences were inspiring giving him the visualizations to write realism-fiction and non-fiction stories. He has always enjoyed writing but never published his work until 2008 – he wrote a book on his younger son, Matt, *Noza: A True Basketball Success Story*. In 2011 he published his second book, *Poor Kid, Wealthy Kid*. In 2013 he published his third book, *The Professor - Grayson Boucher Plus More NW Sports Stories*. In 2015 he published his fourth book, *Poor Kid, Wealthy Kid II*, the sequel. In 2017 he published his fifth book, *Parenting The Athlete*. He now has six books published with this one, *Half Blind with Full Vision*.

He enjoys reading the Bible and puts Jesus before sports. Family is next on his list followed by writing; sports; reading; Oregon coast trips; watching movies; encouraging students, and listening to music (Christian and 1970s hits).

Other Books by David Espinoza
You Might Enjoy

NOZA: A True Basketball Success Story

The Professor Grayson Boucher
Plus More NW Sports Stories

Poor Kid, Wealthy Kid

Poor Kid, Wealthy Kid II

Parenting The Athlete

Books can be ordered at **DavidEspi.com** if you want them autographed. They are also available to order at Amazon or any retail book store.

CPSIA information can be obtained
at www.ICGtesting.com
Printed in the USA
FFOW02n0030130618
47096171-49535FF